W9-CJS-412

Defensive Racism

Edgar J. Steele

Defensive Racism

*An unapologetic examination
of racial differences*

**ProPer
Press**

ProPer Press.

DEFENSIVE RACISM. Copyright © 2004 by Edgar J. Steele

www.DefensiveRacism.com

All Rights Reserved. Printed in the United States of America. No part of this book may be reproduced or transmitted in any form or by any means, graphic, electronic or mechanical, including photocopying, recording, taping or by any information storage retrieval system, except for brief quotations embodied in critical articles or reviews, without the permission in writing. Address inquiries to ProPer Press, PO Box 1255, Sagle, ID 83860.

www.ProPerPress.com

Library of Congress Cataloging-in-Publication Data

Steele, Edgar J.
         Defensive Racism: An Unapologetic Examination of Racial Differences / Edgar
     J. Steele
           p. cm.
     Includes bibliographical references.
     ISBN 0-9761259-0-0
     1. Racism. 2. Civilization, Western – Forecasting. 3. Social prediction – United States.
     4. Social prediction – Europe. 5. United States – Social conditions – 2004 – Forecasting.
     6. Europe – Social conditions – Forecasting. 7. United States – Population – Forecasting.
     8. Europe – Population – Forecasting. 9. United States – Emigration and immigration –
     Social aspects. 10. Europe – Emigration and immigration – Social aspects. I. Title.

First Edition: October 2004

*Dedicated to those brave souls
who have fallen in the struggle
to achieve true equality
for <u>all</u> races*

"Men occasionally stumble over truth, but most of them pick themselves up and hurry off as if nothing had happened."
---Winston Churchill

"It's not the things you don't know what gets you into trouble. It's the things you do know that just ain't so."
--- Will Rogers

Contents

Introduction

"Racism works. Racism is good."
   --- (with apologies to Gordon Gecko, as played by Michael Douglas in the movie *"Wall Street"*)

Of course, whether racism "works" depends upon one's definition. One man's racism is another's multiculturalism, another's hell and yet another's nirvana. I'm not even going to bother with dictionary definitions. Let's deal in today's realities, instead.

"Racist" is a term applied, not only to one who simply prefers his own race to others, but also to those who think their race superior to others and more deserving. Racist is an epithet in almost all contexts. Even those who might properly be called racist prefer to think of themselves as "racialists," as though the slight word change makes a difference to anybody but themselves. Racist connotes bigotry, the unthinking rejection of another based upon his or her skin color. Racist implies stereotyping, whereby certain negative characteristics found in certain members of a race are attributed to all members of that race. Are we on the same page here?

In truth, "racist" is just as quickly applied to many who seek simple equality with others, most notably outspoken White people. In fact, there are those who argue with a straight face that only White people are capable of being racist. Thus, the term has lost much of its currency, together with its legitimacy.

Interestingly, often the very same people quick to accuse one of anti-Semitism are the very ones who label others racist, too.

ix

Racist has become like "Anti-Semite;" applied with a broad brush to swaths of humanity, virtually all White. "Racist" is used pejoratively, in precisely the same manner that "nigger" is used, though without the same consequences.

Accusation, conviction and sentence, all in a single word: racist. There is no defense. Those who bluster about how they are not racists merely become more tightly embraced by that particular tar baby.

At the risk of seeming naive, I believe that certain forms of racism are susceptible of being defended, and with great justification.

Beauty is only skin deep, but ugly goes to the bone, some cynically jest. Many argue that the only difference between the races is skin color. If true, our discussion would end right here, because then racism of any sort truly would be reprehensible conduct. However, they are wrong. Race goes beyond the bone, in fact, and is lodged deeply within our DNA.

A popular current myth has it that there are no intellectual differences between the races, despite contrary results derived in every study of intellect ever done by anybody. This myth also flies in the face of the personal experience of virtually every human being alive.

If one can inherit a superior muscle structure, readily confirmed by the barest of glances at the racial makeup of pro sports rosters, then why is it such a stretch for so many to believe that superior intellect is genetically encoded, as well? Because those same myth purveyors believe that superior intellect makes for superiority, *period*, that's why. The good news is that they are wrong about the superiority thing. The bad news is that they are wrong about the lack of racial intellectual differences. The worse news is that they are in charge.

Because raw intellect is measured so easily, there really can be no rational contesting of the obvious differences in racial IQs. For me, IQ has become a singularly uninteresting question. For those who might take issue with me and become disappointed in my disinterest, there are many books and research study reports. Perhaps the best is *"The Bell Curve."* Read it. Though we will cover some of the more significant IQ studies later in this book, do your own research. Think it out for yourself. Until you can overcome your programming by this simple precursor, the rest of my discussion will be a waste of time for you.

The more interesting questions concern differences brought about by racial culture, on the one hand, and one's genetic structure, on the other. IQ merely is one aspect of genetic determination, after all, as is skin color.

Character, for lack of a better term, is a far more important result, one that only recently is being recognized as having a genetic component. We come to life with a full set of matching luggage, already partially filled on the day we are born; indeed, on the day we are conceived. As we grow up, our culture, composed of those around us, especially those with whom we identify, allows us to complete the packing of our luggage, which we drag with us through every moment of our lives.

Culture and genetic predisposition or proclivity are mere kissing cousins, in my opinion. I like to think of genetics as being culture and prior behavior gone to seed. By the way, this outlook works whether one believes in evolution or creation as the source of man.

In animals, we call this culture-gone-to-seed "instinct," of course. We humans often confuse it with reincarnation or various forms of extrasensory perception. It is a far more important cause of racial differences than intellect and has led to some, if not most, of the national disasters throughout history.

By now, you should be agreeing with how irrelevant skin color differences are, incidentally, yet another uninteresting question. We have much bigger fish to fry in this book.

I know – some reading this wonder if I am a racist. Well, it depends, of course. *The more interesting question is whether you are a racist.* Stick around and find out. By the end of this book, the answer to both questions should be more than apparent.

Chapter 1

Semantics

"What is in a name? A rose by any other name would smell as sweet."
--- William Shakespeare

Names and labels are funny things. Used as a form of shorthand, to facilitate communication, names often accomplish exactly the opposite. Worse, the damage is done in stealth, with nobody the wiser.

A good deal of the world's conflict assuredly can be attributed to those who walk away from an ostensible agreement with very different understandings of what just took place. Marriage merely is one of the easiest-to-recognize occurrences of stealth conflict.

The problem is one of semantics, in other words.

It is critical to this book's central thesis to decide at the outset precisely what is meant by the words "racism" and "racist."

Ask most to define the term "racist" and they will use words such as "bigot," "hate" and "intolerance." Even many who admit to being racist will employ negatively-charged words in describing themselves.

Those who admit to having racist tendencies often try to distinguish themselves as being "racialist," rather than "racist," without realizing that makes no difference to most. They are kin to those who categorically deny being racist, all the while comporting themselves in classically racist ways.

13

Racism is a sort of "gateway" concept, too. Once one sees oneself as a racist, one falls prey to a host of attitudes that simply are adopted whole cloth, with no rational examination. Kind of like how Democrats believe themselves to be liberal and Republicans think themselves conservative (another set of self-defeating shorthand words, to be sure). That is why self-avowed racists almost universally cannot give a rational explanation for disliking (for example) Asians and fall back on skin color as their sole mode of distinguishing others.

I have come generally to believe that two rational people, after a full and complete discussion, can never disagree about anything. At the very least, they can agree to disagree because of some fundamental schism which cannot be resolved.

A good example of an irresolvable conflict is the abortion debate, which is a direct extension of how one views one's unprovable and unknowable role in the universe. No amount of debate will sway one side to adopt the other's point of view without first getting both sides to agree on the origin and purpose of humanity, an impossible task.

Of course, many self-avowed racists hew to a religious basis for their racial outlooks, as well. Followers of Christian Identity, for example, believe all non-Caucasian races to be the spawn either of Satan or of creatures lesser than Man. These people cannot rationally debate the concept of racism.

Similarly, there is no reasoning with those who have adopted secular humanism as a form of personal religion and therefore refuse to believe the manifest proof of there being racial differences other than mere skin color.

There simply is no reasoning with people unwilling to place all underlying beliefs on the table for examination and alteration.

Nor can one get these disparate irrational (for lack of a better word) factions to agree on a definition for the word "racist." If you are one of these, please keep in mind how you have hobbled yourself as you move through the pages of this book. Remember that you have refused to come to grips with the basic definitions necessary to examine racism.

I submit that, ultimately, one can define racism solely as a belief in the mere existence of racial differences. Other words are sufficient to distinguish attitudes and beliefs apart from a fundamentally racist outlook ("hateful racist" or "intolerant racist," for example).

Yes, believing in skin color differences amongst the races is a racist belief. Mind you, if that were the only racial difference that existed, as some would have us believe, then the concept of racism becomes singularly uninteresting and ceases altogether for blind people.

However, ultimately we must deal with the baggage that the term "racist" carries as it is flung about by one person or another. Without realizing it, all the people using the word really aren't even on the same page.

What everybody might agree upon is that "racist" is a negative descriptor. What of those who believe in racial differences without the negative freight attendant to the word "racist?" For example, does stereotyping mean the same thing as bigotry? Is a police profiler a bigot?

Don't we really use the term "racist" as a means to vilify those with whom we disagree and/or dislike? Doesn't that mean the negative implication actually resides within the one using the label, not the other way around?

The label "racist" really has more to do with the labeler than with the labelee, doesn't it?

Consider: Why is it racist to form a White civil rights group, yet it is not racist to support the NAACP? Why can Blacks agitate for preferences which come at the expense of Whites, yet such is not known as racism? Why does opposing affirmative action get many White people labeled hateful and bigoted racists?

Some argue that indulging one race at the expense of another is necessary to redress past societal wrongs. Aside from the obvious inequity of penalizing those who merely possess the same color skin as those who might have acted wrongly in the past, there is the issue of the very real racial caste system that becomes institutionalized once one begins dispensing race-based favors.

If somehow we could subtract all the pejorative meaning from the word racist, we could get on with the real job before us, that of determining if there is any merit to the attitudes and beliefs of those we call racist. A daunting task, yes, but not one to be avoided merely because of apparent difficulty.

For the purpose of this book's discussion, please agree to set aside all the negative outlooks you might have toward racism and racists. Try writing those negative attributes inside the back cover as a symbolic means of setting them aside for the moment. After you have finished the book, then you may pick them up and reinstall them, if you wish. Should you choose to continue with them, after all, you might just have gained a much more rational and logical basis for shunning racists.

I won't hide the ball: There exists the danger that you might abandon your attitudes about racism, in whole or in part. You might even end up unabashedly viewing yourself as a racist, albeit a very special sort, one with none of the negative characteristics you might have listed inside the back cover, as suggested above. On the other hand, some skinheads might start growing hair again.

At the very least, I guarantee you will be thinking about the subject in ways that you never have before. The intellectual exercise, alone, will be worth the journey. I promise.

Let's get on with it...

Chapter 2

Intellectual Myths

"A dollar for your thoughts...."
--- Marilyn Monroe

I have a theory about IQ: One cannot directly perceive intelligence in another beyond the limit of one's own.

It's kind of like the human eye, which sees well, up to point. Beyond that point, however, radiation every bit as viable as visible light is invisible. Infrared, ultraviolet, x-rays, gamma rays and so on.

And there are emanations below the visible light spectrum, as well, physically identical in every way with visible light, save only wavelength, except that they cannot be seen with the human eye: radio, TV, microwave, for example.

These radiations all comprise the electromagnetic spectrum. Think of intelligence as being limited in the same way that the eye is limited.

Why else do we fail to see the obvious intelligence possessed by every living creature? So that we can feel justified in enslaving and eating them is the easy answer, but I think the truth is more fundamental.

There are hints about the presence of electromagnetic radiation, to be sure, such as the warmth generated by unseen infrared radiation. But the eye hasn't a clue.

Neither do so many people walking around out there, despite

manifest hints. Every time some dolt tries to best me with his haphazard logic and regurgitated borrowed ideology, bereft of personal examination and integration, this point is driven home with a vengeance. Arguing with his ilk is like doing battle with an unarmed opponent. Like America versus Grenada. Generally, I have the good sense merely to walk away without proving what is so dreadfully apparent to my own eye, yet oblivious to the other – *because they simply are incapable of perceiving the disparity.*

Seems like they would feel something akin to the heat of infrared light, somehow, and catch a clue from it.

Generally, I can size up another's IQ within a minute or so of conversation, provided it is less than my own. I have known a number of people in my life that I regarded as intellectual equals. Simple logic suggests that some of them were my superior, but I had no way of discerning their intellectual ability beyond the limit of my own. Some of them hadn't even gone to college, to acknowledge the dedicated Mensans reading this.

Come on, admit it. When another is below your own intelligence level, you know it for a fact, though you might ignore that fact – and should, in your dealings with that person, if you know what is good for you. You knew who were the scholars and who were the dummies in school and you had them ranked. I'd wager that ranking was identical to the actual distribution of their IQs. Witness the fact that some of the grasshopper-like layabouts ranked higher in your eyes than some of the ant-like scholars. Today, of course, those scholars work for the former layabouts.

It has become politically incorrect to speak of IQ tests. Why? Because there are racial differences, else there would be no need to obfuscate. For the life of me, I cannot understand why. Perhaps it is a manifestation of thinking by intelligence in excess of my own, but I doubt it. I suppose it is because so many consider intellectual superiority to denote superiority in all respects. Kind of like thinking women with large breasts are better overall – or blondes, I suppose. Or good-looking people. Or tall men.

Whatever the match up, however, I have noticed that intellect seems to trump all else, as illustrated perfectly by Marilyn Monroe's attraction and marriage to playwright Arthur Miller, a man in almost every respect her opposite. Her subsequent divorce from Miller, who treated her with such disdain, then underscored the fact that character is what endures, what really matters.

I've lived with the obvious difference between my own intellect and many others all my life and honestly do not consider that to make me one whit superior to anybody. It is merely an attribute which I have learned to use in making my way through life, much as any professional has learned to marshal his or her particular talents. Or the way in which a pretty girl learns to use a smile to open doors.

Occasionally I have resorted to beating up another intellectually, usually with a relish of which I was not entirely proud, and almost always when I saw that person intellectually brutalizing another about whom I felt protective. Didn't make me better, any more than some schoolyard bully pushing around another, smaller kid thereby is made superior.

Think in terms of the bar scene early in the movie *"Good Will Hunting,"* in which one intellectual bully pushes around another in defending a friend. Though that movie was a caricature, in that it overplayed the intellect of the leading character, the basic thrust was right on the money. I commend it to those who labor under the delusion that members of the intellectual elite of the world consider themselves elite in anything save a single, narrow aspect of existence, an aspect that they, themselves, deem far less important than do others.

Consider intellectual pretenders you have known, galumphing about in the shoes of true giants, trumpeting their self-professed superiority, in a vainglorious attempt to impress the rest of us. You

know who you are. The bad news is that *we* know who you are, too –
we've just been too polite to mention it. The full range of pretension,
unlike intellect, is apparent to all. Arrogance is least attractive in the
company of stupidity.

Truly beautiful people are taken far less with their own
appearance than others. When cornered, their vanity and desperation
always arises from a fear that they have nothing but their appearance
to commend themselves, and that, for only a limited time. Picture the
aging debutante, formerly beautiful, knowing that never will she be
doyenne of her circle.

Others have been more attractive than I, yet I denied them
superiority over myself – something of which most of America seems
incapable in these days of celebrity by media appearance. Others
have been taller – that didn't make them better. Despite what
commonly is called "short man's complex," tall men are not better
than short men. Running faster doesn't do it, either. Nor does the
accumulation of wealth. Nor, even, power.

Why, just look at President George W. Bush, an individual who
all but demands that we feel superior as a direct consequence of all
that he says and does. In fact, perhaps that is why we elected him,
after experiencing the duplicity that accompanied the genuinely
towering intellect of Bill Clinton. Oh, that's right – for a moment
there, I forgot that we *didn't* elect Bush, *the Supreme Court did.*

More than anybody else in the public eye lately, perhaps, George
W. Bush illustrates the adage that, to take the measure of a man's
character, it is necessary only to give him some power. Unlike
intelligence, character is a personal characteristic with which to make
truly meaningful differentiations among people, a subject to which we
will return, with a vengeance, later in this book.

Why is there such a blindness regarding intelligence? Because,
otherwise, there would be no need to cover up the obvious racial
differences in IQ. The politically-incorrect truth, in other words.

Those promoting the PC myth of intellectual equality among the races are of two types: First, those who feel inadequate intellectually and therefore accord intellect far more importance than it really deserves and even deny it in hopes that nobody will notice their own inadequacy. Second, many of those who possess true intellectual superiority are ashamed to be seen in possession of riches they believe they do not deserve, yet another compensation for feelings of inadequacy. Bottom line: virtually everybody conspires with virtually everybody else to pretend there are no intellectual differences. This highlights what I call the basic human condition, by the way: *feeling inferior to others.*

Even when we acknowledge intellectual differentials between individuals, still we blindly insist that there are no racial differences similar to the obvious physical racial differences which make professional sports such a Black endeavor these days.

Saying the earth was flat did not make it so. The establishment once thought the Sun revolved around the Earth, but that did not make it so. Neither does denying racial differences in IQ.

There have been extensive studies of intelligence, privately and within both academia and the military. The discipline of those studies has been refined through the years. Intelligence in individuals can be measured precisely and with ease. And, contrary to establishment pronouncements, without the results being degraded due to cultural differences. Some of the most dramatic proofs have been generated by liberals in pursuit of opposite conclusions. Indeed, it is that very search which has so refined the study of intelligence.

"The Bell Curve," by Herrnstein and Murray (1994), is one of the very best recent overviews of intelligence and class structure, especially racial class structure. You will find this book remaindered all over the country, because it is held in disdain by the establishment. Like the flat-earth misconception of years gone by, though, pushing an ideological point of view does not make the

establishment correct.

Herrnstein and Murray meticulously cover the field of intellectual differences in American society and review the historical studies performed by all manner of persons and organizations. They note that, while there exists a 15-point IQ gap between Whites and Blacks in American society, that fact masks a more substantial difference, caused by the 6:1 White:Black disparity in population numbers: *"At the lower end of the IQ range (55-85), there are approximately equal numbers of blacks and whites. But throughout the upper half of the range, the disproportions between the number whites and blacks at any given IQ level are huge."* (*Ibid*, pp. 279 – 280) While there are a handful of high-IQ Blacks, as a percentage of the total number of high-IQ individuals, those Blacks are statistically insignificant. *This is the reason why affirmative action has not worked and will never work.* So long as we promote by population percentages, we always will have a staggering number of Black supervisors and professionals grossly in over their heads and promoted ahead of more-deserving Whites. More on this later, too.

Elitists like to sniff that IQ tests are culturally biased, otherwise the races would score equally. They are wrong. IQ tests have been devised of every type possible: written, spatial, verbal, cultural, *etc.* In every instance, Blacks consistently score at about the same level, *vis-à-vis* American Whites. What to do? Well, the elitists simply define themselves out of their corner: *"Had the first IQ tests been devised in a hunting culture, "general intelligence" might well have turned out to involved visual acuity and running speed, rather than vocabulary and symbol manipulation."* (O. D. Duncan, 1968, quoted by A. R. Jensen, "How much can we boost IQ and scholastic achievement?," *Harvard Education Review*, 39-1) We might just as well give the points for skin color, as the US Supreme Court says we must, if we employ this sort of rationale.

The US Army conducted extensive IQ testing once WWI was

underway, in an attempt to ascertain how best to help the war effort by allocation of personnel. The Army's findings were consistent with every other study done: American Blacks average an IQ of about 85, with Whites averaging 100. A further refinement was made by the army in grading the relative percentage of White blood possessed by the Blacks studied and learned that, again, there existed a direct correlation, with the pure Blacks scoring even lower, at about the range of 70, a level which has been determined to approximate that of the average native African Black by a great many other studies. (John Baker, *Race and Cognitive Ability*, pp. 470-490, 1974).

There is an average 15-point IQ difference between American Whites and American Blacks. Take it to the bank. All the studies confirm this. My own life experience bears witness to this fact *and so does yours, if you are honest,* regardless of your skin color. More about this later.

That does not make Whites superior to Blacks.

Year in and year out, Kenyans win the Boston Marathon because they are superior long distance runners. Whites have IQs superior to those possessed by Blacks, on average. Which racial characteristic is better? The honest answer depends upon a great many things, not the least of which is whether you are being chased by a lion.

Let me say it again: *Whites are not superior to Blacks because the average White IQ is 15 points higher.*

Just as Blacks are not superior because the average Black can run faster and jump higher than the average White.

Just as a different skin color does not make one person superior to another.

Nor are Jews superior because their average IQ is about 10 points higher than the average White.

Nor are Asians superior because their average IQ is about 5 points higher than the average White.

Just as I am not superior to any of the members of those races because my personal IQ is higher than the vast majority of theirs.

It takes a towering intellect to create a towering house of cards. Only the highly intelligent can manifest stupidity at a truly world-class level. Consider the economic house of cards that America has erected while in the grip of the One Worlders. Its collapse due to all the truly criminal government deficit spending and outlandishly negative international trade deficits, coupled with the unprecedented fiscal intemperateness of the Federal Reserve System, will put to shame the economic chaos wrought by real dummies all through history. Disasters like that about to happen make a compelling argument that superior intellect might actually be a liability, but that is a topic for another time and place.

It is a myth that superior intellect makes one person better than another. Recognizing this myth is key to dispelling the next: *It is a myth that there are no intellectual differences between the races.*

Recognizing the falsity of these two myths is key to understanding and dealing with the true differences between races which affect us all.

Not that raw intellect does not play a role in things that truly do matter. As we shall see later in this book, the degree to which we are ruled by our inborn behavioral tendencies ("nature" vs. "nurture") is related inversely to our IQ. Since behavioral response patterns are what make up character, then those of lesser intellect are less capable of altering their responses to the world. Makes sense, if you think about it a bit. Being unable to think through to consequences precludes one from seeing a need to alter behavior in the first place.

Chapter 3

Genetic Realities

"Birds do it, bees do it,
Even educated fleas do it.."
  ---*"Let's Do It, Let's Fall in Love," Cole Porter*

"I will put My law within them and on their heart I will write it..."
  --- *Jeremiah 31:33*

When we brought my youngest daughter home from the hospital for the first time, she fussed and cried all the time. This was in stark contrast to her older brother, who let us sleep through the night after only a couple of days. It went on so long that we had her examined repeatedly for problems. Most doctors theorized that she had colic. They were wrong. She was just being bitchy.

She's been sort of like that ever since. It's like the old joke: *The doctor tells his patient: "Lola, I have some good news and some bad news." Lola asks for the good news first. "Well, the test results are in, and the good news is that you aren't suffering from Pre-menstrual Syndrome, as you'd feared." "And the bad news?" Lola asks. To which the Doc replies: "I'm afraid there's no cure for being a natural bitch."*

My youngest daughter's IQ is very high, clearly. Worse, now 14 years old, she shows signs of turning out to be genuinely beautiful. I predict hard times for her in life. Intellect is enough of a curse, in its

25

own way, but physical beauty truly is a cross to be borne. And she has been "high maintenance" since Day One. I pity the poor guy she marries. Don't get me wrong: Every time I see her, my heart jumps up. I love her so – more than I could ever say.

A side note for those who have yet to have children of their own: the greatest reward of having children, in my opinion, is in learning that it is possible to love another more than you love yourself. Too late? It's never too late. My youngest daughter was born when I was 45. If possible, I would have more today, to anticipate your next question.

The point is that my youngest daughter arrived in life with quite a load of baggage, baggage she inherited on the day she was conceived. She gets both her intellect and her disposition from me; her looks from her mother. My son got only my intellect and was fortunate to receive both his disposition and looks from his mother. They both got their skin colors, hair, height and body builds from us, too. But that's not all. As they have grown, I have been astounded to see flashes of behavior in both of them that I outgrew and cast aside as I matured; behavior so remarkably like my own at their current ages as to be statistically impossible to come by unless inherited directly.

My wife and I raise registered horses. In addition to bloodlines, coloration and physical structure, we breed specifically for demeanor and disposition, as it is called in the business. Everybody does. Demeanor is a major component of a horse's makeup and clearly is passed from one generation to the next. Not always, of course, but consistent with the basic rules of genetics.

You recall all that business with the peas in high school science class, right? Given the tenor of the times, I doubt they teach genetics in high school anymore. I have red hair. My wife has blonde/brown. Her hair color is dominant and mine is recessive. Statistically, one out of four of our children should have red hair. We didn't have that many children, unfortunately, so I am unable to prove genetics with my family members' hair color. I can prove the laws of genetics in spades with our horses, though. And demeanor is every bit as predictable as coloration and physical build.

The same is true for dogs, according to breeders. In fact, the same seems to be true for all creatures. Like Noah before us, we have a menagerie of creatures here on our ranch in Idaho. In particular, we like cats. So do the coyotes and raccoons. Always, it seems, we are breeding litters of barn cats to control the mice. My current objective in our cat breeding program is a Manx (no tail) Siamese with 6 or 7 toes on each foot and a sweetheart disposition. We are close. We consistently get the multi-toed Siamese with great demeanor. Grafting in the Manx characteristic is proving difficult, however. I expect to get there eventually. The laws of genetics say that I will.

In the lower animals, we call inherited demeanor, or behavior, instinct, a concept for which, you may recall from that science class I mentioned earlier, we have no definition. And instinct is not limited to the lower animals, either.

Baby horses are on their feet and able to run within hours of their birth. In the distant past, those who weren't able to do so were eaten by coyotes and mountain lions, of course, so their flavor of DNA was lost, to put it in evolutionist terms, leaving only those who could. I have watched countless numbers of newborn horses and not a single mother had to show them how to stand, walk or run. They knew automatically...instinctively.

Human babies crawl on all fours automatically but must be taught to walk upright. What does that suggest?

Officially, we don't know what instinct is. Not a clue. Tons of government money is spent every year, studying migrating whales and birds.

Here's a flash for all you scientists and it won't cost the government a half billion dollars in study grants, either: *instinct is*

27

genetically-encoded behavior.

I figured it out. You wouldn't think it would be all that difficult for the government wizards whose job it is merely to sit around all day and think deep thoughts. But it is, in yet another triumph of intellect over common sense. Your tax dollars at work.

I mentioned at the outset that I envision genetics as the study of culture gone to seed. In other words, behavior of one's forebears that sank into their DNA, the same DNA now walking around in an all-new skin suit. Do something often enough and it becomes second nature. Or, saying the same thing from an evolutionary point of view: certain behavior gets rewarded with life and others with death, such that the proclivity for some behavior gets passed along. Eventually, it looks just like behavior sinking into one's DNA, though the DNA produced it in the first place, then got naturally selected for perpetuation. Same thing from two different viewpoints. Of course, for evolutionists the question remains: Where did the DNA get the encoded behavior in the first place? Maybe that's where the creation part comes in, fellas.

Obviously, I do not see any inconsistency between Creationism and the Theory of Evolution. Why couldn't evolution have been a part of God's plan, once He created the Universe? And, there is a reason that evolution still is referred to as a theory, after all. There are very powerful arguments that can be made, refuting the possibility of our having evolved from some overly-bright paramecium. But, just because evolution might not have occurred exactly as taught in public schools doesn't mean there isn't some validity to the concept.

Birds fly south in the winter because of DNA. Fish swim upstream because of it. Ants organize themselves into a strict hierarchical structure, just as do so many insects, because of DNA. Calling it instinct is an easy way of ignoring the real answer: Behavior that is encoded genetically and written on DNA. Nurture become nature.

Why do you suppose human beings would be any different? This would be a good time to reread that quote from Jeremiah placed at the start of this chapter.

The obvious answer is that we aren't much different from the lower animals. Not really. We inherit our physical components from our forebears. As discussed in Chapter 2, *Intellectual Myths*, we inherit our intellect just as readily. What now is being conceded by researchers around the world is what parents and animal breeders knew all along: *behavior also is inherited.* What surprises is just *how much* of our behavior is inherited.

We are all familiar with the twins studies, where the behavior of identical twins separated at birth is compared with that of those who lived together, as well as that of ordinary siblings. There is an astoundingly high, statistically-significant correlation of behavior within each pair of twins, whether separated or not and regardless of how disparate were the environments into which separated twins were thrust. Clearly, when their egg split in two, more than just the DNA controlling physical appearance was duplicated. Clearly, DNA controls a lot of behavior.

"Breeding shows," as they say, when speaking of character in people. And there is more than a grain of truth to all those redneck jokes. And fill-in-your-favorite-ethnic-group slur jokes, as well. In fact, it is only *because* of that element of truth that any of those jokes are funny in the first place.

I used to joke with people that I became a lawyer so that I would have an excuse for being the way that I was. Turns out, the joke was on me. It was true. Once it happened, never again did I ever hear words to the effect of: "Why on earth are you *being* this way?" I was born to be a lawyer, sad to say. Today, I refer to myself as a recovering lawyer, yet another joke that really isn't.

Yes, character is partially developed or learned, just as some behavior also is developed extrinsic to one's DNA encoding. That's

29

the nurture part of the old "nature vs. nurture" argument.

Character simply is a bundle of related behavioral response patterns. Ethics, a fancy term that the moralists among us like to employ, is the verbal description of still smaller groups of certain behavioral patterns which are a part of the character groupings. We don't need fancy legal proofs or scientific studies for concepts such as these – they resonate internally with their authenticity.

And it isn't necessary for behavior to be inherited directly; we need receive merely the encoded proclivity for a behavioral response. The behavioral response could be triggered by an external life event, much as a strong memory might come flooding back or like epilepsy, which often is precipitated by a blow to the head. In a very real sense, we all are Manchurian Candidates, walking around, ready to manifest behavior in response to a particular stimulus that may never come. Behavior passed down from our forebears.

Proclivities without the actual condition manifesting are proven inheritable in the field of disease: some Blacks pass along sickle-cell anemia without falling prey, themselves, and some Jews are merely carriers of Tay-Sachs disease, for example. Certainly, it is no stretch to conceive of a similar proclivity existing for other inherited characteristics, including behavior.

The adrenaline rush that accompanies purely social anxiety is a good example of the inherited "fight or flight" predisposition responsible for so many juvenile dustups. You might say that this merely is a matter of our bodies reacting to chemicals being generated, but that ignores the purely perceptual/behavioral nature of the stimulus that causes those chemicals to be released into our bloodstreams in the first place.

Sexual response is another obvious area of inherited stimulus/response patterns in action. Always, kids are way ahead of their parents' explanations.

How many other response patterns lie dormant in our DNA, just awaiting a stimulus that may or may not come?

Since we can't do much about mere proclivities that lie hidden, the sole remaining interesting question is how much behavior is learned and how much is inherited and whether the inherited component can be trumped by education and/or environment: the classic "nature vs. nurture" debate. In other words, this field of endeavor really is about where to draw the line, not whether it is a valid field of study. More self-evident truth.

A joke about pigs comes to mind: Never try to teach a pig to dance – it wastes your time and annoys the pig. There are some behaviors that cannot be taught and there are some behaviors that will not be overcome by any amount of training or environment. The failing social experiment that America has become is proof positive. More on this later.

Without turning this into an X-Files episode script, I would like to note, also, that certain paranormal phenomena, such as experiences of past lives (reincarnation) could well be mere mental conjuring based upon the genetic encoding of behavioral patterns. Did the child who played the piano like a virtuoso without a single lesson really manifest the spirit of another or did he manifest the specific behavior of a forebear, indelibly encoded in his genes and retrieved intact? How much behavior is encoded that might be tapped into, if we just knew how? Is it possible that we might literally stand on the shoulders of our ancestors?

What role does genetically-encoded behavioral response pattern research have in explaining the variety of extraordinary talents displayed by *idiots savant*?

Studies have shown that worms fed other worms that have learned certain behaviors will manifest, with no training whatsoever, a statistically-significant degree of the behavior learned by the worm that was eaten. Maybe there was something to that business about the Aztec priests eating the hearts of their enemies, after all.

31

This is a genuinely exciting scientific field of endeavor that has, until now, been foreclosed by the narrow-minded, control-freak political commissars of our time: legions of the politically correct for whom it is necessary that reality conform to their ideologically driven desires that we all be seen as just the same. For whom "diversity" is Newspeak for conformity. Astronomy once was held in check by their ancestors, whose stupidity seems to have been genetically encoded and now is being remanifested in the social arena.

Bottom line: *Behavior is inherited, just like intellect and all physical characteristics.* Indeed, a high degree of our behavior seems to be genetically predetermined. And there are very serious racial differences, the implications of which we will examine shortly.

You didn't know that 50% of human DNA is identical with that of bananas, did you? Or that bananas actually have 10% more DNA in common with humans than do worms? I wouldn't be surprised to learn, next, that rocks have DNA – everything else certainly possesses it. Chimpanzees possess 98.4% of our DNA, by the way. Reportedly, there is only .2% variation in DNA within the entire human race, with most (85%) of that .2% variance determining individual differences rather than racial differences. So, according to the scientists, only .03% of DNA differences are racial. Considering that bananas possess half our DNA, however, that small a difference in accounting for races isn't surprising.

There is a good reason why the same DNA is shared by all living organisms, including plants. Biochemistry is pretty much the same, whether in a plant or an animal – the same cellular processes need to occur for life to continue. Oxygen has to be transported and used. Nutrients have to be taken up and consumed. Waste products need to be excreted. All this requires genetically-encoded processes, whether in a chimpanzee, a human or a carrot. It makes sense that the DNA which controls essential functions will be much the same for all life forms. On the other hand, just because we have a lot of DNA in common with a banana doesn't mean I want my daughter to marry one.

Arguing over how minimal interracial DNA differences might be misses the point altogether, however. It is agreed that there *are* racial DNA differences. Whatever DNA differences *do* exist are precisely what create the *racial differences* that exist – physical, intellectual and behavioral. It doesn't take much to make a big difference. After all, there isn't much DNA difference between siblings, yet the physical, intellectual and behavioral differences are, more often than not, remarkably divergent.

Consider the pro golf tour: it takes very little difference in ability among the participants for one golfer to end up completely out of the money and another to win it all. The same is true in virtually all human endeavor, whether competitive sports, business, romance or sandbox politics. Again, a fundamental truth that self verifies in that it rings true internally.

The modern researcher gets funded only if his results match up with the politically-correct outlook maintained by the establishment. Recall how unusual it was for a round-worlder like Christopher Columbus to get funded at the time? Queen Isabella apparently was somewhat taken with him, since it was only her jewels being hocked that financed his little expedition in 1492. Thus, there is a great deal of noise about the DNA differences between individuals being greater than that between races, leading to a rather strained conclusion that, therefore, racial differences are *de minimis* or, even, that races don't really exist.

After all, there are any number of researchers claiming there are no interracial IQ differences, when the plain facts and everybody's personal experience prove otherwise. The entire scientific establishment's credibility is called into question by this single issue, yet there are so many other politically-correct conclusions being pushed by so-called scientists, much as the flat-earth "reality" once was pushed. We simply cannot trust them, folks.

I don't mean to sound like a Luddite with my indictment of modern science, however. As with all evidence in a courtroom, we merely should keep motivations in mind and accord weight appropriate to the evidence.

I am no researcher and have no way of validating whether interracial DNA differences quantitatively are less than those between individuals. Even if true, however, it does not negate the validity of taking stock of interracial differences and acting accordingly. After all, the differences are...different.

For example, there is a pretty extreme variation in hair color within Caucasians. No striking hair-color variation occurs in Asians and Africans, however. And plenty of Caucasians have Black hair, as well. So, there is more inter-individual difference in hair color genes than interracial. Does that mean that hair color differentiation is more significant than racial differentiation in predicting behavior? Obviously not.

What I wish to focus upon in this book in drawing racial distinctions, ultimately, is behavior. And that is where the critical DNA differences lie. As I said before, to discriminate based upon skin color makes no rational sense. To discriminate based upon behavior, however, makes a great deal of sense. After all, in society we discriminate against criminals in the name of public safety, retribution and rehabilitation by keeping them locked away.

Behavior is a composite of genetics, including intellect, and current culture, which includes the entirety of one's environment (nature *plus* nurture). Those who deny genetic racial differences point to culture as being the source of all racial differences. With that, I am in partial agreement. Because I view genetics as culture gone to seed, the results are precisely the same: ultimately, we all manifest behavior that is entirely a product of culture, or accumulated experience. Nurture, in other words, since nature simply is nurture gone to seed and, thus, hard wired into our DNA.

Genetics provides part of the explanation of racial differences. Active, contemporaneous culture gives us the rest, as we will see.

Chapter 4

Cultural Imperatives

*"You can take the boy out of the country,
but you can't take the country out of the boy."*
  --- Proverb

*"All are kneaded from the same dough –
 not all are baked in the same oven."*
  --- Proverb

Thus far, we have covered some basic concepts essential to development of the idea that some racism, in one form or another, might actually be a good thing.

We have dispelled *the myth that there are no intellectual differences between the races,* leading us to the inescapable conclusion that *intellect, as well as the more obvious physical characteristics, is passed from one generation to the next via DNA.* We have discussed *the importance of character over intellect and how character is a composite of a number of behavioral response patterns, only some of which are learned.* We have discussed how *behavior becomes genetically encoded in DNA, either directly or through natural selection, and also is passed on.* These concepts are neither trivial nor widely appreciated.

We inherit our appearance, our intellect and a good deal of our behavior from our ancestors, with there being substantial racial differences in all three areas. Accepting these self-evident truths is all but impossible for many, yet essential if we are to understand how the world really works and what inevitably must surface within a multicultural society such as the one America has become.

Nature vs. Nurture

Having surmounted the relative insignificance of differences in skin color among the races, we now focus on behavior as the prime basis upon which to examine racism; behavior that, as we have seen, is a product of both heredity and culture. The inherited component of behavior is double natured: DNA-encoded behavioral response patterns, called instinct in the lower forms of life, and intellect, which assists in producing behavior based upon perception of one's culture and environment.

Clearly, it is possible to go against one's hard wiring, the encoded behavioral response patterns, as a result of current experience (when I stare at another woman's breasts, my wife gets angry) and intellect (if I kill this guy, I will go to prison). The more interesting question is, *"How much inherited behavior can be unlearned?"* Another interesting question concerns the relative proportion of inherited versus learned behavior.

"Nature versus nurture" is how researchers characterize the tension between inherited and learned behavior. Perhaps in resignation, though they cloak their results in a great deal of statistics, those same researchers tend to ascribe a 50/50 role between the two for humans of average intellect. If you agree with my assertion that inherited behavior is "culture gone to seed," then it is easy to appreciate why it is difficult to separate out the two influences, because they appear to manifest in precisely the same way to a student of human behavior.

Interestingly, these same researchers also postulate that the nature/nurture ratio varies inversely with IQ. In fact, they extend the analysis to other life forms, as well. Here's their bottom line: *the lower the intellect, the greater the role of nature* (manifestation of inherited behavioral response patterns). Thus, the lower life forms, such as ants, are totally at the mercy of their DNA, operating entirely from what we choose to call instinct. Consider the poor dragonfly, who lives but a single day. Hard to accumulate much learned behavior in one day, yet they get their job of reproduction done.

IQ's Role in Behavior

Similarly, low-IQ humans are ruled by their inherited behavioral responses to a degree far greater than those of us with greater reasoning and analytical capacity. That just restates the obvious, though, because one clearly requires the mental capacity to foresee that one course of action leads to better results than a course dictated by simple human chemistry (the way DNA gets us to do its bidding, as with adrenaline, *a la* the "fight or flight" syndrome response).

There is, of course, no direct correlate with IQ, *per se,* just a general tendency, because of the way in which we measure intellect. IQ merely is an overall estimate of one's intelligence, based upon an assessment of several different intellectual abilities. People with the same IQ can have disparate spreads in abilities. The IQ number alone seems to say that verbal comprehension, for example, is interchangeable with spatial reasoning and any of another ten or so different characteristics. Fact is, different capabilities serve us in different spheres of life and we all have different mixtures of capabilities.

Not surprisingly, there also are racial differences in the mix and relative proportions of the different intellectual abilities like verbal comprehension and spatial reasoning that make up what we call IQ, differences that are quite profound.

Racial intellectual capability mixture differences explain the Asian gravitation toward math and the sciences. Though Asian average IQs are about 5 points higher than that of the average White, the standard deviation (a measure of how spread out data is) for Asian IQs is exceedingly tight when compared to that of Whites. In other words, there is a pretty small variation from the average for most Asians. This explains why they can have higher average IQs with a much lower incidence of genius (and fewer morons, for that matter). This might also explain why Asians excel at copying and assembly line work, whereas Caucasians, with a much wider standard deviation (and a correspondingly higher incidence of both true geniuses and genuine dolts) provide most of the world's innovation. Because Asians are more homogeneous intellectually, we might expect that their societies also would be more homogeneous, just as they clearly seem to be.

Racial intellectual capability mixture differences also seem to explain why Jews disproportionately hold sway in areas of human endeavor that reward verbal skills (*e.g.,* sales, law, media), the very same skills which some say excessively influence calculation of overall IQ. An absolute IQ differential, taken together with a skew toward the verbal skills, goes a long way toward explaining Jewish ownership of the world, but the Jewish cultural ethic fills in the gap.

Jewish sharp dealing in business and money matters is legion down through history and in modern times, as examined in some detail later in this book, particularly Chapters 16 and 17, *World War III* and *Money's End Game: Depression II*. The following concept is a bit premature for our discussion, but bears mention: those willing to do anything to get ahead, all other things being equal, usually will be the ones getting ahead. Think of being burdened with ethics as akin to barefisted fighting with one hand tied behind your back. Behavior, again. Character, if you like.

Evolution vs. Creation

IQ and its various components are inherited. If you are an Evolutionist, then you explain this by pointing out that the environment rewards those with characteristics which favor survival by granting them continued life. Creationists would argue that intellect comes packaged with the soul or, at minimum, is genetically encoded and passed along. Evolutionists, on the other hand, still are left with an issue about ultimate origins, even if we accept, *arguendo*, their belief that man evolved from a primordial soup. Query: *From whence came that soup?*

Evolutionism is not proven, as evidenced by the fact that it properly is referred to as *"The Theory of Evolution."* In truth, the usual thrust of the Theory of Evolution incorrectly refers to the *creation* of man, not man's development thereafter. That is why the debate is billed as Evolutionism vs. Creationism.

Debating whether life started via evolution or divine creation is a chicken/egg inquiry and thus not susceptible of human resolution - not on this plane of existence, in any event.

Imagining the Unimaginable

By analogy, contemplate infinity. Space can't just stop, as the flat earthers once believed - wherever there is an end, by definition, there must be something just beyond that end. But, nothing can go on forever. Can it? This paradox, as it is referred to by scientists, demonstrates the edge of our reality – the outer limits of this plane of existence – and itself demonstrates that there are other realms.

How do we conceive of other realms, as I put it? We don't. Imagine yourself a two-dimensional creature without a hint as to the nature of a third dimension and you get a glint of the difficulty involved. *Flatland, A Romance of Many Dimensions*, a marvelous

41

little novel written by Edwin A. Abbot in the late 1800s, examines this very premise. (*Flatland* is available in full on line, I believe, as it now is in the public domain.)

Even if one plops down solidly on the side of Creationism, there is the nagging question as to who created the Creator. Or His Creator, for that matter. Or... You get the idea.

Even the Bible makes the concept clear...er, clear that it can never be clear to us mere mortals, that is. *"I am that I am."* Parse that. *"Thou cannot look upon me."* Another golden oldie. God usually is depicted in the movies as being a light too bright to be perceived. If understood to be a literary device, then such a surrogate is fine. Problem is, people always want to take things literally, which is another way of saying they will believe what they want to believe, based solely upon their own preconceptions of the meanings of words before them.

I, for one, have no problem with the Bible's description of God as being indescribable. We have no correlates in this reality with which to properly comprehend God. Or infinity of either the spatial or temporal variety, for that matter. We quite literally cannot look upon God because we don't have the right equipment. More accurately, we cannot properly contemplate the nature of God.

Consider the possibility that time does not exist everywhere. Consider a universe organized according to the Dewey Decimal System, rather than the linearity of time. Can't do it, can you? Is time really just Nature's way of keeping everything from happening all at once? Is it possible that things really do happen all at once and we simply choose to perceive them in a temporally linear fashion?

It is important to realize that there are things beyond our capacity to comprehend. Things that always will be beyond our comprehension, in fact.

All religions posit the existence of alternate realities. Some religions argue that this life is but a dream, dreamt by us while we sleep in those other realities. Tough to dispute that. Impossible, in fact, as French philosopher Rene Descartes finally concluded (*cogito, ergo sum*: "*I think, therefore I am*," being as far as he got).

The one constant concept, common to all religions, is a belief in other realities. Realities that we cannot comprehend; not fully, in any event.

I bring all this up simply to illustrate the futility of trying to prove Creationism over Evolutionism...or the reverse, for that matter. Frankly, I see no particular conflict between the two.

Evolution as a Universal Concept

Once created, biological entities evolve; that is, we respond to our environment and adjust accordingly to better survive. In order for something to evolve, something must exist in the first place, from which to evolve, else evolution cannot take place. *Duh.* Yes, an elementary concept, but one that gets lost in all the shouting, and which shows that evolution is not really a creation concept, at all. Besides, creation is a concept beyond our ken, like infinity.

So many Creationists throw the Evolution baby out with the bathwater. Evolution is a fact of life. Always has been. Always will be. Merely because we see only what we are today does not mean we always have been this way or that we always will be. Explain the human appendix, for example, a singularly useless and troublesome organ seemingly left over from some earlier stage of human evolution. Or freckles, for that matter.

Evolution is influenced heavily, if not entirely, by environment and experience. For example, loud noises evoke a startle response from everybody. Why? Because loud noises generally are made by large things. Often, hostile things. Things that might eat you. Only those who possessed and heeded a startle response ran for cover and thereby survived to pass on genes which included that startle response. Eventually, it became ingrained for everybody, since those without it got eaten by large things that made loud noises.

Again, there is no necessary inconsistency between the two ways of looking at the same phenomena. Once created, it seems perfectly reasonable that some evolution will take place in any biological organism.

Winter, a Cog in the Gears of Evolution

IQ ultimately is a product of environment and culture. We hypothesize that a harsher environment naturally selects the more intelligent, those with the ability to foresee hard times in the way of bad winter weather and lay up stores in anticipation. Those who survived nurtured their young and protected them during their formative years. Those who didn't simply perished. Those who survived were naturally selected for further propagation and passed along their DNA-encoded intellect. This scenario supports the IQ breakdown of the races, as those with higher IQs originated in harsher climes.

Blacks, with lower overall IQs, originated in areas where physical prowess ensured one's survival. Intellect only secondarily was rewarded. Even after hundreds of years of interbreeding, the average American Black's IQ still is 10-15 points shy of the average American Caucasian's.

In Africa proper, the average Black IQ falls by another 15-20 points, more reflective of the Black race's true genetic intellect. 30 points is a gulf. No wonder the wheel never occurred to any of them. No wonder that so many still live as they did a thousand years ago, barely eking out a living, eating off the land and eluding predators – some of them still eating one another, in fact. They evolved in the African veldt, where strength and swiftness were rewarded with life, while natural selection doomed lesser physical specimens. Broad, flared nostrils enhance the intake of oxygen, which is used in prodigious quantities by oversize gluteal and thigh muscles in jumping and running, the very physical characteristics that allow Blacks to dominate American sports today.

Again, whether IQ or speediness or a host of other racially differentiable characteristics marks one as superior to another is a situational issue, dependent upon one's needs. Outrunning a lion is much more important in the African savannah than planning for a harsh winter that never comes.

Do you suppose that this fundamental difference is why White people created the greatest civilization known to man? Simply as a byproduct of getting ready for winter each year? After all, without the press of winter, there are lots of projects I simply never would get around to.

Without harsh weather, would we have developed the drive and need to accomplish what now is the hallmark of White civilization? I doubt it. Just as our skin color is a result of northern climates and the lack of a need for lots of melanin, so, too, is our drive a product of fighting the elements simply to survive. The long-term thinking necessary to survive the demands of a harsh winter has become genetic for White people, who still get things done when they move to tropical climates.

Evolution also explains why so little gets done in the ghettos of American cities and why they are such a disaster, every day looking more and more like, well...a jungle. Despite the presence of winter, the response to it - and the concomitant drive and long-term outlook - is not genetically encoded in Blacks.

Instead, evolution explains the short-term mentality and physical aggression of Blacks, who evolved in tropical climes and whose prime environmental adversaries were immediate, in the form of animals, only some of which made loud noises. Their survival mechanisms involved lots of posturing, running and fighting, traits on ready display in America's ghettos.

This disparity in racial evolution also explains why violent interracial crime throughout Western civilization almost exclusively is a one-way proposition: Black on White. For Blacks, Whites represent easy prey, compared to that which evolution provided them previously. As time goes by, Blacks can only soften and become less effective at their ingrained genetic response to their new environments.

For modern Whites, however, Blacks have become but another element in an already hostile environment and likely will make Whites stronger. The White response will be long term, thus lag behind the Black provocation, just as it has seemed to do. The thoughtful and considered White response, evolution tells us, also will be most effective...and permanent. Eventually, simple self preservation will rule.

All because we had to get ready for winter. Imagine.

Culture Gone to Seed

Getting back to our primary discussion, behavior patterns also played a role in natural selection. The foolhardy died and the prudent survived. The brave prevailed and the cowardly fell. There are countless response patterns encoded in each person's DNA, with similar DNA producing similar behavior. It is no surprise that there are racial differences. Here is where cultural stereotypes truly provide a beacon. The Irish predilection for strong drink. German technological superiority. Japanese industriousness and group cohesion. The Black propensity for violence and primal physical satisfaction without regard for consequences.

Caucasians who didn't take care of their mates and young may have survived, but their DNA didn't. Family is a part of White heredity. Without a protective male, the pregnant female would not have made it through the winter. In Africa, family is of far less importance because the constant climate and natural bounty provide ongoing sustenance. This racial difference has been genetically encoded and manifests itself throughout America, despite a similar environment and culture for the two races. But, I get ahead of myself with this line of thinking, properly reserved for Chapter 5, *National Disaster*.

Similarly, *current* environment plays a role in developing one's behavioral responses. Witness the difference in aggressive survival skills demonstrated by street-smart city children, versus their guileless country cousins, though born of the same racial stock.

Even with superior weaponry, American soldiers repeatedly have been bested by guerilla fighters defending their own countries, stark examples of the advantage of a complementarity of environment with man. Think of the Sherpas, able to function at altitudes where others cannot even breathe. Practiced often enough, through sufficient generations, adaptive behavior sinks into one's DNA and is passed along automatically, enabling one to adapt to one's historical culture and environment effortlessly.

Akin to the twins studies, there have been studies of families which have adopted children born of other races, both as babies and some already partially raised, both within America and without. Predictably, trouble comes packaged with children from other cultures far in excess of that generated by the parents' natural children. Results suggest that racial differences are of far more significance than culture. In other words, a White family can expect far greater difficulty after adopting a Black child from within America than a European child of Caucasian heritage. Imagine that same family with a Bantu adolescent, possessed of a less-than-room-temperature IQ and eons of jungle-bred DNA, fresh off the plane.

Intellect, Yet Again

Admittedly, some racial behavior differences are the direct result of racial intellectual disparity. But that is only part of the answer, exemplified by test scores. Nor are intracultural racial differences attributable to economics except in the dreams of dedicated leftists. Extreme example: Whites in America from families with incomes below $10,000 have average SAT test scores that are 46 points higher than American Blacks whose family incomes range from $80,000 to $100,000. See Chapter 5, *National Disaster,* for an extended discussion of racial differences in SAT scoring.

Early beliefs and experiences are the most powerful, as they provide the lens through which all future experience is perceived. And perception is everything, as they say. Hayakawa's landmark work, *"Language in Thought and Action,"* makes this point eloquently and convincingly. What Hayakawa missed, however, was the role played by genetically-encoded behavioral responses, which provide the very first lenses through which reality is filtered. Easy to miss, since they function the same as behavioral response patterns acquired from one's current environment.

To recap:

Behavior is the product of genetics, culture and environment.

The genetic component gives rise to profound racial differences.

Very little intellectual influence can be expected to overwhelm established behavioral response patterns, whether learned or inherited, even less as one's IQ declines.

Character is the manifestation of certain behavioral response patterns and, thus, differs markedly between the races.

Character is of far greater import than mere IQ.

While variations in character make life interesting, character traits such as those leading to violent outbursts can be quite dangerous.

In early 2003, the American Food and Drug Administration ordered that racial information be collected by researchers conducting clinical trials. Even before that, however, medical studies repeatedly showed numerous interracial differences between Whites and Blacks.

For example, tests have proven conclusively that Black men produce testosterone at levels higher than that produced by White men. This is why Blacks are so much more prone to prostate cancer, the fuel for which is testosterone. This also is why Black men are much more aggressive than Whites. Doctors profile Blacks. This is both reasonable and proper. So should the police, of course. Blacks do it to themselves, with justification, and are far more concerned about violence at the hands of their fellow Blacks than from Whites.

Descendants of races brought together from different cultures and environments must live with the consequences of differing genetic backgrounds, though they share a similar milieu from birth. This is the state in which White and Black America find themselves today, standing literally on the brink of a national disaster the likes of which has occurred repeatedly down through history...as we shall talk about next.

Chapter 5

National Disaster

"I am not, nor ever have been in favor of bringing about in any way the social and political equality of the White and Black races. I am not nor ever have been in favor of making voters or jurors of negroes, nor qualifying them to hold office, nor to intermarry with White people; and I will say in addition to this that there is a physical difference between the White and Black races which I believe will ever forbid the two races living together on terms of social and political equality."
--- President Abraham Lincoln, the "Great Emancipator," *Fourth Debate with Stephen Douglas* at Charleston, Illinois, September 18, 1858

"As flies to wanton boys, are we to the gods;
They kill us for their sport."
--- William Shakespeare, *King Lear*

To some, racism arises from the simple preference of the company of those of one's own ethnic background over that of others. *Of course, such conduct is racist only when engaged in by White people.* Most imply an element of false superiority when invoking the term *"racist,"* thus it has fallen from favor among even the politically incorrect. That is why some who so unabashedly speak of racial differences as the basis for favoring one's own nonetheless prefer the term "racialist."

Most of us prefer the company of members of our own family to that of others. Showing racial preference is the logical extension of showing family or community preference. Stand by your man. Be true to your school. That sort of thing. Why must it be any different as the circle widens enough to encompass one's own racial group? "I love Mom and Dad" doesn't threaten other parents. "I love the human race" isn't a despised sentiment. How did something on the same continuum, "I love the white race," come to be invested with such negative freight?

Thought Criminals

The politically correct see no difference between "racist" and "racialist," because they pretend there are no differences among the races except skin color and economic class. In fact, the politically correct dismiss all who dare speak of obvious racial differences as being racist. Thus, the entire topic is set off limits to discussion or investigation, with the consequence that serious scientific researchers either adjust their findings to the establishment viewpoint (their predecessors condemned Galileo and proclaimed the Earth to be flat in the face of overwhelming evidence to the contrary) or become marginalized (defunded, in the case of researchers, or fired, in the case of employees, or simply killed, in the case of so many down through the ages). The most glaring example of political correctness erecting a false ideological construct astride science today might well be found in the area of IQ measurement.

The sole exception to the racist "no-go zone" is invocation of the term "racist" to vilify another, either socially or judicially. Baseless vilification of this sort has been done repeatedly down through history, as in Salem with the witch hunts or in the Middle Ages, via the Inquisition. The parallels are aptly made, since those guilty today of racism, via hate crimes or "Holocaust denial," for example, are routinely sent to prison throughout the Western world. Executions have resulted from the enhancement of criminal penalties, engendered by laws governing racism.

Thus, a charge of racism is seen for what it really is: thought crime – thinking and expressing thoughts inconsistent with the establishment's point of view, though such thoughts were perfectly legal until very recently.

Racist Pressures Building

The politically correct believe that their approach is working, due to an apparent decrease in overt racism. They are wrong, as the politically incorrect are well aware. Racism merely has gone underground in polite society and is building pressure, like a steam boiler without a release valve – a release valve plugged by societal condemnation and repressive hate crime laws. Witness the ever-growing resentment of affirmative action on both the left and the right in America. The pressure is aggravated by a sense of entitlement and victimhood engendered in so many minority groups. A disaster of mythical proportions looms over the American landscape, awaiting only the spark of ignition.

Simultaneously, there is a growing recognition in America that White separatists might not be the racists that the media would have us believe. Separatism merely is the act of being or living apart from others possessing specified characteristics. Want to live in a low-crime area? Near good schools? Then you are a separatist, because those are characteristics that do not exist in multiethnic neighborhoods. Separatism might be racism, but if it is, then most Whites are racist. Removing separatist tendencies and forcing full integration upon society is a very recent phenomenon in America, but not to the rest of the world, whose experience would be instructive, if only we were inclined to pay attention.

Recipe for Disaster

Race mixing has led to many national disasters down through

history, the most noteworthy of which involve the fall of empires, a topic we will take up in Chapter 7, *The Price of Empire*. Lesser national disasters look a lot like today's South Africa and Zimbabwe (*nee* Rhodesia). Both countries were founded by European expatriates and both were sparsely populated by indigenous populations at their founding. Both grew to substantial size and wealth, exporting agricultural products and natural resources, the most prized being gold and diamonds.

Blacks were imported to Southern Africa from other parts of the continent to provide labor and prospered as well, albeit at a pace far behind that of the resident White population. With a good deal of help from liberal elements in both America and Europe, Blacks seized political power. Thus began the downfall of two formerly great countries.

Today, White farmers are extinct in Zimbabwe and becoming extinct in South Africa. With the backing of anti-White governments, Blacks have invaded White-owned farms and slaughtered White farmers and their families. Crime has become rampant in both countries, with violent Black-on-White crime, especially rape and murder, being the most pervasive and most ignored. This is nothing short of genocide, with Whites who do not flee reduced to living in bunkers which are proving not to be the safe havens intended.

Moreover, both countries have become net consumer states, versus net providers a short time ago. White-owned farms have been broken up and rendered nonproductive, with both livestock and seed corn consumed by the Black squatters, who have no apparent concern for the future. The native population is...well, going native.

Let Them Eat Cake

In 2002, Brian Williams, the MSNBC anchor slated to replace Tom Brokaw as NBC's network news anchor, penned an article posted on MSNBC's web site entitled, *"The Struggle to Survive in Malawi,"* about a small country near the southern tip of the African continent. He attributed the rampant starvation there to *"years of bad harvest, erratic weather and the devastation of AIDS."* He noted that those conditions were becoming endemic throughout Africa.

But, as is so typical of the controlled media today, Mr. Williams neglected to note that this famine has been self-inflicted. He didn't say a word about how the vast farms of Zimbabwe, *nee* Rhodesia, in particular, which fed so many Africans until recently, have been lain fallow. Why? Because it is the Black Africans who are responsible, you see.

Zimbabwean farmers, so productive that they had been supporting far more than the population of their own country, have been removed from their farms, if not killed outright, due to the racist policies of their Black government rulers.

"Kill the Boer, kill the farmer," a phrase first uttered by ANC member of Parliament Peter Mokaba, was the mantra shouted aloft by crowds of Blacks at all manner of public meetings and demonstrations. The South African Human Rights Commission called this slogan, not hate speech, but merely an exercise of *"the constitutional right to free speech."*

Thousands of South African and Zimbabwean farmers and farm workers and their families now have been murdered by roving bands of young African Blacks, while authorities have stood by and literally watched, in what is nothing more than "ethnic cleansing," a euphemism for genocide.

The remaining White farmers are unable to leave their country because other countries, notably America, erect impassable immigration barriers to Whites, while allowing a flood of nonWhites across their borders.

You don't hear about the carnage in Zimbabwe because it is politically incorrect to note the murder of Whites by Blacks anywhere in the world today. Zimbabwe President Thabo Mbeki calls the execution of White farm owners and workers, *"the final stage of the revolution."* Final because, presumably, they are running out of White people to slaughter.

In the article referenced above, Mr. Williams stated that, *"donations keep these people alive. The U.S. is the single largest donor, but there is only enough food to feed 500,000 people, just one sixth of what they need."* Touching, indeed, but not nearly the whole story, as we see by bringing in the South African connection.

And, of course, those TV commercials depicting the fly-ridden, emaciated Black children of Africa fail to note that these kids would be well fed if the White African farmers had been left alone.

I know, those kids didn't kill the farmers and slaughter the livestock and cut up the farms to squat on and eat the seed corn in the sheds and so on, but there is a limit to those for whom I will feel responsible. Just now, we have malnourished children in America, for example.

African Blacks, both those in government and those in the death squads, are responsible. They have killed their golden-egg-laying goose and have nobody to blame but themselves for today's lack of food.

Of course, we in America who were so instrumental in driving Whites out of political power in Africa must shoulder some responsibility, too. All the American liberals formerly so adamant about boycotting companies doing business with South Africa have morphed into neoconservatives and now care only about killing the enemies of Israel (including hundreds of thousands of Arab children). They certainly show no concern about the murder of White children in Africa.

Now we are expected to feed Africa, though that continent possesses the most verdant soil in the world which, if cultivated properly, could serve as breadbasket to the rest of the human race.

Just as we have created a welfare class in America, which will persist so long as we continue the handouts, and which is an undeniable magnet to hordes of illegal immigrants, now we are expected to extend that mentality to other countries, as well. It isn't working here. It won't work there.

They wanted total self determination. Now they want all Whites killed or driven from their countries while we open our borders to them and feed their starving populations.

Let them eat cake.

The African Lesson Ignored

I have heard the African tragedies dismissed by liberals who sniff, "Well, this is the first time the African Blacks have experienced real freedom, so a few missteps are to be expected." These people ignore reality.

For example, Liberia was founded shortly after Australia, with a constitution modeled on America's. Today, Australia ranks in the first tier of nations. Recently, Liberia once again collapsed into widespread anarchy. Or Ethiopia. Independent since 1855, save only four years when it was occupied by Italy (1936-1940), Ethiopia was host to the single greatest man-made famine ever known, in 1985.

What is taking place in Africa today was as predictable as night following day. One need only have observed the behavior of Blacks in the rest of Africa to foresee precisely how things might go in South Africa and Zimbabwe. Tragically, nobody took notice. More tragically, that lesson, played out all over again in Southern Africa, seems lost on modern America.

After all is said and done, the best way to tell where you are going is to turn around and look at where you are coming from. Based on that analysis, things are going to get much worse in southern Africa, more akin to what is taking place elsewhere on the continent, where superstition is rampant and cannibalism still exists. South Africa's experience may loom on the horizon for America, as well. Could cannibalism actually come to North America, do you suppose?

America's Looming Disaster

Thus far, we have seen that we inherit appearance, intellect and a good deal of behavior from our ancestors, with there being substantial racial differences in all three areas. We know that character is a collection of behavioral response patterns, most of which are directly inherited (breeding shows, as they say). Now we also know that there is an inverse relationship between IQ and the degree to which our DNA governs our behavior, with the result that those of lesser intellects are bound to repeat the behavior of their forebears to a degree far greater than those of higher intellect.

The average African Black's IQ is about 70, thereby placing a significant portion of the African population into the range of the mentally retarded. It is scarcely surprising that they are almost entirely governed by inherited behavioral response patterns, passed to them from their ancestors via DNA.

Even the Blacks now ruling South Africa and Zimbabwe agree that they preside over burgeoning national disasters, while simultaneously seeking aid of all forms from Europe and America. Whereas once they exported food in abundance, now their populations are starving. All this on the continent that arguably is the richest in natural resources on the planet. The reason is obvious to those willing to see.

What is less clear is that America , too, stands on the edge of its own racial national disaster, and for the same reasons. The American disaster will take a different form, if for no other reason than the fact that Blacks comprise only 13% of the total American population. Then, too, the average Black IQ is higher than that of their African cousins, though 15 points less than the White average of 100...still a gulf.

Brown vs. the Bored

Fifty years. Two generations. That's all it took to transform the leading public educational system of all time into something on a par with third-world countries. After hundreds of thousands, even millions, of years of evolution, it took just fifty years for America to devolve its educational miracle into something on par with Senegal.

And now, the remaining human capital of America's former educational investment is being tossed on the scrap heap, thanks to NAFTA, GATT, WTO and the New World Order of America.

Meanwhile, the last gasp of America's intellectual prowess, its great University system, increasingly is reserved for foreigners (who pay more in tuition), illegal immigrants (who pay little or nothing) and, of course, "minority" students, upon whom endless advanced placement (all out of proportion to anything resembling merit) and full-ride scholarships are lavished. Jews, who comprise fully half the students at many American Ivy League schools like Harvard, are counted as White, therefore the reported figures for true European Whites are skewed well beyond their true nature. What is happening to White Americans of European extraction certainly rhymes with "skewed."

White Americans, descendants of those who created America's great Universities and for whom they specifically were created, either are shunted aside in favor of far-less-qualified "minority" students or simply cannot afford the cost of attendance. Public schools today cost what private colleges did in my day. Today, many college Graduate School classes, both public and private, are conducted without a single White face present! In my day, I would have been relegated to menial labor, but for the facts that (1) college was cheap enough for

59

me to attend by working part time and (2) I was granted entry based upon my intellectual and academic merit.

In fifty years, virtually all of America's top industrial and professional positions held today by qualified White Americans will be filled by multi-hued beneficiaries of that odd form of racism called affirmative action. Except for those held by Jews, of course, which will continue to be held by, you guessed it - Jews. Long before then, however, America will self destruct through sheer incompetence, because you simply cannot keep savages out of the seed corn.

Think not? Look at what is happening today in Zimbabwe (*nee* Rhodesia) and South Africa, wherein the White intelligentsia recently was replaced by Blacks (often through murder, quite often accompanied by rape and, occasionally, even cannibalism). The first thing they did upon stealing the White farms was, literally, to eat the seed corn and butcher the production livestock. Today, they have the hubris to exclaim that they haven't enough to eat and then demand that the UN (America, that is) feed them. Think it can't happen here?

If the controlled media would report it, you would hear of the staggering levels of Black-on-White murder and rape that occurs already in America, at a rate in excess of fifty times that committed by White Americans. Of course, it won't be reported, because they know that the wholesale slaughter of America's Black population would begin the next morning.

To think, it all began with a single US Supreme Court case, issued fifty years ago on May 17, 1954: *Brown vs. The Board of Education of Topeka*, which overturned the "separate but equal" mandate of its prior ruling in *Plessy vs. Ferguson*, which itself was issued fifty years prior to that day. In denying appellant Plessy's claim that racial separation marked Blacks as inferior, *per se*, the previous Court quite accurately stated, *"The argument also assumes that social prejudices may be overcome by legislation, and that equal rights cannot be secured to the negro except by an enforced*

60

commingling of the two races. We cannot accept this proposition. If the two races are to meet upon terms of social equality, it must be the result of natural affinities, a mutual appreciation of each other's merits and a voluntary consent of individuals." In both my personal and professional opinion, the *Plessy* decision was one of the last rational statements on race uttered by an American court.

In 1954, the *Brown* court stood the *Plessy* decision on its head, ruling that, after all, equal rights could result only from an "enforced commingling," in an end run straight out of the Marxist playbook.

Legislation by Judicial Fiat Begins

The *Brown* court also marked a sea change in American jurisprudence. At long last, the US Constitution simply was cast aside and the court directly engaged in what it, itself, previously had referred to as "legislating." What's more, its legislation was based upon specious sociological theorizing, too, not law, not evidence and not facts. Absolutely without a legal basis, fifty years of history have disproven the possibility of there having been any factual basis for the *Brown* decision. Meanwhile, the Supreme Court has moved well into the territory of nonstop legislation, especially the legislation of morality (actually, the lack of morality, some would argue). Marx and Lenin must be smiling down...er, up...on America, from wherever they are these days.

Fifty years. You be the judge. Supporters of the *Brown* ruling maintain that the American racial gap has been partially closed during the ensuing fifty years. That appears to be true, but is illusory. One of the enduring legacies of the *Brown* decision: America's white children have been dumbed down due to an emphasis upon teaching to the bottom of all classes, a bottom that is much lower as a result of full integration. In that regard, the gap actually has narrowed, but not in the direction they would have you believe. As we will see later in this chapter, the rest of the illusion derives from the jiggering of SAT scores along racial lines.

Never mind that the American educational system has been destroyed in the process. Never mind that American White European history has been rewritten, nay, erased. Never mind that the birthright, the legacy, the very promise of White American youth all have been sacrificed on the altar of political correctness.

Brown vs. the Bored, that's how the case really should be remembered. No, not as in the disinterested, but as in the *screwed*.

Here's a fact that you can take to the bank: There are differences in the races quite aside from the obvious physical appearance and capability differences. Those differences result primarily from genetics, not environment (nature, not nurture). And I am not the first, simply among the more vocal, to say so just lately.

Racial IQ Differences

Hernnstein and Murray conclusively documented racial IQ differences in their landmark work, *The Bell Curve* (1994). No, it has not been discredited, despite media propaganda to the contrary. To the everlasting chagrin of the liberal establishment, every study and test designed to discredit *The Bell Curve* has served only to buttress its results. IQ tests devised by Blacks, for Blacks, employing exclusively Black references, idioms and imagery, when given to both Whites and Blacks, reveal precisely the same IQ differences between the races as traditional IQ tests. Facts are facts.

Does this make Blacks inferior to Whites as human beings? Absolutely not. That is a conclusion pressed only by the very racist leftists in America today, in explanation of why they demand that racial parity in test scores be achieved. That is like White America demanding that White runners finish in a photo tie with the Kenyans at the Boston Marathon. Facts are facts. Wishes will not make things any different. Get over it.

Oddly enough, the very right wingers who get accused of being racist are, in fact, the least racist because they generally do not see lesser IQs as being a mark of inferiority. Yet another demonstration of how far through the Looking Glass America has come, such that so many things are precisely the opposite of what they may seem...and regardless of what the Red Queen educational establishment might declare, as well.

Ignoring racial IQ differences and demanding proportionate representation of all races in all of society's venues has produced a monumental tragedy in the making. Because of the huge disparity between white and black IQs, clearly unqualified blacks get propelled into positions of responsibility well beyond their ability to cope, let alone succeed. And we have yet to discuss the very substantial behavioral differences between the races, differences which ultimately prove to be so critical.

It has been estimated that an IQ of 130 is required to be senior executive material in both the private sector and governmental service. Blacks with an IQ at or above 130 virtually do not exist, understandable when you consider that 130 is over 4 full standard deviations above the mean Black IQ of 85 in America.

The authors of *The Bell Curve,* noted above, concluded that there are just 4,500 American Blacks in the entire American population with a college degree and an IQ of 130+, with over 15 *million* companies vying to hire them.

The IQ level for Blacks which evens them up proportionally (though not numerically) with Whites who have IQs of 130+ is 115, which still produces very few qualified candidates, each and every one of whom gets promoted well above his or her ability level. Only 2% of Blacks, about 1300 *total* each year, even possess an IQ that makes them proper college material. That compares to 25% of Whites, or about 650,000 would-be students.

The Legacy of Affirmative Action

In 2002, only 29 *total* American Black students qualified for a top-ten law school without any sort of boost from diversity programs, versus 4,500 White students nationwide. 420 Black students found places at a top-ten law school that year, however. This story is repeated at all colleges and universities, of every level and in every discipline, with the result that virtually *every* Black is in over his or her head.

Predictably, virtually all Black law students are at the bottoms of their classes and have much lower bar exam passage rates. The same is true of all professional programs. Once admitted to their respective professions, these same Blacks fall far short of the standards set by their White colleagues. Of course, *these indicia of failure are attributed to white racism and unwillingness to recruit,* leading to yet more governmental intrusion via the court system. Advanced placement begets relative failure, which begets still more judicially-mandated advanced placement, in a neverending vicious cycle. How can smart people be so dumb?

The competition among colleges, where "diversity" has attained the status of a religion, to confer scholarships and other benefits upon qualified Blacks is ferocious.

The greatest tragedy, perhaps, is found in the large number of Blacks who are hired over the heads of more-qualified Whites, yet who function only slightly above the level of what is considered mentally retarded in America.

What's more, in virtually all these cases, *the Blacks involved become convinced that active white racism is the real problem,* not their own lack of aptitude or skills. It is, after all, only human to psychologically project our failures onto those around us. This is made especially easy when national leaders of every skin color join the media in vilifying White Americans for their pernicious and pervasive racism. White managers know better, of course, but prefer to take the rap rather than tell the truth and get fired outright.

One can only wonder at the role this over-promotion of blacks has had upon America's industry fleeing overseas altogether, either shipping its assembly lines there or agitating for the immigration of foreigners to be granted H-1B visas as knowledge workers. During 2001 and 2002, nearly 800,000 H-1B visas were issued or renewed, during a time of rapidly rising US employment, particularly in the very category for which low-paid H-1B workers primarily are imported: high technology.

Racial SAT Differences

Not surprisingly, racial differences in IQ are what result in the very real and generally intractable racial differences in educational achievement. No amount of busing, no reduction in the teacher/student ratio and no amount of money thrown at schools will make the slightest difference in this outcome. Facts are facts, as the past fifty years have proven.

In Washington, DC, which has the highest per-student expenditures on public schooling, the best-paid teachers and some of the lowest teacher/student ratios in the country, the 1998 SAT disclosed that, while 54% of Whites scored at or above proficiency in reading...only 9% of the Blacks and 11% of the Mestizos did so, per the US Department of Education. This result is duplicated all over America, and at all grade levels.

Yes, this is the same testing regimen that has shown a narrowing of the gap between Whites and Blacks in recent years: The SAT, or Scholastic Assessment Test, the new, politically-correct name for what used to be known as the Scholastic *Aptitude* Test, a title which had to be changed to reflect the political ideology that there are no racial aptitude differences. But, the narrowing did not come about as a result of Black improvement. On the contrary.

White achievement scores have declined, to be sure, consistent with the abysmal decline in educational quality received in America's public schools over the past fifty years (no child left behind means no child out in front). In the past 40 years, SAT scores overall have declined by over 100 points, a decline which does not include adjustments for jiggering the SAT's scoring template to create the illusion of a narrowing gap.

In 1995, the SAT scoring approach was "recentered," a purposely convoluted process designed to mask the abject failure of America's educational system. The "recentering," a euphemism for the jiggering, resulted in the arbitrary addition to White scores of 100 points, while Black scores were elevated by 130 points (Asians got 90 points and Mestizos 120 points). This overall increase, aside from the absolute advantage awarded to skin color alone, *caused the percentage differences to decline*, which is what is crowed over by the liberal educational establishment.

The rejiggering of test scores in 1995 to narrow the percentage gap highlights yet another important element of SAT scoring: padding. Each student receives 400 points simply for showing up...another device with the sole purpose of masking the percentage differentials in racial SAT scores. When the 400-point padding and the 90-130-point "recentering" bulges are removed, the percentage difference between Whites and Blacks mushrooms from 39% (a significant number in its own right) to a staggering 69%, or *a raw score of 328 for Blacks and 554 for Whites, an astounding and insurmountable gap*.

Incredible, isn't it? Actually, the truly incredible thing is how far the Red Queen educational establishment is willing to go in order to delude the American public, not to mention itself, into believing that it is doing its job, when the test results lead one to precisely the opposite conclusion.

Nor does the myth about family income hold water. Parents' income has next to no effect upon the outcome of their children's test scores (see, generally, *The Black-White Test Score Gap*, by Jencks and Phillips, 1988).

Intellectual Ghettos

In the not-so-distant past, there was a pretty even distribution of intellects all through American society.   Before the Industrial Revolution, very few jobs required high intelligence.   All that changed during the past few generations, with the change accelerating as the "Information Age" swept through America.

Today, the professions draw the most intelligent and concentrate them in urban centers. From the ghettos of the cities escape the more intelligent minorities, who move into white surroundings. As the new, highly-paid elite, they can afford to buy their way into the best neighborhoods and place their children in private schools.

Today, the economic middle class, even with two bread-winners the day's standard, cannot match the elite, either for themselves or for their children.

An American underclass, earmarked by lesser intelligence and low income, has been created. Serfs, if you will. But worse than in times past. Since the upward mobility available to the intellectually accomplished and ambitious moves the smarter serfs out, those left behind are astoundingly dull. The underclass is composed of many races, including poor whites, though lower- and middle-class Blacks and Mexicans predominate. The American underclass is notable for low intellect, low education and hostility. Respect for authority is nonexistent and a "you owe me" attitude has been inculcated by the burgeoning welfare system of the past fifty years.

Though the rural areas have been in decline for years because the best and brightest left for the city, crime in the rural areas did not increase until the Mexicans began to arrive in significant numbers. In other words, the crime associated with city ghettos is due not to the generally-lesser intellects found there, but rather to something else altogether, something which I prefer to call character.

The intellectually accomplished have become the elite and financially privileged. They have become divorced from their much duller countrymen and absolutely fail to comprehend the mentality extant in America's underclass. The bright cannot conceive of someone who might never have read a single book, for example, and labor under the delusion that anybody can learn anything and can get ahead in life, just as did they, if only they want it strongly enough. None so dumb as those so bright.

It is the elite who push multiculturalism, diversity and affirmative action. They are out of touch and intellectually untouchable. They will be warned away from this book and others like it by America's Zionist masters, in an attempt to keep the elite just as they are, locked away in a fairy-tale castle of multi-hued harmony, unaware of the gritty subtext of reality which resides just outside their zone of awareness.

The elite seem blissfully unaware of the growing resentment in all segments of society beyond their own inbred world, a resentment that one day will erupt and result in a massive restructuring of American society. It will be the intellectually elite, concentrated in cities, who will be the first to pay the ultimate price when their elaborate house of cards falls to the ground. Not even the right skin color will protect the "haves" in those days from the wrath of the "have-nots."

The American Coup

Is the dumbing down of White America and the smokescreen covering racial test score differences accidental? No. Nothing is accidental. Designed to compensate for racial inequity? No, that never was the intent, as even a cursory glance at testing scores both then and now discloses. Why, then? Because fifty years ago is about when the coup that now is reaching completion in America began in earnest.

Fifty years ago the Zionist financial cabal decided it was possible to take over America as completely and thoroughly as it had Russia a mere half century prior to that time. Of course, America had been targeted a hundred years ago, along with so many European nations. Key to the goal of taking America was removal from power of the White European stock that founded America and had been firmly in control ever since. Much, much more on this is coming up in the final chapters of this book.

As was true in Jewish-controlled Russia of the 1920s, the next step for America is adoption of laws mandating prison for expressions of anti-Semitism (several now pend before Congress). Death for anti-Semitism will follow, mark my words, just as it did in Russia. At first, it will be masked, as other laws are misapplied, just as today's hate crime laws are misapplied as hate speech laws.

Now that the average American has come to believe that hate speech is illegal, the laws (also pending before Congress) outlawing pure speech are being put into place. It will happen the same way until "Say the J-word and die" becomes a reality. Just ask 20-80 million Russian Christians - oh, sorry, you can't ask them *because they are all dead*, killed by Russia's Jewish masters last century, many if not most simply for being anti-Semitic (and being Christian is all that it ever has taken to be called anti-Semitic). Much more on this in Chapter 12, *The Truth Hurts*.

The First Victims

Aside from the people felled every day in the street by the race war already raging throughout America, the first victims of the failing social experiment that America has become are those least able to protect themselves: the very young and the very old.

Illegal immigration effectively has led to denial of required medical treatment, drugs and emergency care to the elderly throughout America. Though symptomatic throughout America, this shortfall is most acutely felt by those trapped "behind enemy lines," in areas that see the greatest influx of illegals.

In California, major HMOs have pulled out of the MediCal system, resulting in the effective denial to our elderly of necessary services which now must be used, by judicial fiat, for those here illegally. By 2004, over half of Los Angeles County's emergency rooms, trauma centers and healthcare clinics had been forced to close down due to lack of funding, leading to still more elderly denied necessary treatment and drugs. Resultant cost increases mean that our elderly sometimes must choose between necessary medication or food when allocating their already-meager fixed incomes.

Children of the "almost poor," who do not qualify for the medical care mandated free for illegals, also do without.

This scenario is being repeated all through the states that border Mexico and, increasingly, in other states where immigrants have flocked. Health insurance premiums throughout America rise in direct response to losses and cost increases suffered in the states most affected.

The elderly and the children are but the first victims of a health-care crisis that will affect all but the richest Americans before it runs its course.

Equal Outcome, not Equal Opportunity

I like to preach about dealing with root causes, not symptoms. Black American supremacy is but a symptom of what is wrong with America. Black supremacy has been used to weaken White America, to loosen its grip on the levers of power.

Black and Jewish racism both have been erected against White America, producing the affirmative action, quotas and racial preferences which resulted from decisions such as *Brown vs. Board of Education.*

Simple racial equality is all that is sought today by White America, simple equality in opportunity, despite what the controlled media would have you believe.

What we are being forced to shoulder is equality of outcome. Problem is, it's the Black outcome that Whites are receiving, not the other way around. Used to be, Johnny could read and 'Rastus couldn't. Now, Johnny can barely read, while 'Rastus still can't.

By insisting upon equal outcomes, the cabal astride America demonstrates that it will not be happy until neither Johnny nor 'Rastus can read, since it simply is not genetically in the cards for both to be able to read well. Only then will we have true racial equality, to their way of thinking. In truth, then is when we will be too stupid to challenge their authority over us. Then is when our enslavement will be complete.

It is no crime to demand racial equality in America...unless you are White, of course. That is what must change.

Criminal Behavior

A goodly portion of the behavioral response patterns encoded in DNA by Africa's jungle habitat still remains in America's Blacks. We see it manifested in Black street gang behavior on a daily basis.

Paved With Good Intentions is a masterpiece written by Jared Taylor in 1993 and subtitled *"The Failure of Race Relations in Contemporary America."* Taylor shreds the lie placed upon racial criminal statistics in America. His extensive studies of published government figures and statistics, particularly those of the US Justice Department, found that:

60% of all those killed by police are Black.

58% of all arrests for weapons violations are of Blacks.

64% of all violent crime arrests are of Blacks.

73% of all "self-defense" killings are by Blacks (and almost exclusively *of* Blacks, too).

60% of all Blacks are armed with a weapon at all times.

Blacks commit 8 times the number of assaults committed by Whites.

Blacks commit 9 times the rapes committed by Whites.

Blacks commit 14 times the murders committed by Whites.

Blacks commit 19 times the armed robberies committed by Whites.

Black neighborhoods are 35 times as violent as those of Whites.

If you believe what you see and hear in America's controlled media, you believe that Whites commit the vast majority of interracial crime. The truth overwhelmingly is just the opposite: *Blacks commit 90% of interracial crime.*

Australian journalist Paul Sheehan's researches disclosed that *Blacks murder Whites at 18 times the rate that Whites murder Blacks* (*The Race War of Black Against White,* Sydney Morning Herald, May 20, 1995). Since Blacks comprise only 13% of the American population, *a White American is an incredible 126 times more likely to be murdered by a Black* than *vice versa.* Sheehan also found that *Blacks are raping or attempting to rape one-half million White American women each year.*

Interestingly, Sheehan also learned that, in the thirty years since

72

the civil rights marches of the 1960s, *violent Black crime committed against White Americans increased at a rate four times the rate of increase of that against Blacks!* In that same time period, Blacks murdered 45,000 White Americans, less than the 58,000 men lost in the Viet Nam war, but significantly more than the 34,000 killed during the Korean War. Keep in mind that now, eleven years later, the Viet Nam total certainly has been surpassed.

Already, a racial war of epic proportions is raging in the streets of America, with its existence and extent masked by both the controlled media and the American government at all levels. *And this has been during good economic times!* It has become an increasingly bad joke in the Patriot community that perpetrators are identified in they media only when they are White, while Black crimes largely go unreported altogether.

As America slides into what now seems inevitable – a second economic Depression – the underclass will take to the streets *en masse* because government will prove incapable of providing, as in the past. South Central LA riots writ large, all across America.

America has operated under the assumption that White/Black differences are socioeconomic only, thus wrongly assuming that interracial problems would respond to socioeconomic stratagems. That was a grave error, akin to the relatively recent medical practice of treating disease with leaches and bloodletting. Out goes the bad air, in comes the good air. Sure. America is doomed as surely as so many who died in times past from similarly arrogant medical blundering.

We erroneously believed that affirmative action, quotas, set asides, preferences and welfare would provide a temporary bandaid, a hand up for Blacks to attain socioeconomic parity with Whites. Then, such programs could be discarded and we would live in multi-hued bliss. This literally was the rationale taught in law school in the seventies (and today, probably) for favoring one racial class over another.

I recall hearing my Constitutional Law professor muse that the new century would be one of true equality, allowing us to dispense with preferential treatment after a single generation. A recent US Supreme Court decision saw Justice O'Connor make the same argument, extending the time line by another 25 years, however, yet another generation.

Because of the inherent racial differences between Whites and Blacks, Whites always will have to be handicapped in order to provide equal outcomes for Blacks. Get used to affirmative action, because it is here to stay. The good news is that "here to stay" won't be long, because America simply won't last that long. At least, not America as currently comprised. Of course, *that is the bad news, as well.*

Prison Planet

America jails more of its citizenry, by far, than any other nation in the history of the planet. Currently, our rate is 600% higher than the nation considered the most repressive by America's current ruling elite: China. Well over 2 million people now languish in cells throughout America. Canada, actually leading America in the Police State sweepstakes, matches only China in its rate of incarceration, but, then, Canada does not yet possess the minorities roaming the streets of America.

While America's Black population has doubled in the last fifty years, *the Black prison population has jumped by 900%.* A result of White racism, many like to say, though the truth is that fewer Blacks go to jail who deserve such than do Whites, in a manifestation of the reverse racism that has swept America with a vengeance.

Consider what the Black on White crime statistics, already outlandish, might be if so many Black criminals weren't locked up right this minute.

Today America outlaws so many things that weren't crimes even a single generation ago, a fact that contributes to the large number of Americans in jail. America now has an extensive population of political prisoners, mostly Whites, targeted by various governmental agencies for speaking out against a government increasingly out of control. They have been taken down on charges that can be characterized only as thought crimes and then so vilified in the media that they dare not stand before a jury eager to demonstrate its commitment to political correctness. Thus, they are forced to plead out to sentences in cases that would never even be brought against ordinary citizens. The pretextual convictions are of real crimes either altogether trumped up or fomented by governmental *agents provocateur*.

The cost of imprisonment is crushing American governments at every level, each of which already is overspending its budget in record amounts. California estimates that each prisoner costs it $35,000 per year to incarcerate, with juvenile offenders costing even more.

Like war suppliers, the crime "industry" has become so large that now it is self perpetuating. Crime has become altogether too important to the government and too profitable to the government's suppliers of prisons and related goods and services ever to be reduced in terms of punishment meted out. Meanwhile, being "tough on crime" has become the touchstone of most election campaigns, what with the differences in political parties having been reduced to a minimum.

Racial Separation by Right

Remember, with this book I construct the thesis that some forms of racism might be a good thing, at least some of the time. For that to be true requires good reasons and a rationale that withstands the charge of "Hate" for its own sake. I propose that rationale to be twofold: personal preference, on the one hand, and safety, on the other.

All will agree that we have the right to associate with our own family members, to the exclusion of others. So, too, is it our constitutional right to associate freely within our society. As a corollary, we should have a right not to associate with others, as well. Just as outsiders have no right to enter my family's home and associate with us in that setting, so should Americans have a right to band together and live apart from others, solely because of desire. The US Supreme court disagrees. So much for personal preference and individual rights.

Racial Separation for Physical Safety

However, the US Supreme Court *does* agree that a certain class of people should be segregated from the rest of us for our physical protection: criminals. Therefore, even America's current society allows for the separation of classes of people for certain purposes if physical safety of the population is threatened. I submit that a simple extension of this court-approved logic demands that Blacks be separated from Whites.

American Blacks comprise about $1/7^{th}$ the total population. American Blacks commit seven times the total violent interracial crime that American Whites commit. Do the math: Blacks are fifty times as likely to commit violent interracial crimes as are Whites. Interracial crime, overwhelmingly Black on White, has claimed more American lives in the past generation than the Korean war and nearly as many as did Viet Nam. Already, there is a racial war being waged in the streets of America.

The Inevitable Race War

Psychological testing has revealed that, in addition to differing IQs, there are a great many other interracial differences, which relate directly to the issue of character. To me, character is a far greater determinant of behavior than intellect. In that regard, Blacks have demonstrated markedly lower levels of empathy, personal responsibility, behavioral inhibitions and parental investment in children, among a great many other things. At the same time, Blacks manifest higher levels of sociopathy, impulsiveness, sexual activity, aggression, hostility, violence, posturing and psychosis. These attributes all are a part of what I refer to as character and lead inexorably to the Black proclivity for violence.

As developed at length in this book, the Black tendency for violence, like all other behavioral response patterns, largely is genetic. No amount of education, affirmative action, racial preference or welfare is going to change this disparity between White and Black Americans. Only thousands, if not millions, of years of evolution will change things. Since the danger cannot be neutralized or eradicated, physical separation is required for the safety of White America.

Here is where many step up and say, "But, they're not all like that. You can't condemn them all because of the acts of some, even if the miscreants do make up a sizable portion of the entire population." Or, better yet, "I judge people one by one, not in groups." There is truth to these viewpoints, but they ignore the reality of genetics and DNA-encoded behavioral response patterns.

Alan Keyes may never steal my hubcaps, *but his grandchildren will.* (Keyes was a 2000 Black candidate for president who clearly was the best of an otherwise vapid field of Whites.) Even Keyes will pass along his jungle-evolved DNA to children and grandchildren, some of whom will rape and kill my children and grandchildren in numbers consistent with their cousins across America. Yes, there must be full racial separation, else we are right back where we started, and in only a generation or two.

Racial Separation by Preference

Separation hardly will be a tragedy. After all, the races in America already show distinct preferences for their own kind in all situations: school, work and domestic. All but the White race already are permitted to separate themselves in America. Whites can't do it because that would be racist, of course. Fact is, other races want to invade White space only when it gives them some advantage which they cannot otherwise obtain for themselves.

The same rationale can be employed with regard to the hordes of Mexican illegals now occupying southwest America, given their demonstrated predilection for criminal behavior. And some Pacific Islanders, such as Tongans and Samoans. Possibly Filipinos and Puerto Ricans, as well.

However, and this is where the rationale truly loses its ability to be called racism, other races need not be segregated for reasons of physical safety. There is no demonstrated disproportionate proclivity for violence on the part of Asians, for example. Or Russians. Or Eskimos. Or Indians. Or any of a host of other racial groups.

Whether they know it or not, the real beef that most racists and racialists have is over the issue of safety. Without the Black and Mexican elements of American society, most racists would live blissfully unaware of there being any racial differences that matter, just as so many other Americans pretend to do at present.

There is another racial group in America that is less obvious because of a lack of physical markers, but which presents an even greater menace to the safety and well being of White Americans on many levels, not just that of physical safety. Indeed, this group has made it possible, through Black civil rights and unchecked illegal

78

immigration, for both Blacks and Mexicans to threaten the physical well being of White America and thus are to be held accountable for that harm, as well. We take up examination of that racial group and the rationale for its exclusion, as well, in the very next chapter.

Chapter 6

Masters of Disaster

"The Jew and the Goy are like wolf and lamb; if you want the Wolf to dwell with the Lamb, please provide a fresh lamb every day."
--- *"Wolf, Lamb and Ouroboros,"* Internet essay by Israel Shamir, a rare Israeli voice of reason, 2004.

"The White race is the cancer of human history."
--- Susan Sontag, Jewish-American recipient of MacArthur Foundation genius grant, *Partisan Review*, Winter 1967, pg. 57.

"Jewish blood and a goy's (Gentile's) blood are not the same."
--- Israeli Rabbi Yitzhak Ginsburg, inferring that killing isn't murder if the victim is Gentile, *Jerusalem Post*, June 19,1989.

We have come a long way in this book so far – much further than many might suppose. The pace may have seemed pedestrian to those who find the concepts we have developed to be elementary. Methodical logic is like that. Each step seems almost trivial in light of one's current context. It is only when one stops and looks back to the beginning that the distance traveled becomes apparent.

In Review

Let's look back for a moment:

1. *It is a myth that higher intellect confers superiority* over those possessing lesser intellects, just as *it is a myth that there are no*

81

interracial intellectual differences.

2. Just as with the more obvious physical characteristics, *intellect is passed from one generation to the next via DNA.*

3. *Behavior "goes to seed" and becomes genetically encoded in DNA*, either directly or through natural selection, to be passed on from one generation to the next. In lower animals, genetically-encoded behavior is called instinct. In humans, genetically-encoded behavior passes for intuition, sixth sense, spirit guides, reincarnation and a host of other misinterpreted experiences.

4. *A good deal of the average person's behavioral responses are generated from genetic encoding*, such as the "fight or flight" response which manifests as social anxiety. The rest comes from learned responses, most of which derive directly from one's environment and culture. *Very little behavioral response is the result of the exercise of one's intellect.*

5. *As one's IQ declines, one is ruled more extensively by one's genetically-encoded behavioral response patterns.* Lower animals, such as ants, are ruled totally by instinct.

6. *Character*, a composite of a number of behavioral response patterns, only some of which are learned, *is significantly more important than pure intelligence in determining behavioral response in any given situation.*

7. Because character is so important a determinant of violence, *merely possessing a low average IQ does not make one prone to violence,* as shown by many relatively peaceful, low-average-IQ cultures, such as India's. Nor does a higher average IQ ensure that a culture will be peaceful – witness North Korea.

8. *Separation of classes of people, such as convicts, is a necessary and acceptable practice for the safety of the general population.*

9. *Certain racial groups show a marked proclivity for physical violence.* Generally, those racial groups possess lower IQs, therefore

are responding to, and are at the mercy of, their genetic behavioral response patterns far more than others. Very little learning, welfare, affirmative action or socialization will interfere with the behavioral response patterns of lower-IQ races. *Nothing, other than generations of interbreeding with other races, will ameliorate a proclivity on the part of a given race for violence.* Blacks, Mexicans and certain Pacific Islanders are among these groups.

10. Because all members of a race carry the DNA for that race's particular behavioral response patterns, *even the proven peaceful members of a generally violent race will bear offspring with a high propensity for violence.* Therefore, for the ongoing safety of other, less violent races, total racial separation is required. In times past, that racial separation occurred naturally, imposed by the realities of geography.

These ten points constitute the premise of this book, logically leading one that some forms of racism might well be desirable at times. Note that the end result is an unapologetic argument for racial separation only, without making any sort of value judgment as to the worth of one race versus another.

If you define racism as requiring something more than a simple preference for one's own and a desire for the safety and protection of one's own, then I am not a racist. Neither are you, I suspect.

However, the vast majority of Americans will call you racist for believing any or all of the foregoing. They are hypocrites, because they also are racist by their own reckoning, due to having opted for safe neighborhoods, good shopping and good schools, all code phrases for racial separation.

Race War

When America implodes economically, which even the most simple-minded Keynesians (but I repeat myself) concede likely, the eruption of street violence will result in a massive geographical realignment along racial lines. Even the Whites who continue to refuse to believe in the inherently violent nature of Blacks will be forced back across the line by Blacks who see their skin color as their uniform.

Blacks consider Whites to be advantaged as a race, creating resentment among even those Blacks who have earned their place in society. *Those with little believe that all deserve the same. Those with much believe that only those who work deserve to get ahead and then based solely on relative merit.* Thus, Whites resent Blacks, even those who earned their way through merit, for demanding and getting "something for nothing." This unaddressed difference in racial outlooks increasingly polarizes American society. This bilateral, brooding resentment has been growing in recent years, with no release allowed in an increasingly politically-correct society. When the building pressure finally is released, the result will be spectacular...and fatal for many.

Already, the carnage in the streets of America is outlandish. Annually, 1.2 million violent crimes occur nationwide, involving Blacks and Whites. In 90 percent of those cases, according to U.S. Justice Department figures, the perps are Black and the victims White. Since Blacks comprise only 12% of the total population of America, they are, therefore, *at least 50 times more likely to commit violent crimes than Whites*. I say "at least" because Latinos are considered "White" when reported by the US Justice Department to be perpetrators of crimes. They magically become Latino when they are victims, however. Don't forget about the huge segment of America's Black population which is behind bars, either, else the ratio would be even higher.

In the three months following the "official" end of the most recent Iraq war (marked by President Bush's outlandish visit to an aircraft carrier displaying that ridiculous *"Mission Accomplished"* banner), 52 Americans were killed in Iraq. During that same three months, 66 Americans were killed in Washington, D.C. alone.

In a deluded effort to reduce crime, Washington, D.C. outlawed the private ownership of guns. That, of course, merely led to a higher body count because criminals then knew they had absolutely nothing to fear from their mostly law-abiding victims-to-be. Incidentally, the gun grabbers in America, mostly Jewish Zionists, are not stupid and are well aware of this relationship. For extra points, guess why they want *your* guns next?

All by themselves, truthful crime statistics by race make a conclusive argument in favor of a move toward physical separation of Blacks from Whites.

Almost Invisible

When the time comes, it will be more difficult to see and exclude a racial group more pernicious and harmful, by far, than those discussed so far: *Jews*. More pernicious because the Jewish grasp of power at all levels of American society is much broader, stronger and irresistible than the overwhelming majority of Americans suspect. More harmful, not just because they have facilitated, through massive immigration and the hijacking of America's legal system, the physical harm which now requires the racial separation outlined above – but also because they repeatedly harm us economically and socially.

Thanks to the magic of genetics, however, the harm will prove neither fatal nor lasting to the White race, though the current White generation pretty much is toast.

Truly the Masters of Disaster on a national scale, Jews have been ejected from society after society down through the ages – always for the same reasons and always claiming to be the victims of unjustified persecution.

In Defense of Anti-Semitism

The silence in America concerning Jews is simply deafening, isn't it? The old adage has it that, when visiting a foreign country, to ascertain who really runs things, one need determine only who is spoken about in whispers, if at all.

What gets lost in all the saber rattling and bellicosity concerning the Middle East is the WHY of America's involvement. Because the Arabs "hate our freedom?" No, obviously not. Because they are too evil to exist? Come on. Because they have used awful weapons, still possess them and will use them again? Give me a break – on the basis of that rationale, we should be marching on every member of NATO.

The Muslims are right, you know. This is a war against Islam, pure and simple. Not Christianity vs. Islam. Not America vs. Islam. Not the West vs. Islam. This is a war between Judaism and Islam. Palestine writ large. Not a religious war, either, despite the rhetoric of the Arabs. It is a racial war and Americans are the cannon fodder.

"But Israel is our friend," you say, "The best friend we have in that hostile quarter of the world." Our only friend, more like it. Israel is our friend so long as we serve its purposes. Indeed, "friend" is too kind a word. "Svengali" is more to the point. While Israel is America's only friend in the Middle East today, *before Israel, America had no enemies in that part of the world.*

Proof abounds of Israel acting against America's interests at every turn, many of which we will review below. No, Israel does not run America, but the shadowy cartel that does run America is solidly behind Israel. Israel is that cartel's mistress, America its dowdy wife. No, not every member of that cartel is Jewish, but so many are that it might as well be exclusive.

There was a time, in the not-too-distant past, when I thought that Jewishness was religious and cultural, possibly racial, too – but so

86

what? After all, American Jews are generally well off, well educated, well spoken, a little clannish and well connected. Just like you and me, only better dressed and with trust funds – like rich Mormons, maybe. It is an outlook shared by most Americans. It is wrong. This common misperception will prove fatal to America, just as it has to so many nations down through time.

This is where I am supposed to utter the obligatory, *"I'm not anti-Semitic, I'm really just anti-Zionist."* That is a cop-out and I refuse to do it, even though strictly true. I am appalled that all Jews allow the Zionists among them to fall back into their ranks, hiding behind their Jewishness, while hurling charges of anti-Semitism at those they dislike – and their fellow Jews don't say a word about it. In the law, we call that a conspiracy and we lock up the co-conspirators just like the perps. Ok, I'll play. I'm anti-Semitic. *So what?* Do you really blame me, after all that you have done to me, my family and my country – nay, the world?

Let's get the terms straight. Pundit Joe Sobran really is right on the money regarding "anti-Semite," first of all: *"An Anti-Semite used to mean a man who hated Jews. Now it means a man who is hated by Jews."* (*Sobran's*, Sep. 2002.) Ultimately an Anti-Semite is whatever a Jew says – whoever a Jew dislikes – and, ultimately, Jews seem to dislike everybody. In fact, I have heard Jews argue that everybody who isn't a Jew is, by definition, anti-Semitic. Kind of like the rationale underlying hate crime laws, which are applied only against White people, because all White people are deemed racist, *per se.*

"Jew." It's a race, not a religion. Facts are facts. The majority of Israelis are atheist and there are distinguishable DNA markers. At this moment, Jews doggedly are trying to craft a deadly virus that will select people, such as Arabs, for their DNA differences from Jewish DNA. And I don't want to hear all this buzz about Khazar versus Sephardic Jews or who deserves to claim to be descended from the

Biblical family of Abraham. There is a group of people scattered throughout the world that calls itself Jewish. We all know who they are, just as they do. They are racially identifiable, even if of two or three flavors. They get the label "Jew," and that is reality, history aside.

"Zionist." Used to mean those who worked toward the establishment of a Jewish homeland. Now it means Jewish supremacist, pure and simple. Kind of like White supremacist, only kosher. Zionists are the real problem and they are found among the ranks of Jews everywhere. They are the ones who always cross the line and get the whole lot of them thrown out of a country. You don't believe this? Ok, then you offer a single logical reason why it has happened, time and again, in all the European countries. *Zionism is racism of the first order.*

Yes, Jews do get persecuted. What gets overlooked is the reason. Kind of like focusing on the rights of the murderer and not his victim. No, not "kind of." That's exactly what it is. *"Oy! Foist Egypt, den Germany, now here. Vhy are dey poisecuting us so?"* Trust me, they know precisely why.

Generally, it appears to me that someone has to have had a trigger event of some sort happen to themselves or someone close before that person is willing to see Jews as predatory. A trigger event wherein a Jew played the role of victimizer. Like how being raped will make any woman a rabid defender of the Second Amendment. Without a trigger event, people generally are willing to dismiss those who speak out as being nuts, racists and White supremacists. Like saying the raped woman was asking for it, that's how that treatment feels, believe me.

My trigger event actually was twofold. First, when I hired a lawyer, hoping that he would work hard and eventually take over my thriving San Francisco law practice, allowing me to retire. He was Jewish, of course. Most lawyers are, you know. The idea was to let the firm buy itself from me for him while he still drew a comfortable salary, since I had my life's work tied up in its assets, name recognition and caseload. Within six months, he tried to steal everything, by lying, cheating and stealing...literally. His intent was to leave me with nothing. *"They come as 'foreigners,' as 'beggars,' slinking and groveling, with false humility and dishonest respect. Once they have swindled their way to something, they become thieves and bloodsuckers, either openly or in secret. They turn into thieving and murderous Bolshevist hordes for their host peoples. That happens everywhere."* (Esser, *Ibid,* pg. 12)

Only after I picked up the pieces of my firm did I begin to suspect that my hireling's ethnicity had anything to do with it. After all, he did it so naturally, so matter of course, without a shred of remorse – just like he was entitled to the fruits of my life's hard work. Then I began to think back over my business and professional life and all the people who had been crooked, sharp dealers or mean businessmen – they all had names like Von Stein, Goldberg, Ganz, Silverman, Goldman, Stein, Weinstein and Cohen, to name just a few. The lawyers and judges were legion. I realized then why they stuck together and how some got ahead inexplicably. *My awakening had begun.*

However, my key trigger event occurred when my children received death threats from a Jewish telephone caller – merely because I had dared to represent Richard Butler and the Aryan Nations against a set of false charges. There have been lots of other events since then, but I will never forget the look in my little girl's tear-filled eyes as she told me about the woman who was going to kill her. In the seconds that passed while I heard her story, in between sobs, my life changed. They crossed the line with me then and there was no going back. *I was wide awake and, ever since that day, I have been committed to awakening others.*

What happened to me would make an anti-Semite of anyone. Similarly, killing a man's child will make a suicide bomber of anyone, I am sure. I understand, at last, why Palestinians strap on dynamite and step aboard Israeli buses loaded with soldiers.

One's trigger event serves as a personalized wake up call. Once awake, the evidence of what is being done to America and the world becomes apparent. None so blind as those who will not see, and all that. And that evidence is everywhere.

Supposedly, Jews account for 2-1/2 per cent of the American population. Why, then, is half the student body at Harvard Jewish? Statistics simply are not kept as to the percentage of Jews in this profession or that, but when was the last time you saw a doctor whose name did not end in "berg," "man" or "stein?" I'm not sure I have ever met a psychiatrist who wasn't Jewish. On the other hand, how often do you see a Jewish farmer or mechanic?

Rarely do I appear in court, but what the guy on the other side of the courtroom – and often as not, the judge, too – is Jewish. And, it is incredible the deference paid by the bench to the Jewish DA, or whoever, sitting at the other counsel table. There has been more than one trial where I merely could have phoned in my participation, for all the good it mattered that I was even there.

Many complain about what the international and central bankers are doing to our country. Yet, hardly anybody seems to have noticed that those people are almost exclusively Jewish.

They are everywhere in the media, particularly Hollywood. Talking heads, movie stars and the like. Curly hair, hook nose and names that rhyme. Pay attention and you will be amazed. The names won't always be a good guideline, however, given how many changed their names at the start of the last century, so as to meld into the American population of the time.

Jews seem to comprise about 50% of America's population, based upon those in visible positions. Looks can be deceiving, though, because they are drawn to those positions by their money, their intelligence and, most importantly, the indulgence of their kosher comrades.

People refuse to notice the Jewish hands on virtually every power lever in the US Federal government. Or at the helm of virtually every media organization that exists, and throughout the executive and editorial ranks. And, it's not just Jews that control America – they are Zionists. Even Ariel Sharon, Israel's current Prime Minister, has said openly, *"Every time we do something you tell me America will do this and will do that . . . I want to tell you something very clear: Don't worry about American pressure on Israel. We, the Jewish people, control America, and the Americans know it."* (October 3, 2001, to Shimon Peres, as reported on *Kol Yisrael* radio). Problem is, most of us seem *not* to know it.

Books have been written on the subject, but, essentially, a group of late 19th-century elites, comprised of Rockefeller, Morgan and others, mostly Jewish, established an organization designed to consolidate their control of America and, eventually, the entire world. It was called the Council on Foreign Relations (CFR). Offshoots, such as the Bilderbergers, have formed since then, but the objective has never slipped from their sight.

One of the first acts of CFR's members was to survey the newspaper field, the sole mass media of the time, and conclude that purchasing control of only 25 major newspapers would give them effective control of news dissemination. They bought those papers and, since then, many, many more. Today, members of these shadowy organizations literally run virtually all of the media, control the political structure in America and most other Western countries, own or manage much of world business and are firmly in control of world banking.

That is why the two political parties in America have become identical, so as to provide us rubes with the illusion of throwing the

91

rascals out come election time, yet with the same old agenda not missing a beat. Did you really see a difference from Bush to Clinton to Bush? They knew what NAFTA would do to America's manufacturing base and job structure, yet both parties embraced it. We are firmly on a path to one-world government. America writ large, but without individual civil rights, not the America of the 20th Century. And it's largely kosher.

Read "*The Israeli Spy Ring Scandal*" at the Internet web site http:// people.msoe.edu/ ~taylorm /mirror/www.whatreallyhappened. com/spyring.html for a particularly chilling look into the extent of the Israeli spy ring uncovered in America during 2002 and Israel's extensive US telephone network ownership.

It is not my purpose herein to prove Jewish control of America. There is ample material available on the Internet for those who wish to prove it for themselves. Rather, it is my purpose to show that there are perfectly valid and understandable, even laudable, reasons for being anti-Semitic. Resenting those who manipulate us on a daily basis, against our own best interests, is primary among them.

2-1/2% Jews versus 70% Caucasian (used to be 95%, not too long ago), yet they set the agenda domestically and internationally. Why else do you think we are even in the Middle East? The oil is the excuse that allows us cynically to stop and look no deeper. Notice the extreme difference between US policy in the Middle East versus elsewhere, exemplified by the fact that we invaded and did our best to destroy Iraq, a country with nothing, while we give a pass to both China and North Korea, countries which have threatened to nuke America.

And it is not enough that Zionists control America. They have to reshape it to suit themselves.

As previously noted, virtually every recent case that involves the removal of Christian symbols from society is brought and/or prosecuted by a Jew, usually with a Jewish judge presiding.

Hate laws, written by the ADL, the organization that lobbies for their adoption, state by state, are designed to stifle dissent and speaking out. Even now, the ADL seeks to broaden their sweep to include Holocaust revisionism, as has occurred in Canada and most of Europe, where many people sit in jail for publicly stating true facts about the so-called Holocaust that Jews simply do not want publicized. More on this in Chapter 12, *The Truth Hurts*.

America's borders purposely are kept wide open to a flood of illegal immigrants, purposely, apparently to dilute the population (why else?), thereby making us more easily controlled. Yet, there is a furious struggle to expel and jail those who criticize Jews.

The money that Israel has cost us, facilitated by their Jewish brethren, is nothing short of breathtaking. For a particularly good discussion of those costs, see the article *"Costs of U.S. Middle East Policy: An Economic Overview,"* by Dr. Thomas R. Stauffer at the Internet web site http://www.jfjfp.org/backgroundF4_stauffer.htm. A couple of particularly salient paragraphs from Dr. Stauffer's work:

> "Policy in the Middle East has been very costly to the US, as well as to the rest of world. The cost to the US of its policies in the region has accumulated to over $2.5 trillion, an amount greater than the cost of the Vietnam war...About two-thirds of those costs – circa $1,600 billion – arose from the US defense of Israel since 1973...

> "Since 1973, however, protection of Israel and subsidies to countries such as Egypt and Jordan, willing to sign peace treaties with Israel, has been the prime driver of US outlays or the trigger for crisis costs."

$2.5 trillion. Boggles the mind, doesn't it? Lessee now, America has a population of 290 million and about 80 million households, so that amounts to $31,250 from your family to Israel. And that doesn't include some other items which could easily double that figure, as Dr. Stauffer continues:

> "Rescue of Israel in 1973 by President Nixon cost the US almost $900 billion in lost GDP, resulting from the Arab oil embargo, and higher oil import costs...Worsening political relations resulted in the loss of hundreds of thousands of US jobs...

> "Hundreds of billions additionally were spent on 'Project Independence,' ostensibly to emancipate the US from reliance upon ME oil. The projects were largely co-opted by domestic lobbies of diverse colorations, and little imported oil was actually displaced."

Nor do these figures include the costs of America's most recent "pre-emptive" wars waged in Afghanistan and Iraq.

What is ironic, if not pathetic, is what an incredible amount of our own tax dollars, given to Israel, come back in the form of campaign contributions to American politicians, funneled through American Jewish hands and foundations, making Israeli/Jewish interests the single largest lobby in Washington, DC. Any politician that dares vote or speak against Zionist interests faces a withering campaign at election time, ultimately *funded by America's own taxpayers*, in the main. Now you see why Sharon's statement about controlling the US is true, quite aside from the considerable direct control exercised by American Jews.

Zionists will do anything to advance their own interests. For example, the 1967 extended Israeli attempt to sink the USS Liberty in international waters off the coast of Gaza, killing 37 US sailors and injuring another 174. It is unclear whether the Israelis were attempting to eliminate witnesses to atrocities they were committing during the "Six-Days War" or attempting to create their own "Reichstag Fire" event by blaming Egypt for sinking the Liberty with all hands. False flag operations are particularly favorite Israeli ploys, however, so as to curry support from others, *especially* Americans.

There are far too many problems with the official 9-ll story. The only real question is whether the US or Israel was really behind it. John Kaminski sums up a number of them eloquently in his essay "*Billions are wondering why,*" to be found at this Internet web site: http://disc.server.com/discussion.cgi?id=149495;article=37490:

"Few people are raising questions about the obviously false statements we have been told about 9/11? Why did it take 28 minutes for flight controllers to notify NORAD two planes had been hijacked when the average time to do so in such a case is 3 minutes? Why were fighters scrambled from a base 180 miles away when seven other bases had fighter jets ready that could have done the job in a fraction of the time? Why was FEMA in New York the night before the crashes? Why did those fires at the base of the towers burn for 100 days? Why did Bush read a book for a half hour when he knew two planes had hit and two more were hijacked? Why was the bin Ladin family flown out of the country when all flights were grounded? Why did the FBI chief say we had no warning this was coming and everybody else in the FBI say we had plenty of warning? Who did make the billions of dollars from all those put options on two airlines the day before the attacks? These are only a fraction of the questions the government continues to cover up, as several billions of people know."

Even Mr. Kaminski stays away from the obvious Jewish

involvement, however. Not a mention of the Israeli "art students" caught celebrating on a rooftop nearby while they photographed the ghastly spectacle. Nor of all the missing Israeli executives and workers that day, people who otherwise would have died. Nor of the two-hour advance warning provided to the employees of Odigo (a Jewish telephone firm) in the building. Nor of many other indicators of Israeli involvement.

In particular, hardly anybody wants to discuss who benefited from 9-11. The Afghanis? Iraq? Al Qaeda? *Not a chance.* What country was plummeting in world, especially American, opinion at the time, whose fortunes in that regard turned around 180 degrees overnight? *Israel*, of course.

And we haven't even discussed what Israel has done to the hapless Palestinians.

As if the provisions of Patriot Acts I and II, whereby Americans can be jailed without hearings, stripped of their citizenship and deported for "further processing," aren't enough, recently Israeli hit squads were given the go ahead to roam the entire world, including America, all the better to protect Israel's interests.

Yes, there are an abundance of reasons to be offended by Israelis, Zionists and, even, the Jews who provide cover for their brethren. Most people deny the existence of most of those reasons, and ignore the rest, until they suffer their own "trigger event."

Every time I talk about Zionists, or Jews, or Israel, I come under an incredible assault on my web site and my email servers, some from Lebanon, where Israel maintains internet servers, and even more from American Jews. False claims to my ISPs, in an attempt to get me shut up. Viruses...you wouldn't believe how many. And hate speech! You haven't seen hate speech until you have seen what righteously indignant Jews can deliver.

But, it is important that these things be said. Out loud, not in whispers. People have to wake up. It is almost too late. You see, they are on the verge of adapting the Hate Crime laws to outlaw such discussions altogether.

I am prepared to be called anti-Semitic, of course. After all, some Jews view all non-Jews as inherently anti-Semitic. Why, some Jews consider lots of *other* Jews to be anti-Semitic. My response to those who hurl the label "Anti-Semite" my way, in the expectation that it will shut me up or get me apologizing: "That's *Mr.* Anti-Semite to you!"

Jewish Overreaching

"Throughout history the poets and philosophers, the leaders of industry and science, the leading lights of art and culture, statesmen and economists whose blood was not infected by the Jews have warned against the Jew in every century. They proclaimed openly and clearly what he is: the plague. From Tacitus to Schopenauer, from Giordano Bruno to Mommsen and Treitscke, the intellectual heroes of every age have called the Jew the demon of decay, the ferment of decomposition, as the misfortune of the peoples or of humanity. In the New Testament, the Jews were in Christ's words the "sons of the Devil."" (*The Jewish World Plague,* Hermann Esser, 1939, pg. 10)

Here is the biblical quote to which Esser refers: *"Ye are of your father the devil, and the lusts of your father ye will do."* (Jesus Christ, speaking of the Jews, *John* 8:44)

Most have had personal experiences of Jewish overreaching consistent with Esser's point of view, but have never connected the dots. I have...and didn't. Not until I hired that glib and patronizing Jewish lawyer, that is.

Why do they so overreach? Because they really do consider

themselves superior – *"Chosen,"* even. As they will tell you themselves, just as they have told me: *"It's cultural."* It is. With a healthy assist from that form of culture gone to seed: genetics.

They teach and take to heart Biblical passages like that from *Deuteronomy* 6:10: *"I shall lead you to the land of your fathers and give you large and beautiful cities that you did not build, and houses full of things that you did not gather, and fallen trees that you did not cut, vineyards and olive groves that you did not plant, and you will eat and be satisfied."* So, you see - all this stuff? It isn't *our* stuff – it is *their* stuff. God said so. Of course, you know who wrote the Old Testament, don't you?

Today, they are engineering a disaster global in its reach – their "final solution," if you will: the New World Order. And America is their intended vehicle. Just as before, it will fail because their ambition always exceeds their reach. This time, however, since they're going for all the marbles, *they better have a new planet picked out.*

America's founders were well aware of the dangers presented by the Jewish race. Following is an excerpt from the written records of Charles Pinckney of South Carolina, of proceedings during the drafting of the Constitution in 1789, memorializing a statement made by Benjamin Franklin at the Constitutional Convention, concerning Jewish immigration (original in *The Franklin Institute*, Philadelphia):

> "There is a great danger for the United States of America. That great danger is the Jew. Gentlemen, in whichever land the Jews have settled, they have depressed the moral level and lowered the degree of commercial honesty. They have created a State within a State, and when they are opposed, they attempted to strangle the nation financially as in the case of Portugal and Spain.
>
> "For more than 1700 years they have lamented their

sorrowful fate, namely that they were driven out of the motherland; but, gentlemen, if the civilized world today should give them back Palestine as their property, they would immediately find pressing reasons for not returning there. Why? Because they are vampires and cannot live on other vampires. They cannot live among themselves. They must live among Christians and others who do not belong to their race.

"If they are not excluded from the United States by the Constitution, within less than a hundred years they will stream into our country in such numbers that they will rule and destroy us, and change our form of government for which Americans have shed their blood and sacrificed life, property and personal freedom. If the Jews are not excluded, within 200 years our children will be working in the fields to feed the Jews, while they remain in the Counting House gleefully rubbing their hands.

"I warn you, gentlemen, if you do not exclude the Jew forever, your children's children will curse you in your grave.

"Their ideas are not those of Americans. The leopard cannot change his spots. The Jews are a danger to this land, and if they are allowed to enter, they will imperil its institutions.

"They should be excluded by the Constitution."

Jews claim this Franklin quote is a forgery, just as they claim *The Protocols of the Learned Elders of Zion* is a fake. Of course, these are the same Jews who still claim that Jews were made into lampshades and soap by the Nazis (both disproven and acknowledged by Jewish historians themselves), along with a host of other "Holocaust" lies (see Chapter 16, *World War III*). The same Jews

99

who deny most of the proven and provable allegations made later in this very chapter, in fact. The same Jews who scour America's libraries to steal and destroy so many books written during the past century that disclose them for what they are. The same Jews who...well, you get the idea.

The Protocols is a scathing indictment of Jewish avarice and ambition, allegedly written by one of their own at least one hundred years ago and laying out the path that Jewry must take enroute to total world domination. The best way to dispute both claims of forgery is to respond with, *"So why are they so dead-on accurate?"* Especially, *The Protocols*, which reads like a script for Jews enroute to the New World Order on the back of America. I was going to include an extended discussion of *The Protocols* at this juncture, but have decided to leave that to the reader as a form of independent research. Do an Internet search and read them. Note that, though written over one hundred years ago, whether by the person to whom they are attributed or not, *every single aspect of The Protocols has thus far come true.*

"It's Cultural"

The Jewish IQ differential noted previously, both absolute and in the manner in which it is skewed toward manipulative capabilities, goes a long way toward explaining Jewish ownership of the world, but the Jewish cultural ethic (or lack thereof) is what really explains Jewish world hegemony. Those willing to do anything to get ahead, all other things being equal, always will be the ones getting ahead.

Jews themselves point to their culture as being the source of their drive. True enough. Problem is, that culture "went to seed" long ago, such that today's Jews are governed by a genetically-encoded need to get atop others at any cost.

Even the seemingly amenable Jew carries the DNA which will

cause his progeny to want to control our offspring. And today's Jews will pass along the wealth they inherited from their ancestors, which will ensure their descendants' continuing stranglehold, all other things being equal. Fortunately, all other things never remain equal.

One thing the Jews have done, time and again, and which has been their undoing, time and again, is to allow their ambition to exceed their reach, leading to their expulsion from one country after another. Today will be no exception.

Many Jewish Internet web sites carry lists of the expulsion of Jews from various countries. From www.eretzyisroel.org:

 415 A.D. - Expelled from Alexandria.
1012 A.D. - Emperor of Germany expels Jews from Mainz.
1290 A.D. - Expelled from England.
1306 A.D. - Expelled from France.
1483 A.D. - Expelled from Warsaw, Sicily, Lithuania, Portugal.
1492 A.D. - Expelled from Spain.
1510 A.D. - Expelled from Brandenburg, Germany.
1569 A.D. - Pope Pius V ordered all Jews out of the Papal states.
1593 A.D. - Expelled from Italy and Bavaria.
1614 A.D. - Expelled from Frankfurt, Germany.
1715 A.D. - Pope Pius VI issues edict against Jews.
1941 A.D. - Expelled from the German Reich to Poland.
1942 A.D. - Mass transport of Jews to Belgium & Holland.
1956 A.D. - Expelled from Egypt.
1970 A.D. - The Jewish exodus from Russia begins.

What never gets discussed on the Jewish web sites is *why* they get expelled, time and again. Always, the excuse is "Persecution." You have to ask yourself, based upon the world's experience with Jews, both down through the ages and in modern times, just how likely is it that it was simply "persecution?" And, persecution for *what*, incidentally? They never provide answers to those questions. Trust me, however, *they know.*

Many Jews are fond of referring to anti-Semitism as a disease. I agree. Anti-Semitism *is* a disease – *you catch it from Jews.*

Beneath Every Rock

Yes, there is a conspiracy. Yes, it is being run by Jews. Yes, it is being condoned by our government, which has become Jewish.

It isn't benign, either. Witness noted Harvard Law Professor (and Jew) Alan Dershowitz' serious suggestion about legalizing torture in America for dissidents. His preferred method: antiseptic needles inserted beneath one's fingernails. By the way, just how does Harvard end up having half its student body being Jewish, particularly when most of us can't afford to send our kids to state colleges?

And who, exactly, do you suppose is behind the recent eradication of the Bill of Rights in America? And, with most of the legal profession's power positions now in Jewish hands, there is nobody to set things right.

California's state government is sinking into a morass of red ink, clearly leading the nation into the depression. So, why do even the most ridiculous Jewish interests still get all the state funding they want, led by the Simon Wiesenthal Center in LA, as evident from the most recently-approved California state budget?

Just as they were in Russia last century, Jews have become the American ruling class. Just as they did in Russia, they are bleeding America dry. What, you didn't know Communism was a Jewish invention? Just what do you think Lenin, Marx and Trotsky were? Just who do you think funded the Russian "Revolution?" What do you think an Israeli kibbutz is? Just who you do think was responsible for killing between 20 and 80 million Russian Christians in the early 1900s?

Who do you think is behind the move to eradicate Christianity from America, starting with every public venue? Check out the names of the plaintiffs, attorneys and judges involved with those Pledge of Allegiance, Ten Commandments, Christmas lights, cross cases...they rhyme.

The Russian mafia? No, the Jewish mafia. And the mob in America is, and has been for the past hundred years, Jewish.

Flush with the success of forcing court-ordered removal of crosses from county seals, now the Jewish-controlled California chapter of the ACLU wants to change the names of cities like San Francisco, claiming those names violate the Constitutional mandate of church/state separation, a mandate which does not exist, by the way. "Excessive entanglement" is what is prohibited, as our forefathers did their best to prevent establishment in America of anything so powerful as the Church of England. In one of the great ironies of all time, as Christianity is rooted out of every nook and cranny of American society by Jews, Judaism (which really amounts to a form of secular humanism: *the worship of self*) increasingly becomes America's *de facto* religion.

Judeo-Christian? What a sick joke. This was a Christian country when founded. It has become a Zionist country. Judaism is anathema to Christianity. Read the Talmud before you reject this line of thinking. I have. You will be shocked, I promise you. Read the New Testament. Christ said it straight out: *"Ye are of your father the devil..."* (*John* 8:44). Things have not changed in two thousand years.

Who do you think has been behind the racial polarization in America during the last forty years? Do your research. Dig out the names of the civil rights "leaders" and lawyers. You'll be surprised, I guarantee you, to find that...they rhyme.

What, you didn't know that all the Jews in political power in the US today also are Israeli citizens? Just ask Fleischer, Wolfowitz, Perle, Libby, Adelman, Satloff, Kissinger, Luttwak, Feith, Zakheim,

Abrams, Grossman, Haass, Zoelick, Schlesinger, Sembler, Chertoff, Bolton, Greenspan, Goldsmith, Golden, Gersten, Gildenhorn, Weinberger, Bodman, Cohen, Davis, Bloomfield, Lefkowitz, Frum, Melman, and Blakeman...all Jewish and all running things in Washington. Names from today's newspapers. What's the only ethnic group allowed by America to hold dual citizenship with another country? That's right – *Jews...with Israel, of course.*

Even Colin Powell has a Jewish forebear; he grew up in a Jewish neighborhood and speaks Yiddish (didn't know that, did you?). His family was *Shabbats goy* for the Jews (those who do the Jews' forbidden work on the Sabbath).

The price for the White House? Selling out to Jewish interests. That's why the so-called War on Terror. That's how Bush came from nowhere and coasted to the Presidency. He, Clinton before him and most of the presidents of modern times are traitors, pure and simple. Just as will be Kerry if he unseats Bush in 2004, as seems likely at the time of this writing, so vexed by the media has become Bush's presidency. They sold their country, including you and me, for a turn at the trough. Yes, you heard me right: George Bush is a traitor.

Why in the world does America have to share Israel's fate, simply because the Jews want to eject the Palestinians from all of Palestine today? Why do American boys have to die to advance Israel's interests, when Israel's boys do everything they can to shirk the call of duty during war (did you know the malingering coward slapped by General Patton in that WWII hospital tent was Jewish)?

Why does America lionize people like Clinton and Bush, both of whom dodged the draft? *Shabbats goy*...that's all they are.

Jewish Zionists started both World Wars (see Chapter 16, *World War III*).

Jewish bankers were behind the 1929 stock market crash and the Great Depression (See Chapter 17, *Money's End Game: Depression II*). Jews also are behind the economic meltdown just around the corner, which will cause us to start numbering our Depressions, just as WWII caused "The Great War" to be renamed WWI.

Jews were predominant in the Council on Foreign Relations (CFR) and its many progeny, including today's Bilderberg Group, wherein the course of world events is set.

Jews have a monopoly on American media and a stranglehold on foreign media. Jews literally own Hollywood.

Jews control the international banking system through ownership of all central banks.

Jews own most of Wall Street.

Jews monopolize the American pornography and drug industries. The "Russian Mafia" is really all those Russian Jewish criminals, come looking for fresh meat.

Jews are disproportionately homosexual and pedophilic (research NAMBLA, the North American Man-Boy Love Association, and see for yourself); thus the push for American society to accept those "lifestyles" as normal.

There is not enough space in this book to take side trips into the who/what/why of all these facts and events, though the balance of our discussion *will* cover a surprising amount of this ground, and more. Plenty of material exists on the Internet, even if public library shelves have been denuded by Jewish groups intent upon rewriting history. Do your own research if you doubt what I say and prepare to be amazed.

Behind Every Tree

Feminism is a singularly Jewish travesty, foisted upon an unsuspecting public in order to weaken white male control of America. Feminism has proven to be the single most significant master stroke of the Zionists, as it has provided the critical mass in an electorate which now allows Zionists to run roughshod over America and her traditional structure.

Jews control America's government at most levels since the silent revolution of the Sixties, after which the antiwar activist leaders (virtually all Jewish) assumed control and have become today's neoconservative warmongers (just count the noses surrounding both Bush and Clinton) - a change in outlook in order to further Israel's Middle East ambitions.

Jewish elements of America's government were behind the massive change in immigration policies which choked off White European immigration and opened the floodgates to non-Whites of every stripe, especially the illegals flooding across America's southern border. Jewish hands are behind most of the civil rights organizations which press for special privileges for ethnic groups at the expense of Whites, part of the overall program to subjugate White America (it was only recently that the NAACP, founded by Jews, even had a Black president, rather than a Jew).

Lest you think that manipulation of other races is anything other than by Jewish design, consider the following:

"We must realize that our party's most powerful weapon is racial tension. By propounding into the consciousness of the dark races that for centuries they have been oppressed by the Whites, we can mould them to the program of the Communist Party. In America we will aim for subtle victory. While inflaming the Negro minority against the Whites, we will endeavor to install in the Whites a guilt complex for their exploitation of the Negroes. We will aid the Negroes to rise in prominence in every walk of life, in the professions and in the world of sports and entertainment. With this prestige, the Negro will be able to intermarry with the Whites and begin a process which will deliver America to our cause." (Israel Cohen, *A Racial Program For The 20th*

Century, 1912, quoted by Congressman Abernathy, *Congressional Record*,1957, p. 8559.)

Now we have the spectacle of thousands of Somalians and Bantus, among the most backward and least intelligent that the human race has to offer, being transplanted to the heart of American cities. Most of these people never even have seen a doorknob or a toilet and all of them will be on full public assistance for their entire lives. Guess who heads up the organizations behind this boondoggle?

The American legal system has been hijacked by Jews. An overpowering presence in any law school (50% of Harvard's *undergraduate* class is Jewish), Jewish lawyers flock to bar association seats, judgeships and public attorney positions, with the result that American law literally has become Jewish law. The *New York Times* quoted Supreme Court Justice Ruth Bader Ginsburg, just the latest in a long string of Jewish Supreme Court Justices, as crediting the Talmud for her professional performance: *"The Talmud is my sacred guide for daily living."*

Thus, we endure the spectacle of things that Jews don't like, especially things Christian or having to do with America's founders, being pushed down the memory hole.

Hate crime laws are being jiggered toward locking up people who criticize Jews, as now is done in Canada (think Ernst Zundel).

Virtually every case involving the removal of Christian symbols is brought by a Jewish lawyer and/or plaintiff, often heard by a Jewish judge.

Rarely do I enter a courtroom where the judge or the prosecutor (often both) are not Jewish.

It was a Jewish judge that led to the censure of Alabama Chief Justice Roy Moore, concerning that Ten Commandments memorial. It was a Jewish lawyer that prompted the 9th Federal Circuit Court to remove "under God" from the Pledge of Allegiance.

Jews even successfully sue to have multicolored Christmas lights removed from all public venues, *including elementary schools during the year-end holidays.*

White America Held Hostage

For some time now, America has held the record for imprisoning the highest percentage of its own population. Many complain of racial profiling in pointing out that over half the prison inmates are Black. They are right. Racial profiling is at work, because the percentage should be much higher.

Lately, however, the envelope is being pushed drastically, with many poor, White, conservative, home-schooling Christians now being incarcerated for felonies that weren't even infractions a few years ago.

Those same poor, White, conservative, home-schooling Christians' families are being ripped apart in record-breaking numbers by a largely Jewish-controlled system of "Child Protective Service" state agencies throughout America that is instrumental in placing White children in foster homes where they are abused, beaten, raped, robbed, humiliated and psychologically scarred. I have handled too many of these cases not to know the real truth, which is kept from the public by courts sitting without juries, in sealed proceedings, closed to the public, without observing classic rules of evidence or due process, in a manner that makes military tribunals seem the epitome of fairness.

The so-called drug war sees a great many poor Whites jailed every year for simple possession, while elements of the US government facilitate the massive international drug trade, perhaps the most visible of which was the 2003 replanting of Afghanistan's opium poppy fields which the routed Taliban previously had lain fallow.

Now there is a roundup and imprisonment on trumped-up charges taking place of the more visible and vocal American White nationalist leaders, such as Matt Hale and David Duke. This is just the way the Soviet Union did things back in its "Evil Empire" days. *And the same people are doing it here as did it there, then.* It is no coincidence that so many of those being jailed these days are highly critical of things Jewish.

Christ is being removed from Christmas and Christmas itself seems on the way out. Crosses are being removed from public property all over America because of Jewish complaints. Amazingly, many formerly Christian churches now are removing crosses from their altars and podiums in rank obeisance to Jewish demands.

Jews uniformly have shirked their duties in serving in the military, preferring to let others die in the place of their own children, though the wars producing the death tolls always have been Jew-inspired. American Jews pulled off the Russian Revolution, which resulted in the death of between 20 and 80 million White Russian Christians. Communism is a Jewish invention, too.

Every time a dollar rounds a turn in the world economy, there is a Jewish hand stretched out, ready to take a slice of it, often in the form of interest (usually at usurious levels) and often hidden, as in the "kosher fees" extracted, Je$$ie Jack$on style, from companies for nonexistent "services" rendered (most consumer products today carry nondescript symbols indicating that a kosher fee has been built into the price), in a blatant update of the old "protection" rackets.

Much of American industry is owned or controlled by Jewish interests, often the same ones determining government policy, *a la* Enron, NAFTA, GATT and the WTO. American labor is being whipsawed, what with upper-level jobs being outsourced to India, mid-level jobs sent wholesale to the Far East, including entire factories, and low-level jobs going to low-paid illegal immigrants. America's employment debacle properly is laid at the doorstep of

Jews who sought to increase their profits, at the expense of American workers, an increasing percentage of whom are jobless today and likely to be jobless tomorrow, as well.

The American "mob" always has been Jewish, not Italian. The Italians merely were errand boys and public fall guys for the likes of Dutch Schultz, Legs Diamond and Meyer Lansky, king of the Jewish mob lords. Lansky's crowd was instrumental, together with rogue elements of the CIA, in engineering the assassination of John F. Kennedy and ushering in the modern era of Jewish dominance of America at all levels (Michael Piper's book, *"Final Judgment,"* is the absolute last word on the JFK assassination).

The "Holocaust" has achieved the status of a state religion in Western civilization, with its "denial" (which doesn't really mean outright denial, but covers merely stating true facts about the so-called Holocaust that Jews don't want circulated) being punished with prison sentences in most western countries. And it is milked for all it is worth, which is billions in "reparations" from countries and companies around the world.

It's in the Scriptures

Jews are taught from their Talmud that crimes against Gentiles, including murder, genocide, child abuse, prostitution, and the like *actually are considered holy services to God*, if you can believe it. Rabbinical exhortations to deceive, rob, hate and even murder non-Jews are required, else Jews ultimately will be punished by God. Look, I couldn't just make stuff like this up.

Elizabeth Dilling, (1894-1966) conducted a 20-year study of Judaism and the Talmud:

> "The non-Jew ranks as an animal, has no property rights and no legal rights under any code whatever... 'Milk the

Gentile' is the Talmudic rule but don't get caught in such a way as to jeopardize Jewish interests. Summarized, Talmudism is the quintessence of distilled hatred and discrimination, without cause, against non-Jews...

"The Talmud is characterized by obscenity and more obscenity, a setting up of laws seemingly for the purpose of inventing circumventions, and evasions; delight in sadistic cruelty; reversal of all Biblical moral teachings on theft, murder, sodomy, perjury, treatment of children and parents; insane hatred of Christ, Christians and every phase of Christianity.

"(The Talmud) characterizes the Virgin Mary as a 'harlot' and adulteress and Jesus as a 'bastard' and sexual pervert who was crucified as a 'blasphemer of Pharisee Judaism.' Jesus' punishment was to be 'lowered into dung up to his armpits' and then strangled. Christians in hell are punished by 'hot boiling excrement...'"

"(The Talmud describes God as being) a nature essence which has no attributes and can neither know nor be known. That is atheism..." (*The Jewish Religion: Its Influence Today*, Elizabeth Dilling, 1964)

A few choice observations from the English translation of *The Soncino Talmud*: Jesus was born a bastard and his mother, Mary, was a harlot (*Mishna Yebamoth* 4,13). Jesus practiced black arts of magic (*Sanhedrin* 1076). Jesus is now suffering eternal punishment in a boiling vat of filthy excrement (*Gittin* 57a). The murder of Gentiles by Jews is said to be a "holy sacrifice" to God (*Zohar*, III, 2276 and I, 38b and 39a). Death of Gentiles by beheading is especially recommended (*Pesachim* 49b).

Moral relativism (if it feels good, do it) and *secular humanism* (an atheistic viewpoint holding that humanity controls its own destiny) are the hallmarks of the modern Jew and are what allow Jews like Harvard Law Professor Alan Dershowitz to advocate torture of prisoners in America. Lacking a moral compass, anything goes. Israel, in fact, acknowledges that a majority of its population profess to be atheists.

The Jew's "religious" studies leave him mentally twisted and often perverted, with significant wounds to his psyche, the result of which is to view all non-Jews as lesser beings, to be used and abused as he desires. Consider the manner in which Palestinians are treated by Israelis, for example.

"The attitude resulting from such teachings has been resented by non-Jews in all countries and centuries. Such resentment, however, is always portrayed by Jews as persecution of the Jews." (Dilling, *Ibid*)

"It's cultural," I hear repeatedly from Jews, a statement with which I wholeheartedly agree. Jewish mothers, and all that. Problem is, evolution has made it genetic, as well, but that is just a different form of culture, albeit far more durable.

Jewish Nature a Disease?

Dr. Arnold Hutschnecker, New York psychiatrist, concludes that Jews have a need for persecution, thus repeatedly create the circumstances which generate their own persecution. This, of course, is the other side of the equation that Jews never wish to discuss: the reasons for their persecution and expulsion from every country in which they have gained dominance. Hutschnecker states that all Jews are born with a predisposition to schizophrenia, a mental disease most notable for the paranoid state of the victim. *"Schizophrenia is the fact that creates in Jews a compulsive desire for persecution,"* says Dr. Hutschnecker, who goes on to note that, *"The world would be more compassionate toward the Jews if it was generally realized that Jews are not responsible for their condition"* (*Mental Illness: The Jewish*

112

Disease, Dr. Arnold A. Hutschnecker, *Psychiatric News*, American Psychiatric Association, October 25, 1972).

Hutschnecker notes that the paranoid schizophrenic is unable to distinguish right from wrong and specifically points to Jewish canonical principles of patience, humility and integrity being disregarded in favor of aggressive, dishonest and vindictive behavior.

Hutschnecker's findings square up with our thesis that behavioral response patterns are inherited and racially differentiable. Culture gone to seed. Always, the avaricious nature of the Jew has led to persecution. Like the abused wife who returns, time and again, for still more abuse, the Jew now seems to need persecution. It no longer matters which came first, persecution or paranoia, because Jewish paranoia now guarantees a degree of overreaching that can end only in persecution. Jewish leaders often note this need, saying it is desirable in that it fosters racial identity and solidarity. Indeed.

Pointing to the explosion of mental illness in America which parallels exactly the increase in America's Jewish population, Dr. Hutschnecker states:

> "The great Jewish migration to the United States began at the end of the nineteenth century. In 1900 there were 1,058,135 Jews in the United States; in 1970 there were 5,868,555, *an increase of 454.8%.*
>
> "In 1900 there were 62,112 persons confined in public mental hospitals in the United States; in 1970 there were 339,027, *an increase of 445.7%.*
>
> "In the same period the U.S. population rose from 76,212,368 to 203,211,926, *an increase of* (only) *166.6%."*

The Jewish compulsion to manipulate and take advantage of others is both cultural and, in a different way of saying the same thing, genetic, since genetics merely is culture gone to seed. Again, only evolution can possibly strip out the compulsion to take advantage of others, a compulsion deadly to other races, coupled as it is to superior intellect. Thousands of years of employment as merchants engrained the behavioral response patterns apparent in all Jews today.

Always, when Jews migrate to a new country, they follow the same pattern: take over communications, become indispensable to the leaders, feed the population what is sensational rather than what is nurturing and, finally, demonize, jail and kill those who protest, until the general population finally rises up and demands their ouster. That time once again has come for them. Again, only physical separation of the Jew from other races will put an end to the ongoing Jewish manipulation, deception, exploitation and fiscal robbery.

The problem is in distinguishing Jews, since they now have so intermarried with other races. The line must be drawn, however, even for those Jews who live in harmony with their neighbors, for they carry in their DNA the seeds for the Jewish mental disorder. Israel Shamir, one of the rare voices of reason emanating from Israel these days, may not cheat me out of my lunch money, but his grandchildren will.

Only Israel

Israel can do no wrong. Israel receives billions in US foreign aid each year, some of which comes back to America in the form of bribes...er, campaign contributions, to keep our elected officials in check.

Only in Israel is interracial marriage illegal if one party is Jewish.

Only in Israel is racial segregation the order of the legitimate government.

Only in Israel is it illegal for foreigners to vote...or hold property.

"Let's boycott Israel," some say upon learning the truth. Guess what? There is only one country in the world which boycotting will get you charged with a crime in America: *Israel.*

Only Israel could have gotten away with the murderous attack on the *USS Liberty* during the Sixties.

Only in Israel is wholesale and widespread trafficking in slaves, mostly Russian women and children, allowed to flourish.

Only Israel could get away with erecting the wall now separating it from Palestinians, built well into Palestinian territory.

Only Israel has an estimated 500 nuclear weapons, many nuclear missile submarines and massive biological/chemical weapon stocks, while officially denying it has any.

Only Israel could threaten to take the rest of the world down with it in the event of a nuclear exchange with Arab states, yet have such a statement be ignored in the West.

Only Israel.

Benjamin Franklin was Right

I could go on for hours in this vein. Books have been written. Examples of the Jewish yen for power, control and wealth at any cost are legion within most countries. Results are the surest way to gauge intent and Jewish results speak for themselves throughout the world. They have attained their desires, time and again, down through the ages, yet each time demanded more. It is cultural, of course. But, they have done it for so long that their culture has gone to seed and it has become genetic with them. Today, they cannot help but do it. *Jews raised by wolves would end up trading in wolf pelts.*

Benjamin Franklin was correct. Though generally I revere America's founding fathers, I do *"curse (them) in (their) grave(s)"* for not having prevented the disaster now looming before us while the solution was within their grasp. Now we will pay a price for that shortsightedness. Unfortunately, a much higher price will be paid by our children, if we don't do something about it now.

Maybe if we become obnoxious enough, the Jews will erect a wall down the middle of America between themselves and the rest of us, as they did in Jerusalem to the Palestinians. Unfortunately, that will happen only after they have taken everything we own, including our dignity, just as they have with the Palestinians. In any event, and one way or another, racial separation from Jews in America is inevitable. It's just a matter of when.

The Jewish tribal thing has become endemic, actually genetic, and, therefore, second nature - like pigeons homing in on the same target without knowing why or who else is enroute.

Without Jews, the CFR never would have come into being or become the force that it has. It merely is the messenger. The message is the death knell of all things goy. The senders of the message...ah, now therein lies the real problem, particularly since they seem individually unaware of the Manchurian Candidate nature of their roles in life.

Say what you will of Francis Parker Yockey's book *"Imperium."* Yes, it is obtuse and turgid. Consider the circumstances of its authorship. However, Yockey correctly perceived that there is something afoot in a supervening racial consciousness or imperative. We may merely be blind men feeling up an elephant, but clearly we have hold of the real perps, nonetheless.

The full extent of Jewish supremacy and control in America becomes evident to the most casual observer who simply is willing to see all that unfolds before his eyes on a daily basis. What is not yet apparent is that, once again, they have overreached themselves and are creating the context for their own comeuppance. Witness the fact that they have gotten people like me proselytizing like this...problem is, since America now has become such a Jewish country, when they go down, we go down *with* them. And the landing will be hard, as we will see in the next chapter, wherein we consider *The Price of Empire.*

Chapter 7

The Price of Empire

"If the doors of perception were cleansed every thing would appear to man as it is: infinite."
--- *"The Marriage of Heaven and Hell,"* Plate 14, William Blake, 1791

"This is the end, beautiful friend
This is the end, my only friend, the end
Of our elaborate plans, the end
Of everything that stands, the end
No safety or surprise, the end
I'll never look into your eyes...again"
--- *"The End,"* The Doors, 1967

"There is no fool like an old fool."
--- Proverb

It has become a trite symbol of middle age: economic and social success well in hand, the 49-year-old guy chucks it all, giving up his wife, his children, everything, for a fling. He buys a red Corvette and leaves town with his 30-something secretary. Only gradually does he begin to appreciate the immensity of his earlier good fortune. But it is too late. No fool like an old fool. *"The end, my friend,"* as Jim Morrison might have said.

Civilizations are like that, too. Nations go through discernible periods. Though the length of time in each phase might vary, the progression is inevitable. And the end is never pretty.

119

I'm reminded of Gail Sheehey's *"Passages,"* an excellent book, the research for which she is accused of having plagiarized extensively, by the way. *"Passages"* describes the seasons of a man's life as he grows older, noting how there are certain stages through which all men go. I started reading it in my late twenties and found it to be eerily accurate – so much so that I closed it when I reached the point where I supposed I actually then was in my life. To this day it sits there on the shelf, daring me. *"Come see how predictable you are,"* it seems to hiss, every time I pass by.

Of course, it is perfectly reasonable that I *would* be predictable, given how greatly I am ruled by my genes. We all are, of course. As we have seen, much of one's behavior is driven by genetic encoding.

The Life Cycle of Empire

Societies go through similarly predictable stages. We can see ourselves reflected in the Roman Empire, to which modern America endlessly is compared. Greece. Carthage. India. Persia. Egypt. Their empires all progressed the same. They all ended the same. *Badly.* Always, in the same way. Always, for the same reasons. Why should we suppose that the demise of the American empire will be any different?

It is far more than simply the insufferable arrogance of empire that leads to its downfall. And more than the economic laziness that develops as a result of having too much. The real key is in the racial makeup of empires, which always end in massive race mixing.

Always, empire starts with a pure strain of overachievers. Always, empire ends with a strongly-diluted populace; diluted by have nots, ne'er do wells and intellectual inferiors.

We often hear it said that the average age of the world's greatest civilizations has been about 200 years. America is overdue.

Always, empire begins with strong leaders. Hard times breed

hard men. Always, empire ends with weak sisters in charge, who import others to do the common labor...who fatally overreach in an attempt to regain past glory, like the guy with the red Corvette who ditched his family in one last grasp for the freedom of youth, yet who lived to regret it. Soft times breed soft men. Look for leadership where the same name repeats: Caesar, for example. Romanov. Bush. Or, God forbid, Clinton. That is a mark of the end of empire.

Once the Western frontier Sheriff cleaned up a town, the next thing on the town's agenda always was to get rid of the Sheriff because his Neanderthal outlook, appearance and methodology offended the gentle town folk. Nations are no different.

Empire attracts and fosters the weak and the spineless, who are drawn to strength for their protection. In their turn, believing themselves to be as strong and capable, they create a survival of the least fit as increasingly weak, often inbred, leaders dispose of potential competitors. The frontier town, rid of its uncontrollable Sheriff, makes the personable and articulate town fop Sheriff, then wonders why the next gang that rides through town lays it waste so easily. *No empire like an old empire.*

Race Dictates the Depth of Empire's Decline

Empire devolves to its lowest common denominator, elevated only slightly by its founders' descendants. No citizen left behind, to paraphrase the ideology that has destroyed America's educational system, and for precisely the same reasons. Usually, that lowest common denominator racially is a gulf apart, else its members would not so easily have been conquered and transported home for involuntary servitude.

"All civilizations rise and fall according to their racial homogeneity and nothing else - a nation can survive wars, defeats, natural catastrophes, but not racial dissolution." (*March of the*

Titans, Arthur Kemp, Introduction, 2003) In *"March of the Titans,"* Rhodesian-born Arthur Kemp painstakingly outlines the rise and fall of empires from the dawn of time until today. A book so big it required two volumes. A truly spectacular work. On the Internet, go to www.white-history.com for information about purchasing both volumes directly from Mr. Kemp.

I will not attempt to paraphrase Mr. Kemp, who so eloquently covers the field, particularly in summing up the reasons for the decline of empire:

> "Politically correct historians blame the rise and fall of the great nations of the past on politics, economics, morals, lawlessness, debt, environment and a host of other superficial reasons...
>
> "Japan, England, Sweden and Germany have gone through crises of these nature scores of times, without those countries falling into decay. It is obvious that there must be some other factor at work - something much more fundamental than just a dip in politics, morals, lawlessness or any of the other hundreds of reasons that historians have attempted to dream up...
>
> "The decline and eventual extinction of the White populations in the Middle East mark the end of the original civilizations in these regions...
>
> "In India, the invading Indo-Aryans established a strict segregation system to keep themselves separate from the local dark-skinned native population. This system was so strict that it has lasted to this day and has become known as the caste system.
>
> "However, even the strictest segregation (and Aryan laws prescribing punishments such as death for miscegenation) did not prevent the majority population from

eventually swallowing up the ruling Aryans until the situation has been reached today when only a very few high caste Brahmin Indians could still pass as Europeans...

"Exactly the same thing happened in Central Asia, Egypt, Sumeria, and to a less marked degree, in modern Turkey. Slowly but surely, as these civilizations relied more and more on others to do their work for them, or were physically conquered by other races, their population makeup became darker and darker...

"Despite several attempts to prevent large numbers of Nubians (African Blacks) from settling in Egypt - one of the first recorded racial separation laws is inscribed on a stone on the banks of the Southern Nile, forbidding Nubians from proceeding north of that point - the use of Nubians for labor of all sorts gradually led to the establishment of a resident non-White population...

"Once again the factors which led to the extinction of the Aryans in India came to work in Egypt - a resident non-White population to do the labor - a natural increase in Nonwhite numbers - physical integration - and a decline in the original White birth rate - all these compounded to produce an eventual Egyptian population makeup of today that is very different to the men and women who had founded Egypt and who had designed the pyramids...

"The Egyptians of today are a completely different people, racially and culturally, living amongst the ruins of another race's civilization...

"Within 100 years of Blacks becoming commonplace in ancient Classical White Greece, that civilization collapsed." (Kemp, *Ibid*, Ch. 9)

The Predictability of Decline

Human society is made up of humans. Humans are eminently predictable by virtue of genetics and culture, which really are the same thing. Therefore, the interplay of humans, known as society, also is predictable, provided one can get one's mental fingers around the concept. Admittedly, it is a complicated model that must be constructed, but complexity *can* be modeled.

We model the stock market and, though we cannot establish exact timing (and timing in the stock market, more than most things, literally *is* everything), we know full well how things will go: the market goes up, then it goes down. Realize this and grow rich. Buy low, sell high. Easy, *n'est-ce pas*? Based on results, no. Most people get caught by the stock market, therefore most must be unable to comprehend that it moves both directions.

It is commonplace for much of humanity to be unable to see trends until they have passed. Forests and trees, and all that. Certainly, we can see *other* forests, however, just as we can see other empires and thereby know what lies ahead for America. But most people won't. That's why Middle America will not march on Washington next week and hang all the politicians from lampposts, as it should.

If only our "doors of perception" could be cleansed, Blake-like.

As an aside, Jim Morrison and friends took the name of their band, *The Doors,* from the Blake snippet quoted at the beginning of this chapter, so impressed were they with the imagery therein contained. Similarly smitten was Aldous Huxley, the philosopher/author (best known for *Brave New World*) who titled his landmark work, *The Doors of Perception*, a book which also served to inspire Morrison and company. Better than most, the Doors managed to fuse existential poetry and improvisation into their rock music and

124

become the spiritual house band to a generation.

The Curse of Success

No longer do people debate whether America's is an empire; that fact is taken for granted. Perhaps that is the surest indicator that we are well past the peak. When I heard cab drivers and hotel doormen in San Francisco discussing their Silicon Valley stock portfolios, I suspected that the end of the high-tech market mania was at hand. It was.

We see the same things at work in America as seen during the decline of empires past. We bring back those we have conquered to till the fields and clean our houses. The borders are thrown open, due to need and external pressure. We import our necessities and indulgences alike because the cost of transport is insufficient to allow our own inflated sense of worth to compete. We indulge in sloth because we can. Comfort becomes our master.

If youth is wasted on the young, then surely money is wasted on the old.

The very perquisites of empire are what inevitably bring it low. The curse of success. With massive immigration comes massive miscegenation. We send the best of our youth to distant lands, there to die while foolishly maintaining our hegemony. We lose our edge, our training, our skills, our will. We become bored and jaded, turning increasingly to frivolous and debauching pastimes.

Unfettered consumption leads to gluttony, an inability to produce and, inevitably, to poverty, which increases the pressure for more war, more conquest, more comforts, in a neverending downward spiral.

We may not be sure of the timing, but we can be certain of the sequence of events. America's sequence clearly is in the downtrend. And empires never recover once they hit the skids.

No empire like an old empire.

Usually, it takes a while for an empire to unravel. But today, times are different. Things move with the speed of jets, as opposed to that of clipper ships or camel caravans in times past.

> "Once (an empire) starts to allow large numbers of other races into its midst (to do the labor and then to integrate with the original population) then that civilization will change - or in many cases, vanish completely. This fact applies equally to all civilizations, no matter who their original creators are, anywhere in the world.
>
> "A civilization - any civilization, be it White, Black, Asian or Aboriginal - stands or falls by the homogeneity of its population, and nothing else. As soon as a society loses its homogeneity, the nature of that society changes.
>
> "In reality, this is a perfectly logical principle and is not even an opinion, but a simple statement of fact and of the obvious." (Kemp, *Ibid*)

Indeed. It *is* obvious.

Loss of Perspective

Today's America finds itself firmly in the grip of a faction which consciously hastens the process of racial devolution in a manner reminiscent of the leaders of declining empires who felt constrained to eliminate potential contenders for their own thrones. The dagger in America's heart, however, has been the opening of her borders to a flood of immigrants, not to mention the excessive sway given to her Black population in the name of diversity and affirmative action.

America is ruled by globalists. It isn't that America's leaders must be globalists, though they seem to have been, of late. After all, they merely do the bidding of their financial masters: the international banking families, the true globalists...Jews mostly and Zionists all.

America is headed where it is because its masters think globally. That always is the problem with an empire – the view of its masters becomes internationally elongated, at the expense of their local perspective. Forests and trees again.

What is good for empire, which is where the globalists mentally dwell, never is good for the country originating empire. Once under way, there is no way to stop an empire gracefully. Always, the source country suffers miserably in the end. America will be no different.

An ancient writer, Plutarch, recounted a conversation involving Pyrrhus, a Greek king near the end of the Grecian empire, who discusses the point of conquest with a friend. *"To be free to do what I wish,"* is a paraphrase of Pyrrhus' reason for marching off to conquer others. *"But,"* inquired the friend, *"you can do that now. Why go to war and risk all this?"* Blinded by the vision of empire, Pyrrhus went off to war anyway and conquered portions of the burgeoning Roman empire, albeit at a colossal cost in men and equipment, thus the origin of the phrase "Pyrrhic victory." Eventually, Pyrrhus was defeated, then killed, by legions of the growing Roman empire.

"The last great Grecian leader, Pericles, actually enacted a law in the year 451 BC, limiting citizenship of the state by racial descent." (Kemp, *Ibid*) Several hundred years later, this law was rescinded in obeisance to the misfortune of reality, but may account for why modern Greeks actually are more homogeneous than occupants of other nearby former empires.

Of course, one piece of the old British Empire did ascend to a position of some importance. We called it America. Might not a piece of today's American empire possibly do the same?

127

Chapter 8

Immigration's True Costs

"We're going to take over all the political institutions of California. California is going to be a Hispanic state and anyone who doesn't like it should leave. If they (Anglos) don't like Mexicans, they ought to go back to Europe."
--- Mario Obledo (former California Secretary of Health and Welfare and co-founder of Mexican American Legal Defense and Educational Fund), interviewed on radio station *KIEV*, Los Angeles, June 17, 1998.

Those who turn a blind eye to the massive immigration which has occurred during the past forty years invoke the mantra that immigrants do the work that White Americans refuse to do and that those same immigrants bring more in productivity and taxes than they and their families take away. That has a nice idealistic and nurturing sound to it, doesn't it?

Nothing could be further from the truth.

Immigrants, both legal and illegal, cost considerably more than they contribute and, particularly in these days of massive outsourcing of American jobs and affirmative action, take jobs that Americans born here gladly would perform. The average wage of the jobs left to Americans gets bid down as a result of all the additional available manpower, of course.

Ultimately, the cost of immigration will be the loss of America and, possibly, Western civilization altogether.

Strong words, I know. Let's see why it must be this way and why it is too late to change things.

129

Who Dropped the Ball?

My generation has dropped the ball. My father's generation is the one that muddled through the first Great Depression and went on to win World War II. They were the heroes.

We are the dissolute offspring, spending our inheritance on needless luxury and wasting the moral legacy bequeathed us.

We are the ones who give up the freedoms our fathers gave so much to secure. Of course, we are the ones taking them away, as well.

We are the ones spending our children's income by saddling the next generation with outlandish debt that cannot be repaid.

To the generations coming after, I apologize on behalf of my own. We were spoiled rotten. We deserve to get little. You do not. Regrettably, *you* will receive the lesson that *we* deserve.

Ultimately, the most valuable thing we could pass on to our children already resides within them: their DNA. That is what will enable our descendants to make their way on their own out of the mess that we continue to create. Fortunately, we had far less to do with the makeup of our children's DNA than did our common ancestors.

A Coup has Taken Place

My generation came of age during the Viet Nam War, which marked a turning point for American society. What has ensued since the assassination of President John F. Kennedy amounts to nothing less than a coup in slow motion, resulting in today's socialistic-cum-fascistic police state.

I recall that JFK was not all that highly thought of during his incumbency. Regardless, I believe that he would have been one of

America's truly great presidents, had he lived and served a second term.

At the time of his death in 1963, JFK was acting on a number of fronts: getting America out of Viet Nam; pulling control of the dollar from the Federal Reserve and back into the US Treasury; demanding that Israel behave itself and stop development of its nuclear arsenal; assaulting organized crime across a broad front. All that changed the moment Lyndon B. Johnson assumed office.

Some say that LBJ was involved in the JFK assassination. I doubt it. He may have had foreknowledge, though, which probably amounts to the same thing. Nor was LBJ the first of a long string of American presidents who have carried water for Zionist interests in America and around the world. A much more reasonable argument can be made, as seen in Chapter 16, *World War III*, that Woodrow Wilson really deserves the honor of being the first to sell his Presidency for 30 pieces of Jewish silver.

JFK was of my father's generation, too. Though he overlooked the deals that were required to secure his election, he was the best of the best. Once elected, JFK represented courage, wisdom and strength of character. Truly, he wished the best for America and possessed both the intellect and the strength of character to follow through. How ironic that his own brother would come to serve as the instrument by which America would be laid low in years to come.

The Flood Begins

In 1965, Ted Kennedy was instrumental in getting Congress to pass the Immigration and Naturalization Reform Act, which increased annual immigration from 175,000 to over one million.

Ted Kennedy and his cohorts said immigration standards would not be lowered. They said they would not deflect immigration away from Europe. They promised not to increase the annual levels of immigration. They guaranteed that the demographic mix in America would not change. *They lied.* What's more, *they knew, all along, that they were lying.*

Almost immediately, the emphasis on immigration shifted from European to third world. Out the window went education, asset, literacy and health requirements that had been in place since the founding of America. Huge increases in immigration were mapped out.

Why? Because American business, losing its battle with organized labor unions, wanted a reliable source of cheap labor. The trickle of illegal immigration began at that time, a trickle that swelled to a flood and today has yawned into a massive tidal wave. Now we see those same businesses relocating to other countries altogether or outsourcing their jobs at all levels, save only the executive suite, though America's immigration flood continues unabated.

The remaining human capital of America's former educational investment is being tossed on the scrap heap, thanks to NAFTA, GATT, WTO and the New World Order of America.

It is easy to argue against illegal immigration and its attendant costs. Principles of fairness appeal to all comers, after all. Why should lawbreakers actually get preferential treatment over those who comply with the law?

However, even the legal immigration that has occurred over the past forty years has exacted a monumental toll upon America. Even without the illegal immigration, America never would have been the same again, anyway, and the result would have been identical, just delayed perhaps a hundred years, at most. Why?

Personal Case Study

Here's an example from my own past. I grew up in a small town in north-central Washington state. The climate was ideal for tree-borne fruit, particularly apples.

With mid-century innovations in irrigation came the ability to bring hundreds of thousands of acres of arid land under cultivation. Small and large land owners alike did so with a vengeance. They chose what then was the big-money crop: apples.

Innovations in storage and transportation at the time made it possible to ship fresh Washington apples to any point in the world. A fever akin to that which accompanied gold strikes gripped the area, I recall, as literally everybody plowed under other crops and planted apple orchards.

The area had only a few orchards as I grew up. Kids were delighted to get work thinning and propping during summer break, earning minimum wage (ninety cents an hour, heady stuff for teenagers at the time).

Apples ripened after school started in the Fall, though, so migrant workers would show up during harvest season. The migrants mostly were White folks who followed the crops around the country, holdovers from the Depression era.

We kids would pick after school and on weekends, too. Even then, several classmates who would like to have had work couldn't get it.

With the huge upsurge in apple orchards, a few of which I helped plant as I finished high school, came a demand for labor that far outstripped what then was available. Mexicans began to show up and brought their families with them. They stayed. At first, they brought a little additional color, but once the trickle became a stampede, they soon overwhelmed the area.

Today, that sleepy little town which never saw any crime other than some Saturday-night rowdiness, regularly deals with murder, rape, robbery, burglary, drugs and a host of related problems.

Today, well over half the local school's student body is Mexican in origin and teachers are required to speak Spanish. In my day, the only foreign language offered was Latin, because that was the only language that one of the teachers happened to know well enough to teach.

In my day, the most grievous sin was running in the halls. Today, there are Hispanic gangs in the school who wear "colors," deal drugs, flash "signs" and terrorize the rest of the student body.

I never had a key to my home, because we never locked the door. There was no need, of course. Today, even the windows of local homes have bars, just as can be seen throughout Mexico.

Today, the apple boom is over, as apples from other parts of the world flood the market. Today, orchards are being plowed under, to lie fallow or be replaced with the wheat crops that preceded them. But the Mexicans who came and multiplied are still there. More come all the time, predominantly illegals.

Today, there is chronic unemployment and crime. County social services are overwhelmed with demands that never used to exist.

The local hospital is on the verge of going out of business, not for lack of patients, but for lack of income.

The main street which once sparkled like a Norman Rockwell painting has become dirty and in extreme disrepair. Store signs are in Spanish and English. It looks just like any other dirty little border town, like so many that line America's border with Mexico. Yet, the Canadian border is but an hour's drive away.

This scene was repeated for one crop or another, all up and down the vast agricultural valley and flatland which stretches north from Mexico and into Canada, between the Sierra/Cascade mountain chain to the West and the Rockies to the East.

Immigration Without Assimilation

These people have made no attempt to assimilate into American culture. They are a subculture unto themselves. A violent subculture that has overwhelmed society on many fronts.

Approximately 40% of illegal aliens are on welfare in America today (53% in California). $55,000 is what The Center for Immigration Studies has calculated that each and every one of the illegal Mexican immigrants costs us in taxes. So much for the myth that they add to America's productivity.

Today, governments at every level are broke. Yet federal laws and judges demand continuation of taxpayer-funded services to illegals.

Where will it end? Absent intervention of some sort, not until American wages and living standards stabilize with Mexico's. The average Mexican's will rise a little. The average American's will drop a lot.

Oh, and the crime rate still has a goodly distance to cover before it equalizes, as well.

So many costs of immigration cannot be quantified – such as the general lowering of the standard of living that now is occurring throughout America.

Even so, let's go through the list.

Education Costs

Education costs are going through the roof, as the immigrant population outbreeds America's, four to one. Schools can't be built fast enough. Add to the construction costs the expense of bilingual education, drug testing, security guards and metal detectors. It becomes easy to see why the load on local property tax rolls has risen to unbearable levels.

The pressure on local property tax rolls does not consider the effect upon the budgets of families that choose to place their children in private schools out of concern for their educational and physical well being, families forced to continue paying for the public schools, as well.

How do we begin to quantify the effect upon our children of teachers forced to communicate in two or more languages and teach to the bottom of the class, as the "No Child Left Behind" programs require? In 1993, the cost of bilingual education in America already had risen to a total of $12 billion per year.

Today, California alone spends $2 billion per year to educate just the illegals in the public schools.

Nobody left behind means nobody out in front. America's test scores in all disciplines have fallen from the top of world standings to the bottom in just two generations. The drop in SAT scores became so alarming that the tests were rescaled, so that historical averages no longer can be compared, as extensively discussed in Chapter 2, *Intellectual Myths*.

Welfare Costs

Social transfer payments, such as monthly welfare doles, food stamps, Social Security disability, survivorship and retirement, are spiraling out of control.

What's more, in addition to the graying of White America, owing to low birth rates, the number of elderly immigrants has risen to three times the level of just a generation ago. Social Security payments have gone up sevenfold and a $30 billion deficit to the program is forecast during just the next ten years. Meanwhile, our government wants to add millions of Mexican citizens to the country's Social Security rolls, in conformance to a policy of "normalization" with Mexico.

The deficit in contribution to America's gross national product is not confined just to immigrants, however. On the contrary. Blacks get $850 billion more than they contribute to GNP, while the Hispanic deficit is less than $300 billion. Women, too, add to the deficit, by getting $100 billion more than they contribute, though their domestic contributions are severely undercounted.

Who pays, then? Men, of course. White and Asian men.

And what gets overlooked while we all complain about the ballooning costs of social services? The share allocated to the non-immigrant American citizen, particularly the elderly, decreases annually.

Medical Costs

Medical care, too, faces unprecedented demands in America due to immigrants, both legal and illegal.

We have all heard about the pregnant Mexican women who cross the border so that their children will be American citizens, thereby entitling them to the full panoply of social services. What isn't generally known, however, is that those hospitals in Southwest America, all along the border with Mexico, are being driven out of business because of it.

Hospitals are *required by law* to treat all comers, unlike private clinics and physicians. Immigrants with no insurance or money to pay for medical services flood hospital emergency rooms for their every ailment. Each illegal immigrant admitted to a hospital ends up leaving behind an *average* unpaid bill of almost $5,000.

Because both the growing Hispanic subculture and the Black subculture are far more violent than White/Asian America's, virtually all trauma patients seen in hospitals are non White. And they overwhelmingly fail to pay their bills.

Like social services, this huge increased demand on social services means that the rest of us get a smaller dose of medical attention when we need it, though we must pay much higher bills and taxes in order to support those who take advantage of America's medical system.

137

Disease of every sort is on the rise in America, including those that essentially were eradicated long ago, such as leprosy and tuberculosis, together with new diseases altogether, such as Chagas. These have been brought to America by immigrants of every stripe, leaving behind their unsanitary countries, but not their unsanitary personal hygiene.

The rates of AIDS and HIV infection, indeed, of all sexually transmitted diseases, are skyrocketing, though half is to be found in America's own Black population.

Insurance Costs

Insurance Costs of every sort are going through the roof.

An individual policy of medical health insurance now costs upwards of $8,000 annually. Very few families with self-employed breadwinners can afford health insurance, which can cost $14,000 per year for a family policy equivalent to that provided groups in government and the workplace.

Many of us haven't seen a doctor in years, because we can't afford to. Yet, the illegal immigrant crows to his relatives in Mexico about the excellent medical treatment he or she receives in America for free.

Auto insurance premiums are spiking upwards, as well, driven by the uninsured immigrant, who has nothing to lose when he injures others. Yet, when they are the victims (of staged accidents, more often than you might imagine), they are quick to line up for their insurance settlement payments.

Excessive drinking is both a tradition and a manifestation of *machismo* in Latin cultures. Mothers against Drunk Driving reports that Hispanics believe it takes 6-8 drinks to affect their driving, well above the 2-4 drinks believed by White Americans and the 1-2 drinks of reality. Drunk drivers cause more accidents than other drivers. A higher percentage of the drunk drivers' accidents are more *serious* than those of normal drivers. Increasingly, drunk drivers are uninsured drivers, simply because today's drunk drivers turn out to be immigrants.

Both home and commercial liability policy premiums have ballooned in response to increases in losses due to crime and vandalism, both attributable in large part to America's immigrant population, though Blacks again must shoulder a significant share of responsibility.

The Cost of Crime

Books could be and have been written about crime in modern America. What inevitably is discussed in low tones and innuendo, if at all, is the role of Blacks and immigrants in the startling increases in crime of every sort.

In Chapter 5, *National Disasters,* we saw the truth about crime's racial divide in America. What gets overlooked, however, is how extensively immigrants are involved in crime. This is particularly important to the thesis of this book, which argues for racial separation based upon inbred proclivities for violence.

The US Justice Department purposely lumps Hispanic crime in with that of Whites, so as to inflate the White numbers, so it is difficult to get accurate counts on immigrant crime. Only when they are victims are Hispanics broken out as a separate racial group. I know how incredible this double standard sounds, but it is absolutely true.

Neither can one infer the proportion of Hispanic crime from prison populations, since they are counted as "White" there, too, where 50% are Black and 40% are "White."

However, one *can* infer racial crime rates from population figures, which strongly imply that the overwhelming majority of crimes are committed by Blacks and Hispanics in America. For example, you are 350 times more likely to be killed in Washington, DC, Detroit and New Orleans than in, say, North Dakota. Similarly, the border states of California, New Mexico, Arizona and Texas have, in the last generation, seen huge increases in all manner of violent crimes.

In the third world, such as Africa and Mexico, corruption, murder, rape, robbery, child prostitution and other crimes are *normal*. Increasingly, America grows to resemble the third world in that regard.

Why are the true figures about interracial crime suppressed by the government and its controlled media? Simply because, if the truth were known by the general population, overnight there would erupt a racial shooting war of epic proportions. Only by maintaining the illusion that Whites commit a proportionate share of crimes can the American public more easily be manipulated through feelings of guilt.

Prisons have been constructed at a record pace, as America has significantly increased its lead over all other countries in jailing its citizens. Currently, America imprisons four times as many people as any other country in the world, taken as a percentage of total population. The costs of constructing and maintaining jails and prisons is mind boggling.

With the increased prison populations, reflective of increased crime rates, has come a "get tough on crime" mentality, with lengthened prison terms and elimination of judicial discretion in sentencing. For the essentially innocent caught up in the judicial system, the first-time offenders (the category into which Whites fall most disproportionately), the resultant sentencing exacts a tragic cost in human suffering.

Consider, as well, the psychic cost of prison rape, overwhelmingly practiced upon Whites by Blacks and illegal immigrants as a form of payback for perceived indignities suffered in

American society.

Employment Costs

Jobs and Wages are taking a serious hit in America from several quarters. First, the huge influx of immigrants, particularly the illegal aliens, creates competition for lesser jobs and a resultant lesser prevailing wage.

Middle-class Americans find themselves whipsawed between the elimination of jobs at the low end, taken by illegal aliens, and the phase out of jobs at the high end, increasingly outsourced to foreign countries by companies required by competitive pressure to do so. The competitive pressure is a result of NAFTA, GATT and the World Trade Organization, of course.

Though these costs spread all through society, to a family hit with unemployment it can seem the end of the world. Only the rich can afford to muse over the unimportance of acquiring wealth.

And it is no small issue that more than $30 billion annually is sent back to the home countries of America's immigrants, this per a recent study by the Inter-American Development Bank.

Taxes

Well, at least all these immigrants must be lightening the load of taxation upon the shoulders of the rest of us, right? Wrong. Taxes at all levels of government are headed up, reflecting the reality that the flood of immigrants takes more in social service costs than it gives in taxes. Government now has become the single most influential segment of society. As government goes, so goes the American economy. That seemed ok in principle...for a while.

However, we are rapidly reaching the point where such a huge segment of society is on "full overhead" that the small portion left doing productive work will collapse under the strain of supporting everybody else. In the State of California, alone, the citizens face a $35 billion annual deficit, which shows no signs of decreasing.

The coming collapse of the dollar, then the American economy, likely will lead to a collapse of America, with a stopover in full-on fascism and world war for a time. Government spending deficits and America's ongoing trade deficit will exact a terrible price from a country that seems simply too dumb to realize that the good times cannot continue forever.

There is no such thing as a free lunch. Eventually, the world will stop lending us the money to buy its products, realizing we cannot repay them without deflating the dollar to near nothing. Then will the government spending and the job losses attributable to immigration show themselves to be the unsustainable expenses that they truly have become.

Affirmative Action

Affirmative Action results in still more job losses by Whites in America. This has become institutionalized, such that now it is being administered by those it favored previously. Now it will never end.

Daily, the resentment mounts, as discussed at length in Chapter 9, *The Real Racists.*

As a citizen, I cannot send my child to college in another state and pay that state's lower tuition rate for residents. But illegal immigrants increasingly can do just that, when necessary. Of course, minorities of every stripe qualify for preferential admission and financial assistance over my children. More resentment.

As we saw in Chapter 2, *Intellectual Myths,* a much smaller proportion of the minority population can muster the talent necessary to compete in college and many professions. Yet, we have a system that demands the proportional representation of minorities, based solely upon population. The one-way nature of racial preferences can be seen in the outlandishly huge Black employment in governmental bureaucracies.

Ironically, in colleges and the professions, the beneficiaries of affirmative action overwhelmingly are the children of privileged minorities, the very ones who *don't* require a leg up in the first place.

Quite aside from increased taxes for affirmative action employment and enforcement, a very real cost is borne by Whites who are directly affected and displaced. This is especially true now that the definition of those encompassed by affirmative action preferences has been expanded to include all non Whites, even those recently arrived in the country.

Housing Costs

A huge new segment of society has been created which is dependent upon government largesse. They must be housed and increasingly are provided housing at the expense of governments at all levels.

The cost of White flight, a direct response to increasing concentrations of minorities, is enormous and incalculable, as Whites move away to gain a measure of the safety lost with the huge upsurge in immigration and forced integration. Similarly incalculable is the value of the talent lost by the cities left behind.

Cultural costs

Traditional European-American heritage is suffering mightily, as well. Fifty years ago, 90% of Americans were White and of European extraction. Immigrants now are over 90% non White. Illegal immigrants are 100% non White, of course, as proven by the 2.7 million granted amnesty in 1986.

143

Immigrants and their offspring now constitute about 75% of the annual population increase in America, with the result that Whites currently comprise just over 70% of the total American population.

In another generation (twenty years), over half the population under 18 will be non White. In two more generations, over half the *entire* American population will be non White.

Between the subcultures about to become America's dominant cultures and the *Masters of Disaster* campaign (see Chapter 6) to neutralize White America, America's traditional culture and heritage is being stripped away. Yet another cost that simply is incalculable.

We put up aid stations in the desert, out of concern for the well being of illegal immigrants sneaking across America's southern border. Meanwhile, we prosecute ranchers who detain the illegal immigrant trespassers who rob them, defecate on their landscaping and invade their homes, enroute to "their" amnesty.

We refuse to seal our own borders, yet spend $300,000 each for 177 checkpoints on the Afghanistan/Pakistan border.

We welcome illegals with open arms, yet treat our own citizens like terrorists at the nation's airports.

Our government seeks to give driver's licenses to illegals. Motor voter laws enable them to vote in American elections.

What is wrong with this picture? Extra points for honesty.

Chapter 9

The Real Racists

"He who fights with monsters should look to it that he himself does not become a monster... when you gaze long into the abyss, the abyss also gazes into you."
--- Friedrich Nietzsche, 1878

"The tactics of smear almost always tell us that the smear's target has offered facts and arguments that can't be answered on their merits—and the only way to answer them at all is to attack the person who brings them up in the first place."
--- Sam Francis, *The Knives are Out for Harvard Immigration Critic*, VDARE Internet essay (March 24, 2004)

"The modern definition of a racist: someone who is winning an argument with a liberal."
--- Peter Brimelow, *Alien Nation* (1996)

If the races are so equal, why do racial disparities exist in so many areas? *"Racism"* is the glib and easy answer offered by both knee-jerk liberals and conservatives throughout the world. It's become an article of faith. An unquestioned and unquestionable mantra.

Economic and academic racial disparities in America have become bootstrapped by conventional wisdom into serving as proof of pernicious White racism. Notice that this conclusion absolutely

145

requires the assumption that all races are identically capable.

"Blacks suffer crime, poverty and illiteracy much more than Whites. Whites are predominantly in charge of American society (wrong, actually, if one views Jews as being a race apart from Whites, precisely as do the Jews, themselves). *Therefore, Whites must be responsible."* Thus goes the logic.

As we have seen, that is wrong. Otherwise, athletics would be a lily-White affair at all levels, whereas the reality is exactly opposite.

Why does racism seem to be so unevenly applied, if conventional wisdom holds true? Why do Asians do so well academically and economically, though the virulent White supremacist sneers at them with a contempt equal to that held for all other non-White races?

No explanation other than White racism is allowed, else we are drawn inevitably to the doorstep of admitting that racial differences exist.

Politically-Correct Racism

Why is it so hard for the politically correct to admit seeing the obvious racial differences? Is it because they believe such differences necessarily create racial pecking orders whereby some races are inherently inferior to others? If so, and this seems the only logical reason, then *just who are the real racists around here?*

Consider the last paragraph carefully. In fact, go back and read it again. I'll wait right here for you.

How ironic. The very people who decry racism in those who readily acknowledge the existence of racial differences actually are the ones possessed of illogical racial attitudes. *They are the real racists.*

This vitally-important concept deserves restatement:

The politically correct refuse to acknowledge racial differences because they believe that such differences would be proof of racial inferiority. They refuse to see differences as being merely different. Theirs is a singularly racist outlook because of the negative implication they insist upon applying to racial differences.

Those who deny racial differences have painted themselves into a corner. If ever they accede to the overwhelming proof of racial differences, then they immediately become the very racists about whom they complain so loudly. That is why they are stuck and unable to accept the overwhelming proof of racial differences, though their position so clearly is lost.

However, the politically correct show they know the real score by the manner in which they handicap races they consider to be superior with such devices as affirmative action, quotas, profiling and diversity programs.

Golfers play with handicaps so as to make their routine game more competitive. Golf handicapping readily acknowledges the ability of some players to play the game better than others. Handicapping makes games like golf more competitive and, therefore, more enjoyable. Handicapping in life merely is unfair for those held back while the less deserving take their places in line.

The Rationale for Affirmative Action

As *Title VII*, the "Civil Rights Act," was forced through Congress, just as with so many other pieces of ideologically-driven legislation, notably the immigration bill that was to follow shortly thereafter, America was deceived. None other than Hubert Humphrey told his colleagues in the Senate: *"Title VII does not require an employer to achieve any sort of racial balance in his work force by giving preferential treatment to any individual or group."* However, when the courts saw that Blacks were not qualifying for jobs in anything approaching that suggested by their relative percentage of the population, they began to require that the number of Blacks hired

147

be increased. It began in the public sector, as do so many unfortunate social ideologies, but quickly spread to private businesses and organizations.

I attended law school in the late 1970s and early 1980s. I recall the rationale put forth in my Constitutional Law classes for affirmative action being necessary to provide a leg up for minorities that unfairly had been held back by pervasive White male discrimination.

William Rehnquist, then the new guy on the US Supreme Court bench and Reagan's first appointment, addressed the assembled student body of UCLA's Law School shortly after he was appointed and recited the rationale for affirmative action: affirmative action was a temporary measure to last a single generation, at the end of which parity would be achieved and the preference systems then being erected would be abandoned.

In late 2003, a full generation (the very generation to which Justice Rehnquist had referred) after racial preferences were installed throughout America, another US Supreme Court justice, Sandra Day O'Connor, said precisely the same thing in justifying continuation of preferences *for at least another generation.*

Sure. We know better, though.

We know what is going on. So do the judges. Once again, I ask you: *Who are the real racists around here?*

It doesn't matter what the courts do, however, because "minority" preferences have become so institutionalized throughout America that they never will be removed without wholesale alteration of the country's government and society. Bureaucracies at all levels of government, corporate and social life have become so entrenched with the favored minorities and their politically-correct patrons that abandoning legally-required preferences would have no effect whatsoever.

Affirmative action says, loud and clear, that the favored

minorities simply don't measure up and will not be competitive without handicapping other, clearly superior, members of society. Talk about a racist outlook!

Diversity, quotas, racial profiling (of Whites only) and the encouragement of multiculturalism all entail the same sort of logic, of course.

Legacy of Resentment

Imagine that you are talented, Black and truly deserving of all that has come your way in life. How can you ever know whether your achievements were born of merit or skin color?

Imagine yourself a Black doctor, every bit as talented as White doctors on staff with you at the hospital at which you practice medicine. Now imagine the rage you feel when both Blacks and Whites express a preference for "another" (White) doctor because of their unstated belief that you couldn't have earned your position and therefore are not qualified to minister to their needs.

Now imagine yourself untalented and Black, knowing that you don't deserve that which has come your way in life, yet resenting having it handed to you in so patronizing a fashion. Can the resentment of the undeserving somehow be denied the same gravity as that possessed by the unrecognized but deserving?

And the racism of the politically correct now has become institutionalized throughout America, such that Blacks are never expected to comport themselves properly, learn adequately or compete without the fix being in.

There are no teachers and no students in America today who are unaware of the intellectual disparity between White and Black (and, to a slightly lesser degree, Mexican) students, save only those yet to occupy integrated classrooms.

Now schools are resegregating, a result that both Blacks and

Whites desire. Yet, America does nothing to address the real problems with Black educational shortfalls, just as it does nothing to deal with the real problems of Black underachievement in all areas of life.

We do not demand that Blacks actually do the homework that Whites regularly turn in. We do not demand that Blacks achieve test scores which show that material has been learned and retained. We do not demand that Blacks comport themselves properly, treating others with respect. No longer, even, do we require that Blacks speak understandable English.

Instead, we provide Blacks with the bare necessities of life, much as we do the family dog, and expect nothing in return except that they lick society's hand. We implicitly expect only second-rate performance of Blacks at home, at school and in the workplace. Blacks know this and have come to expect it of themselves, as well. Is it any wonder that our hands get bitten, not licked?

How demeaning it must be for Blacks of every stripe in today's society, which refuses to expect excellence in minority performance, a refusal born of a very real racist belief in the inherent inferiority of Blacks. A belief held by the very people who claim to be concerned for Black interests.

And the resentment isn't confined to Blacks. Imagine being White and coming to a hospital emergency room, only to find that your attending physician is Black. You don't know if he is qualified to operate on your badly-injured child, yet they refuse your request for another doctor. Your child's life hangs in the balance. *What will you do?*

Imagine your resentment if your store-clerk son just missed out on a spot in the freshman class of medical school because several less academically-qualified minority students were admitted.

Many Blacks, both talented and untalented, are awakening to the legacy of affirmative action and they don't like it.

Some Blacks today speak of the creation, in a single generation, of an entire subculture that cannot stand on its own, so crippled by handouts has it become.

What's more, those Blacks who are awakening resent White America for what has been wrought in the name of equality. They scarcely can be blamed. *They wanted equal opportunity. We gave them equal outcome.*

And we provide equal outcomes with mechanisms that reek of an expectation of failure and inferiority on the part of Blacks. Relative merit is disregarded in favor of skin color. No attempt whatsoever is made to limit society's largesse, either quantitatively or temporally, implying a belief in perpetual, inbred inferiority. All this and more is put in place by the politically correct, who universally accuse others of being racist, all the while showing favoritism in a way that belies their own truly racist beliefs that Blacks are too inferior to earn their own way.

Advanced placement breeds another form of resentment, too: A much higher percentage of Blacks end up "in over their heads," both in college and in business. They know their own work is sub par. Placed with their intellectual equals, likely they would thrive. Instead, society does its best to make as many Blacks as possible taste the bitterness of personal failure. The long-term consequences of such a strategy can be only negative, likely in staggering measure, for *all* races.

This was foreseen by Booker T. Washington, founder of the Tuskegee Institute: *"No greater injury can be done to any youth than to let him feel that because he belongs to this or that race he will be advanced regardless of his own merit or efforts."*

The news gets worse.

Members of the American entitlement subculture, largely Black, but daily swelling with large numbers of illegal immigrants, see nothing wrong with their own ever-increasing entitlement mentality, so immersed in it have they become. These people, too, resent White America for complaining about their getting that which they have come to view as their due.

Meanwhile, resentment on the part of Whites grows daily, as well, resentment of the racial preferences as well as of the growing Black resentment. The explosion in Black-on-White crime, despite being covered up by America's government and media, serves only to aggravate the growing hatred on both sides.

Spread of the Entitlement Mentality

The entitlement mentality isn't restricted to those already in America, either. When President Bush announced his "guest worker" program, the flood across America's southern border swelled to tidal wave levels, comprised of those who literally (and indignantly, when caught by the US Border Patrol) said, *"I am here for my amnesty."* Their demands were made in Spanish, of course.

In a very real sense, we have created an entitlement mentality throughout the world by our actions. Is it any wonder that we face the same animosity everywhere that we have fostered in America proper with our misguided attempts at legislating equality?

Deepening the Divide

Some Blacks and a great many Whites realize that affirmative action and its progeny have created a deeper divide in American culture than ever existed previously, even during periods of slavery. This time, the divide is marked by silent seething and ever-growing resentment.

The media/government coverup serves only to aggravate things. Making Whites feel guilty for their inherent racism (and if you don't think that guilt breeds contempt, then you quite simply do not understand the concept). Making Blacks believe that White racism is at the basis of all Black problems.

More resentment on both sides.

Those who have little (Blacks in this case) always believe that society's output should be divided equally among everybody. Those who have much (Whites) always believe in division according to merit. This fundamental and unrecognized schism exists in America today and grows larger by the day.

Without a pressure release valve, as open racism once provided, an explosion of epic proportions at some time in the future is guaranteed. There will be a race war, the initial skirmishes of which already are being fought in America's streets, that will bring an altogether new meaning to the concepts of race war and genocide, *courtesy of those who claim to abhor racism.* The irony would be amusing if the situation weren't so deadly.

At the highest levels of golf, such as in open tournament play, handicaps are removed. The same is true for the ruling elite, of course. The rules, the handicaps, apply to everybody but themselves. Of course, they can afford to live apart and above the fray, can't they? They can afford to escape the consequences of their very real racism and pretend that, because they don't deal with the issue personally, they are not racists. For now.

This living apart by the elite must not be confused with "White flight" from cities to the suburbs and the rural environs of other states altogether. Whites in general are depicted as the aggressors in the Black/White racial war that is erupting from the cities of America. However, aggressors do not retreat, don't forget. Whites simply are seeking the safety for which they once hunkered together in cities.

Chapter 10

Wag the World

"The real truth of the matter is, as you and I know, that a financial element in the larger centers has owned the government ever since the days of Andrew Jackson."
--- Franklin D. Roosevelt, then Asst. Secretary of the Navy, in a letter written Nov. 21, 1933 to Colonel E. Mandell House.

"Pigs get fat. Hogs get slaughtered."
--- Folk Saying

Many ask why I so condemn the Jews. In truth, it merely is a subset of all Jews to whom I really object: Jewish supremacists. You may know them as Zionists.

If you feel negatively about White supremacism, then picture that same concept, but from the point of view of the oppressed in Palestine; that's Jewish supremacism. Through silence, the rest of the Jews let the Zionists get away with their brand of supremacism; they allow the transgressors to fall back into their ranks and hide behind the hurled epithet of "anti-Semite."

Those who stand silently and wait also serve, as they say, so the Jewish bystanders properly are charged with the crimes of their supremacist brethren. That is why I rail so often against Jews, not just Zionists.

In return, of course, I get labeled an anti-Semite, a term which has lost much of its currency. It has been overused by continuous application to those simply disliked by Jews for any reason.

Incidentally, Jews have co-opted the term "Semite," which refers to those of Middle Eastern origin, just for themselves, just as they previously co-opted even the word "Jew." Ironically, it is the Jewish segment originating in Eastern Europe (Ashkenazi) which most clings to the label, not the true Jewish Semites: Sephardic Jews. Even more ironically, Sephardic Jews are treated as third-class citizens in Israel itself, worse even than immigrant Jews of Ashkenazi origin.

Who Runs the World?

Zionists really do run most of the world. Certainly, all the Western world. If you do not agree with this, then you need to do some basic spadework, work beyond the scope of this book. You might want to skip ahead to Chapter 16, *World War III*, then come back and pick up the book at this point. That should do the trick, all by itself. It is so obvious, once you are willing to see it.

All the power positions in Western-style governments, both here and abroad, are occupied by Jews, generally with only the head of state not being a Jew.

The World's media, virtually every last little scrap of it, is owned and managed by Jews.

Most of business is owned and/or controlled by Jews. The transfer in early 2004 of ownership of the Russian oil empire known as Yukos directly to the Rothschild family, because the ostensible owner was jailed for corruption and fraud, illustrates how true Jewish business ownership exists in many cases without being at all apparent.

The central banks, especially the US Federal Reserve Bank (which is neither Federal nor has any reserves) are owned and operated by Jews. Again, Rothschild is a major player, even in ownership of the US Federal Reserve Bank. In reality, it is the

Zionist international banking cabal that sits at the very top of world control, just as it has for hundreds of years. Most Jews, even most Zionists, merely are tools for implementation of the cabal's exploitation and control of the world.

The legal and medical professions have been taken over by Jews.

These, and more, are facts. Cold, hard, unassailable facts. But they are facts that are unprintable, because they involve Jews.

Jews run most of Western Civilization, and they truly are in the American driver's seat. Mere self preservation demands that White America wake up and start protecting itself, because time is running out. Thus, defense against Jews, the tiny tail wagging all of America and, through her, the rest of the world, probably is the most important type of racism that can and should be practiced.

Christian Zionists, particularly that odd form of Christianity consisting of fundamentalists such as Baptists and Pentacostalists, are as much the problem as any other, if not more so simply because they ostensibly are "of us." They advance the cause of Zionism, including massive support for the murder of any and all Arabs, particularly Palestinians, because of their belief that the Old Testament prophecies must be fulfilled before they can get their tickets punched for the trip to Heaven. You really have to wonder how Jesus Christ might feel about these "Christians," were he to return to Earth today.

Pathetically, Christian Zionists are viewed merely as "useful idiots" by the Jewish Zionists at the top. Of course, those people view *all* of us, even their own Jewish brethren, as being mere useful idiots; sheep to be shorn periodically.

The New World Order isn't coming. The United Nations isn't taking over America. The New World Order already is here. It is America and it is America that is taking over the world, albeit at the behest of its Zionist masters, the tail that wags the American dog and, through it, the world.

Tyranny of the False Majority

A minority often views rule by the majority as tyranny. Modern America has stood this concept on its head, with the result that the true majority now is being tyrannized by a false majority comprised of a variety of minority groupings - feminists, Blacks, Mexicans, the poor and homosexuals, to name just a few.

The primary strategy of the Communist always is implemented as a societal overlay by casting all issues in terms of class struggle. Divisions are created and one side stigmatized while the other is militarized in reaction to the perceived, usually false, stigmatization. Thus, disadvantaged Blacks are turned against their White "oppressors," exploited women are divided against "chauvinistic" men, tireless government workers are made resentful of a thankless public, the poor are driven into a frenzy about anybody who has more than they, disenfranchised (illegal) immigrants are exploited and abused by a harsh, unfeeling host country, *etc.* You get the idea.

As part and parcel of the media propaganda campaign (and we have learned who controls the media), always the group put on the defensive simultaneously is guilt tripped into inaction. The process can happen very quickly, often within a single generation.

Divide, amalgamate into a coalition the groups now convinced they are being victimized, then conquer. That's the tried-and-true approach of the Bolshevik. That, and a bullet to the back of the head, of course.

Majority rule has inherent problems, known to America's founding fathers, who decried a *"tyranny of the majority,"* which is why they created a republic, not a democracy. America became that dreaded democracy long ago. As Benjamin Franklin said so well: *"Democracy is two wolves and a sheep discussing what's for dinner."*

Political associations can occur in different ways, at different levels, belied by the homily that "politics makes strange bedfellows." Accordingly, some minorities in America, considering themselves oppressed, called it a class struggle and enlisted enough of the disenfranchised, such as Blacks, until a controlling majority was formed, a coalition which then proceeded to disenfranchise and torment their former perceived tormentors.

Key to this strategy in America has been the enlistment of women and the consequently necessary development of what is disingenuously called Feminism. That is why we have the spectacle of an America being run by groups that do not accurately reflect the true majority group: Whites. How ironic that a significant portion of the true majority group, White women, was gulled into joining their own oppressors. Now we see other significant subgroupings, such as fundamentalist Christians, also helping in their own demise at the behest of the ruling clique.

With the ruling clique (can you say "Jews," boys and girls?) that formed the new false-majority coalition firmly in place at the head, the new American democracy now is being transformed into a genuine self-perpetuating dictatorship, so as to ensure the long-term rule by America's new masters, despite their small number. Coalition members, most of them viewed as useful idiots by the ruling clique, will be used, abused and abandoned, along with the real majority, as time goes on.

Unbridled Immigration

As discussed in detail earlier in this book, America's Congress set out to turn the immigration statistics on their head back in 1965, with the Hart-Celler Act, also known as the 1965 Immigration Act, prepared and pushed by the Jewish lobby, using Senator Hart as the front man. Virtually all the immigration since then, both legal and illegal, consists of people *not* of White European extraction. Based on results, that was the clear intent, of course, which was directly contrary to the assurances of our elected representatives, particularly Ted Kennedy.

Amazingly, America has taken in huge swaths of populations from every country in which it has meddled during the past forty years. 2003 saw the beginning of a program to immigrate to America virtually all the African Somali Bantu tribespeople that exist. These people were disadvantaged in their home country because they were deemed irremediably deficient there by other Somalis, who themselves would be viewed as marginally retarded, on average, if brought to America. Imagine how the Bantu will be viewed after having been in America for a generation or two. They never will be self sufficient here.

You might ask how this can happen when educated, landowning Whites from South Africa and Zimbabwe are denied anything but short-term visitor visas by the US, despite clearly qualifying for refugee status due to the genocide now being waged against them by ruling Black regimes? There is a reason, of course: they are White.

There is one class of refugee that always is welcomed with open arms by America: Jews. A flood of Russian Jews has been descending upon America in recent years, due to the change of their fortune in the former Soviet Union states. However, that now is beginning to subside. In 1991, 80,000 of a total 120,000 American immigrants taken in under refugee status were Jewish. Just ten years later, only 20,000 of 70,000 refugees were Jewish, according to the New York Association for New Americans, which is a strictly Jewish immigration agency, despite its name.

With the decline in Jewish immigration, an interesting debate has broken out within the Jewish community, concerning whether immigration to America now should be restrained. Thus far, the prevailing view is no, as so well summed up by the Hebrew Immigrant Aid Society's (HIAS) President, Leonard Glickman: *"The more diverse American society is, the safer (Jews) are."* (*Community Questioning 'Open Door,'* by Nacha Cattan, The Forward, November 29, 2002) Indeed, the HIAS puts its considerable money where its mouth is by maintaining offices in Africa to funnel more African "refugees" into America.

The status of "refugee" is critical. Aside from ensuring quick, legal entry to America, refugees are given substantial welfare benefits upon their arrival and continuously thereafter, so long as they subsist beneath the official poverty level. Usually, even the poverty level in America represents a serious increase in their standard of living. Jews are congregated in places outside the country, just as Iranian Jews are being massed in Vienna, Austria, while they await being granted "refugee status," which means an immediate $6,000 in "resettlement" money upon their arrival in America in addition to instant welfare benefits.

As always, some are more equal than others, even when it comes to refugee immigrants. By special legislation, Russian Jews are granted unrestricted entry to America's social security system of payments, despite having never paid a dime into it. *Some collect benefits in excess of those paid to Americans that worked and paid into that system their entire lives.* What's more, now there is a serious effort being made by Jewish lobbyists to get Russian Jewish immigrants grandfathered into America's Veterans' pension program. Why? Because they served in the Soviet armed forces. Never mind that they helped Stalin, Kruschev and Brezhnev to enslave much of eastern Europe and Asia, meanwhile massacring hundreds of thousands, even millions, of Poles, Czechs and Hungarians. After all, they also opposed Germany, boogeymen to the Jews. Clearly, America is the promised land, but only if you are Jewish.

Meanwhile, immigrants are reproducing at numbers far in excess of that of White America. The illegal immigrant reproduction rate alone spells the end of White America, should nothing occur to stem the rising tide.

Blacks on a Leash

"No other public holiday in the United States honors a single individual. Of all the great leaders in our Nation's history - none of them have their own holiday. All of our great war heroes share Memorial Day. All of our great presidents share President's Day. Yet King - a man who was a phony, a cheater, a traitor, and a sexual degenerate - gets a day of his own. I have a big problem with that." (Author unknown)

Black America merely is a symptom of the underlying problem: creeping Jewish supremacy. Blacks are used as straw men, whipping boys and proxies in the Jewish struggle to loosen White America's grip on the levers of power. Even so, as has been extensively developed in earlier chapters, it is entirely appropriate for us to practice defensive racism with regard to those who do harm to White America. Thus, we should defend the sort of racism which has as its sole goal the protection of White America from such destructive elements; indeed, *any* destructive elements.

Perhaps no Black symbolizes the victimization of White America more completely than does Martin Luther King, Jr., though Je$$e Jack$on runs a close second. The truly remarkable thing about King is how thoroughly managed he was by Zionists while still alive and how his memory is equally well managed by them today.

An in-depth look at the myth of Martin Luther King, Jr. provides helpful insight into the extent to which Blacks are used in the Zionist campaign to control White America:

King's history and true behavior are kept secret from Americans. King's widow received a 1977 Federal court order which sealed the huge FBI file on her husband for 50 years, *"because its release would destroy his reputation!"*

162

King incited violence while preaching nonviolence: *"(W)herever King went, violence erupted. He explained it himself, in a piece he wrote for Saturday Review (April 3, 1965), in which he set forth the four steps of his technique: '1. Nonviolent demonstrators go into the streets to exercise their constitutional rights. 2. Racists resist by unleashing violence against them. 3. Americans of conscience in the name of decency demand federal intervention and legislation. 4. The administration, under mass pressure, initiates measures of immediate intervention and remedial legislation.'"* *(Martin Luther King, Jr. - Communist Fraud*, Alan Stang http://www.etherzone.com/2004/ stang011604 .shtml, January 16, 2004)

King ruthlessly stole from others: *"The first public sermon that King ever gave, in 1947 at the Ebenezer Baptist Church, was plagiarized from a homily by Protestant clergyman Harry Emerson Fosdick entitled 'Life is What You Make It,' according to the testimony of King's best friend of that time, Reverend Larry H. Williams."* *(Holiday for a Cheater*, Michael Hoffman, Wiswell Ruffin House, Dresden, New York, 1992)

> *"(N)o less an authoritative source than the four senior editors of The Papers of Martin Luther King, Jr. (an official publication of the Martin Luther King Center for Nonviolent Social Change, Inc., whose staff includes King's widow Coretta), stated of King's writings at both Boston University and Crozer Theological Seminary: 'Judged retroactively by the standards of academic scholarship, (his writings) are tragically flawed by numerous instances of plagiarism.... Appropriated passages are particularly evident in his writings in his major field of graduate study, systematic theology...only 49 per cent of sentences in the section on Tillich (in his doctoral dissertation) contain five or more words that were King's own....'"* (Hoffman, *ibid*)

163

Boston University officials eventually admitted, *"There is no question but that Dr. King plagiarized in the dissertation."* Even so, they concluded that, *"No thought should be given to the revocation of Dr. King's doctoral degree, (because such action) would serve no purpose."* (*New York Times*, October 11, 1991, page 15)

An interesting side note: Lynne Cheney, wife of America's Vice President under George W. Bush, was Chairman of the National Endowment for the Humanities when it purposely and forcefully suppressed knowledge of King's extensive doctoral thesis plagiarism.

The first book that King wrote, *Stride Toward Freedom*, was plagiarized from numerous sources, all unattributed, according to documentation recently assembled by sympathetic King scholars Keith D. Miller, Ira G. Zepp, Jr., and David J. Garrow." (Hoffman, *ibid*)

King never outgrew his need to steal the intellectual work of others. For example, he lifted whole sections of his famous *"I Have A Dream"* speech from a sermon by 1950's Black preacher Archibald Carey.

King stole money from his followers and supporters: *"According to Assistant (FBI) Director Sullivan, who had direct access to the surveillance files on King which are denied the American people, King had embezzled or misapplied substantial amounts of money contributed to the 'civil rights' movement. King used SCLC funds to pay for liquor and numerous prostitutes, both Black and White, who were brought to his hotel rooms, often two at a time, for drunken sex parties which sometimes lasted for several days."* (*The Beast As Saint, The Truth About Martin Luther King*, by Kevin Strom, *http:// www.revilo-oliver.com/Kevin-Strom-personal/Beast_as_Saint .html*)

King even used a phony name. He was born Michael King, but his self-ordained preacher father changed his own name to Martin Luther King in 1935, thereby grandiosely presuming to assume the mantle of the great Protestant reformer, Martin Luther. Thus, his son became Martin Luther King, Jr.

King lied prodigiously. FBI Director J. Edgar Hoover named Martin Luther King, Jr. *"(t)he most notorious liar in the country."*

King liked White hookers, spending his last night on earth in an adulterous liaison with a White prostitute, just one in a long string of such assignations. (*And the Walls Came Tumbling Down*, a biography of King by Rev. Ralph Abernathy, 1989).

King liked brutalizing weaker people. During his last night alive, King was witnessed beating the prostitute he procured for the evening. (Abernathy, *ibid*)

King was a communist: *"According to King's biographer and sympathizer David J. Garrow, 'King privately described himself as a Marxist.' In his 1981 book, The FBI and Martin Luther King, Jr., Garrow quotes King as saying in SCLC staff meetings, '...we have moved into a new era, which must be an era of revolution...The whole structure of American life must be changed...We are engaged in the class struggle.'"* (Strom, *ibid*)

None other than Bobby Kennedy, US Attorney General, had King's office and hotel rooms bugged during the mid-1960s, developing extensive evidence of King's communist affiliations, revealing his communist financing and disclosing his handlers. This is how the shocking discovery of his sexual perversions was made.

> *"Jewish Communist Stanley Levison can best be described as King's behind-the-scenes 'handler.' Levison, who had for years been in charge of the secret funneling of Soviet funds to the Communist Party, USA, was King's mentor and was actually the brains behind many of King's more successful ploys. It was Levison who edited King's book, Stride Toward Freedom. It was Levison who arranged for a publisher. Levison even prepared King's income tax*

returns! It was Levison who really controlled the fund-raising and agitation activities of the SCLC. Levison wrote many of King's speeches. King described Levison as one of his 'closest friends.'" (Strom, *ibid*)

Also, generally, see *Was the Reverend Doctor Martin Luther King Jr. a Communist?* By Chuck Morse at http://www.chuckmorse .com/was_mlk_a_communist.html.

Martin Luther King, Jr., like other Black "leaders," was run by Jews, just as America's government, banking and media are today: *"Jewish Communist Stanley Levison can best be described as King's behind-the-scenes 'handler'...It was Levison who really controlled the fund-raising and agitation activities of the SCLC."* (Strom, *ibid*)

Only in recent years has the NAACP had a Black president. Previously, the leadership always was Jewish, the same people who created the organization in the first place.

Christmas, too, is a national holiday which honors but a single individual. However, Christmas now has been stripped bare of its origins and meaning by American Zionists and their *Shabbats Goyim*, the American Christian fundamentalist Zionists, such that it has become merely a major shopping opportunity, in an uncanny reflection of modern America.

How utterly perfect that the only "religious" holidays left to Americans at year end are one recently created for self profit by a Black American ex-con (*Kwanzaa*) and another which celebrates the massacre of White European ancestors by Jews (*Chanukah*).

The Finlandization of America

Just how far America has come in the past forty years of being wagged by the tail of Zionism is remarkable and perhaps best encapsulated in this quote from President George W. Bush's Address to the AIPAC Policy Conference, given May 18, 2004:

"By defending the freedom and prosperity and security of Israel, you're also serving the cause of America...I know there are buses outside waiting to take you to Capitol Hill. I'm told -- Howard told me there's over 500 meetings scheduled with members of the Senate and the House. That is good news. I'm sure you're going to pass this message on to them: A free, prosperous and secure Israel is in this nation's national interest."

Here's another great line from President Bush, delivered at a Gridiron Club dinner in Washington, D.C., March 2001: *"You can fool some of the people all of the time, and those are the ones you want to concentrate on."* Bush's handlers, of course, were quick to claim that he was joking. That is the same thing they said after he stepped in it with his infamous, *"If this were a dictatorship, it would be a heck of a lot easier, just so long as I'm the dictator,"* delivered on December 18, 2002 to Congressional leadership on Capitol Hill, then, incredibly enough, repeated for CNN's cameras later that same day.

In May 2004, Senator Ernest "Fritz" Hollings dared to say what everybody else in Washington already knew: America dances to Israel's tune, as dispensed through its Washington lobby, the American Israel Public Affairs Committee (AIPAC). *"You can't have an Israel policy other than what AIPAC gives you around here,"* said Mr. Hollings from the floor of the Senate. Of course, then it was safe for him to do so, since his retirement loomed just a few months away.

From the reaction to Mr. Hollings' statement, you would think he had proposed that American Jews be rounded up, tattooed and sent off to death camps. Rabbi Philip Silverstein of Columbia's Beth Shalom synagogue, who claimed to be *"horrified"* by Hollings' remark, hysterically ranted, *"It makes him anti-Israel. It's anti-Semitic...it's dangerous."* Abraham Foxman, National Director of the Anti-Defamation League, then fired off what has become the ADL's standard denunciation of any national figure who even implies that America carries Israel's water: *"To hear such crudeness, such ugliness, such classical anti-Semitism. It's sad."*

The ingratitude apparent in Mr. Hollings' recent statements particularly must rankle AIPAC's membership, since they thought they had bought and paid for him, to the tune of $73,275. Of course, that's peanuts compared to what has been paid for some of AIPAC's favorites, such as the Senators from Pennsylvania (Arlen Spector - $366,123), Iowa (Thomas Harkin - $423,895) and Michigan (Carl Levin - $564,858). (http://www.wrmea.com/html/aipac.htm)

What? You say the Senator from your state won't return your calls? Well, how much did you bribe...er, give in "campaign contributions" to him or her recently? What? Well, no wonder he or she refuses to listen to you. No wonder Israel calls the shots. Is it really any wonder? And AIPAC is just *one* of Israel's seemingly countless lobby groups.

There are lots of other Jewish organizations that also bribe...er, contribute to Congressmen, such as the World Jewish Congress and The Conference of Presidents of Major Jewish American Organizations, just to name a couple. And there are a great many wealthy individual Jews who give serious, *and I do mean serious*, bribes...er, contributions, such as Seagram's heir Edgar Bronfman, a *Canadian* whose work *on behalf of Israel* was recognized with the *American* Presidential Medal of Freedom, awarded by President Bill Clinton on August 11, 1999 (look, you have to admit that this is so off the wall that I couldn't just make up stuff like this). Is it really any surprise for you to learn that well over half of all Congressional bribes...er, campaign contributions now come from Jews?

Getting back to Mr. Hollings for a moment, the 82-year-old

gentleman from South Carolina retired from public office after 38 years in the Senate. That's longer than most Americans have been alive, you know. Oddly enough, 38 years also is almost exactly as long as it took for the coup to take place. What coup? You really haven't been paying attention, have you? Why, the one now reaching its climax in America. You know, the coup that began with JFK's assassination. The coup that put the Zionist International Banker cabal atop America for good.

I appreciate that Hollings came clean at last, but what I really want to know is - where were you during the first 37 years, Fritz? And where were all your colleagues while America was sold down the river? You know, the ones busy shuffling their feet and averting their eyes during your Senate floor speech? Yes, the very ones with whom you took that oath in which you swore allegiance to America and against all enemies, both domestic and foreign.

Early in 2004, bowing to the inevitable, George W. Bush signed off on Israel's campaign of genocide against the Palestinian people whose land Israel steals, inch by mile, on a daily basis. Why? Because he, and every President stretching back nearly one hundred years to Woodrow Wilson, the very first American President to sell America out to Zionist interests, has bowed low before Zionism.

"Israel's governments have mobilized the collective power of US Jewry - which dominates Congress and the media to a large degree - against them. Faced by this vigorous opposition, all the presidents, great and small, football players and movie stars - folded one after another." (Israeli journalist and peace activist, Uri Avnery, *Ha'aretz*, March 6, 1991)

John F. Kennedy reneged on his deal and look what it got him.

Space herein does not permit development of the plot surrounding JFK's assassination, but you can get the absolute last word on the subject from the book *Final Judgment*, by Michael C. Piper, available only from the *American Free Press* web site (www.americanfreepress.net), since it has been banned elsewhere.

President Bush also told the AIPAC audience, in the speech referenced above, that *"(W)e have a duty to expose and confront anti-Semitism, wherever it is found."* He followed that up with *"The demonization of Israel...can be a flimsy cover for anti-Semitism."* With those two statements, President Bush made crystal clear where his loyalties lie with regard to the mushrooming portion of America's population that objects to our Middle Eastern campaign of conquest: With Israel and against America, that's where.

Could it be any more clearly stated, folks? Of course, Bush is the same fellow who gave new life to the phrase, *"yer either with us or agin us."* At least, now we know what he meant by "us," and it most assuredly isn't *us*, fellow Americans.

In contrast to what President Bush thought, I rather liked what Fritz Hollings had to say in response to his Jewish critics from the Senate floor after he came under fire: *"I want them to apologize to me. Talking about 'anti-Semitic.' They're not getting by with it."*

Finland avoided military invasion and conquest by Joseph Stalin's Soviet Union back in the 1940s and 1950s by adopting a Soviet-style government, paying fealty to the USSR and otherwise acting much as it would, had it been conquered by force. Today, the US has gone along with International Zionism in precisely the same fashion: installing Jewish and Christian Zionists in all governmental power points, bowing to the wishes of Israel's lobbyists, removing Christianity from America's culture by edict of an increasingly-Jewish judiciary, fighting Israel's fights and even purging those who disagree with foreign Jews pushing Zionism by imprisoning America's own citizen political dissidents on phony charges.

Of course, Finland had the example of 20-80 million Russian Christians executed right next door early last century, simply for being anti-Semitic, a lesson that America seems to have forgotten. The term *"Finlandization"* has come to refer to quislings like Finland

and, now, America.

America, faithful servant to the Zionist cabal now astride her, is the dog wagged by its Zionist tail, a tail that increasingly, through America, wags the world at large. Keeping America in line is not easy, though. We have seen that Black Americans merely are used to help pry loose White American fingers from the levers of power. Pervasive racist ideologies have been developed through relentless propagandizing to ensure that White America stays under control. We have examined how useful "anti-Semite" can be in that campaign. Now let's take a closer look at racism, itself.

Chapter 11

Racists Everywhere

"Racist: Someone who seems to believe that race really matters."
--- unknown

Thus far, we have labeled the following classes of people "racist," used in the pejorative sense that generally is meant: White supremacists, Jewish supremacists (*aka* Zionists), Black supremacists, Aztlan activists, Mestizos, the world's elite and the politically correct. Let's take care of everybody else now, because *we are all racists of one sort or another.*

It is the most natural thing in the world to want to be with those who seem most like ourselves and to exclude those most dissimilar. Family is the best example of this very universal human desire. Then comes extended family and close friends.   Work and school acquaintances next, closely followed by neighbors. In times past, these people were all of the same race and, often, even of the same clan or family.   In fact, not so long ago, entire countries were composed of the same race. That's what the word "nation" used to mean, after all – a single *race*.

Be true to your school. That sort of thing.

Cats with tails pick on cats without tails. Big horses bully small horses. Schoolyard bullies abound. Exclusion of the dissimilar is an approximation of drawing together with those similar, demonstrating that pecking orders are a manifestation of the desire to be with one's own.

Insecurity might be called the basic human condition, since it has been possessed in abundance by every single human being that ever lived. In the main, insecurity is what causes us to wish to be liked, even loved. And the ones we most want to like us are those that are most like us, starting with family. Otherwise, Mom/Dad stuff would not occupy the bulk of psychotherapy sessions. People most like ourselves put us most at ease.

Neither Blacks nor Whites want integration. This fact shows in the workplace, at schools, in housing and in the military. Whites and Blacks self segregate at every possible opportunity. Only government forces the races together – and then, only temporarily.

The great unspoken fact about interracial relations is that Whites quite simply *lie* about having Black friends. The vast majority of all Whites claim to have Black friends. Based upon that, *statistics alone demand that each and every Black in America must have 4 or 5 close White buddies*. Yeah, right.

Blacks quite simply are a totally different culture in America.

Blacks have the same fear of Black violence that so many Whites possess and which all Whites, in reality, *should* possess. *The Blacks know better.* Profiling and stereotypes are widely used *because they work*.

Whenever sports at American colleges (*e.g.*, golf) become White dominated, they simply put quota restrictions in place. Nothing of the sort happens in reverse, of course.

And the favoritism doesn't end with Blacks, of course, as we already have seen in this book. In 2003, an illegal alien girl named Jessica captured the media's fancy and, before they were done with her, she had received *two* complete heart/lung transplants *for free* (16 Americans die each day while awaiting transplants).

The middle class, that vast slumbering horde planted solidly in the middle of the road, is predominantly racist, though all but a very few deny it. This perhaps is best explained by a letter I wrote some time ago. The thoughts I expressed are even more relevant these days, so I will share it with you.

Letter to a Liberal

You see, I had received a sternly disapproving letter from a liberal friend of mine, one I had known and loved for over 30 years (I was his best man), decrying my representing the Aryan Nations in the trumped-up lawsuit brought by the Southern Poverty Law Center and its founder, Morris Dees.

I'm not a skinhead. I'm not a believer in Christian Identity (the brand of Christianity embraced by adherents of the Aryan Nations). I'm not even uniformly conservative. Though I often describe myself as right wing, that is only because the rest of this country has become so thoroughly socialist-cum-communist. True moderates, such as myself, now appear to be far to the right.

Because those like myself refuse to join the left in condemning those on the right, we get pitched in after them and painted with the same liberal paintbrush (though, honestly, if I had to choose one side over the other, then clearly I have been pitched in with the correct people).

After thinking long and hard, I drafted and sent the following response:

Dear Xxx,

Your letter was unexpected because I thought you had discarded me without further thought once you decided I was too politically incorrect for your intellectual comfort. Since there may actually be some small chance to salvage our friendship, I will respond and attempt to reason with you on the points you raise.

Let's see now...your letter accuses me of having changed from a liberal, becoming a conservative and bigoted, likely due to my apparent affluence, during a period spanning 30 years, during which you changed from conservative to liberal. Because I confess to being a separatist, you equate that with racism. You also state that I must agree with the thinking of the Aryan Nations, since I have it as a client. Having read and reread your letter, perhaps 50 times, I think that's a reasonable summary.

As I look back over my life, you stand out on a number of counts, one of the most profound being the fact that, in the 1960's, you were one of the most bigoted people I have ever known, including all members of the Aryan Nations that I have since met. Have you changed in that regard? Sure, but not exactly in the ways you profess. You're still pretty bigoted...witness the animosity you now feel for me, based strictly on my associations and thinking and not on my basic worth as a human being or my actions toward you.

Though I disagreed with your thinking then, I was pleased to have you as my friend. Now that you perceive our roles to have reversed (your perception only, incidentally, since I have never indulged in the sort of racial vitriol and outlooks you possessed when I met you), you are not inclined to return the favor, however. Funny thing is, though I believe your thinking is pretty muddled politically and your mind as closed as any I have ever seen, I still have no problem with you as a friend. Friendship is, as they say, accepting others *as* they are, not because of *what* they are.

Trite though it may sound, some of my best friends are liberals. Some of my best friends also are conservatives. Some of them are *bona fide* racists. Some are religious zealots. Some are atheists. Some are Mexicans, Jews and Asians. Though I don't currently count any Blacks as more than acquaintances, I have called many of them friends through the years and do currently admire the intellectual acumen of several. My last office manager in California was Black;

176

and there are both Latins and Asians on staff right now. Do you actually have anything but liberals as friends? This is such an issue with you, but doesn't really occupy much of my time. Just who is the bigot here, anyway?

Have I changed through the years? Sure, and it has been for the better in most regards.

Far more profound, however, has been the fundamental societal shift in this country from conservatism to liberalism, undeniable in the face of our having elected a draft dodger (Bill Clinton) to be our President. Compared to that sea change, which has swept you away on its leading swells, I have altered my stance very little, though the apparent relative shift is substantial. As a Berkeley judge I met in my 20's once put it: "If you are not liberal when you are young, you have no heart. But, if you are not conservative as you grow older, you have no head." What a marvelous assessment.

When did the word "conservative" become so dirtied in your lexicon? I have observed the effects of liberalism and increased welfare and entitlements upon this country and its population and been forced to conclude that we are creating and perpetuating that which we profess to be attempting to alleviate and eradicate. "Tough love" is what is required and what works, both at the family level and at all levels of government.

Create a safety net and others of all races always will rely upon it and take it as a given, never becoming self reliant. The current general affluence which overlays this country's outright socialistic government is an anomaly that time will show to have been a product only of the most massive expansion of credit and the money supply ever witnessed, and for which our descendants (and, possibly, we) will pay dearly. There really is no such thing as a free lunch.

Fewer and fewer pay the taxes that support burgeoning governmental bureaucracies, thus the upswell in tax rates, despite the general prosperity. When prosperity gives way to recession or worse, as it always does, then the system will break down.

Fiscal conservatism, which I wholeheartedly believe in, is the only way and I challenge you to say otherwise since I know you personally practice such in your life. You aren't borrowing wildly to finance your current lifestyle. National economics really is no different from that practiced at the personal level.

So, I guess you decry my social conservatism, then, is that correct? Of course, I have supported abortion in the past, however. I also believe in private freedom of religious thinking (no state religions, not even that peculiar brand called atheism). I also believe in true equality. Of course, equality means equality of opportunity to me, not dividing up everything and handing out equal shares - that is socialism, of course. And drugs, well, you know my attitudes in this regard. Pretty liberal thinking, eh? Maybe that means I am still a Libertarian...funny thing, since that is the outlook I subscribed to over 25 years ago. Seem to remember you being there, too, but we will both agree that you no longer are such.

Gosh, maybe "conservative" isn't really what you mean, then. You seem to use that word interchangeably with "bigot," "separatist" and "racist." Of course, I note that most liberals indulge in that sort of broad brush stroking.

I'm surprised you don't accuse me of being a religious fundamentalist, as well, since that is part and parcel of the name calling. Since I am willing to tolerate religious fundamentalists, perhaps I really am one of them to a liberal. Of course, using your logic about my representing the Aryan Nations, if I am willing to defend a religious fundamentalist, then I must think just like them, too. *Ergo*, I must be a religious fundamentalist, which even you will admit is ridiculously off the mark.

Hmmmmm. Do you see the flaw in this sort of reasoning?

You never mentioned the word hate, a favorite of the liberal, left-wing, socialist, commie, tree-hugging, Birkenstock-wearing, fruit-beer-swilling, granola-munching, dirt-eating druids now running America. I'm sure that is implicit in your charge that I am a bigot, however. I'll be happy to deal with that, but first let's get this distilled down to the single real bone you seem to have to pick with me.

Closely allied to the bigotry charge is the separatism/racism duality you propose.

I see you have a new address, though you never have told me you moved. I'll address this letter to that address and see if it comes back. Are you now in a part of your city that is occupied by all manner of different ethnic groups, or is your new neighborhood pretty lily White, just like the last section in which you lived? If the former, then good for you in practicing what you preach. I'll be interested in hearing your assessment in a few years' time. If the latter, however, and I would give long odds on this selection, then you are still a separatist.

I don't care what the rationalization is that you have for living there; the fact remains that you selected it for characteristics that derive from its almost purely Caucasian nature. And I guarantee you that what few ethnics might be there actually are White people, too, in all regards except skin color (and they are the ones you always think of when you are pushing your diversity-is-wonderful message on others, aren't they?).

Separatism is merely the act of being or living apart from others possessing specified characteristics. Want to live in a low-crime area? Near good schools? Then you are a separatist, because those are characteristics that do not exist in multiethnic neighborhoods.

Separatism might be racism, but if it is, then you, too, are a racist and will have to consider that racism may not be an altogether bad thing. I am a separatist; I cannot in honesty profess to be otherwise.

In fact, I don't want my kids associating with White trash or knee-jerk liberals' offspring or the kids of religious extremists, either.

179

I want them physically safe and not being bombarded with propaganda (which I don't spoon-feed them, either). Like you, it is the characteristics that attract or repel me, not the racial makeup; fact is, though, the characteristics accompany and derive from the racial makeup.

Facts are facts. Even the liberal press makes no pretense of crime and ignorance being uniform throughout our society.

So, what are we left with now? Racism, I guess, and the bigotry (hate) charge. But, then, they are the same thing, aren't they? What is racism/bigotry, but the belief that one is better than another (therefore entitled to dislike or hate) due to one's racial history or skin color?

Fair enough? Isn't that really the crux of your dilemma with me? Your assumption/belief that I am someone who hates others due to skin color? Well, guess what? You are wrong and you know it. And my 30+ year history with you deserves better consideration than you have afforded.

Do I possess some attitudes about different races? Sure. Are some of them politically incorrect? You bet. Are they wrong? Show me where and I will change in an instant.

For example, there are differences between races, other than skin color. It isn't just coincidence that sports of every sort are dominated by Blacks; they evolved in the African veldt, where strength and swiftness were rewarded with life and natural selection doomed lesser physical specimens. Broad, flared nostrils enhance the intake of oxygen, which is used in prodigious quantities by those oversize gluteal and thigh muscles in jumping and running.

In the northern climes, where Caucasians evolved, physical prowess was important, to be sure, but intellectual ability was disproportionately necessary in order to make it from one summer to the next by setting aside food for the future and making living accommodations in one season that sustain life in the next. That is why Caucasians so dominate intellectual activity in this country and why affirmative action will never work.

Are Blacks better than Whites because they are physically superior?

The fact is, as shown by even the liberals' hushed-up studies, White IQs exceed Black IQs by an average of 15 to 25 points. Are Whites better than Blacks because they are mentally superior? My own IQ is well in excess of 30 points higher than the average Caucasian's; does that make me superior to any White person beneath that mark? Does that entitle me to hate almost everybody?

Asians and Jews, as races, have higher average IQs than Whites. Does that make them better than us?

There are other differences, including skin colors, but the point is that they are just differences, some of which give some races advantages in certain arenas over other races. There is no inherent superiority to be derived from an assessment of these differences and certainly no privileges that should thereby attach.

However, I am sick to death of political correctness.

I am sick of White people apologizing to Blacks.

I am sick of the very racist attitudes of liberals which results in affirmative action because they fundamentally believe that, otherwise, Black people can never compete as equals.

I am sick of White people being discriminated against, in favor of any ethnic group.

I am sick of the media bias against Whites and in favor of Blacks, which results in the rare White-on-Black crime being headlined and the monstrously-disproportionate Black-on-White crimes being not reported at all or being submerged into the background noise.

I am sick of White children being forced into physically and mentally-unsafe schools and neighborhoods by bleeding-heart liberals.

I am sick of hearing about children of any race being raped and murdered.

I am sick of the hatred being tossed around today by liberals and justified by terms such as anti-Semitic and racist and right wing and conservative, *ad nauseum.*

I am sick of all the hatred, which now seems primarily to be the province of the left-wing.

You want to talk about hatred and dirty tactics and unethical behavior? Then I could talk for hours about Morris Dees and the Southern Poverty Law Center and the JDL and the ADL, in the context of the lawsuit in which I am defending the Aryan Nations. My little girl could tell you of the death threat she received from a Jew, as could my wife and other children about theirs.

I could tell of the multiple threats I have received from the JDL/ADL and from around the globe, especially Israel, for defending the Aryan Nations in this case, brought solely because of their anti-Semitic and racist beliefs.

How about the witnesses being harassed and tampered with, right now, by Dees' minions?

How about my office repeatedly and illegally being searched by someone?

How about the phone taps that I know have been placed on my lines by the FBI/ADL?

How about the tax audits I have all of a sudden had to undergo? The property tax reassessments that have taken place out of sequence with my neighbors? The beer cans in my driveway?

How about the local papers calling me a Nazi because I defend the Aryan Nations (of course, since you, who have known me so well, are willing to stoop to that sort of rationalization, how can I expect more of them)?

How about the loss of my friends (you, for example), now afraid to associate with me because I am standing up to the system?

I am proud of handling the Aryan Nations case, regardless of what the outcome may be. This is the current battlefield for the First Amendment and I am honored to play a part in its defense.

The rest of the Constitution has already been eroded or superseded, and I realize that the First Amendment is on its way out, too. Think not?

2nd Amendment (right to bear arms) - already so limited that it does not exist in most places.

3rd (quartering soldiers) - eliminated by Executive Order, as will be seen when and if martial law is ever declared.

4th (search and seizure) - you or your car can be searched anytime a cop wants. At worst, he can always claim he saw you do or drop something suspicious. Search warrants require merely the flimsiest of affidavits, often perjured, and a friendly magistrate.

5th (due process of law) Fifth Amendment - Government takes what it wants, when it wants, via civil forfeiture, with nothing in the way of due process being observed. Law enforcement now has a stake in the drug trade. It's easier to broker drug deals than to conduct genuine investigations. If the cops arrest a burglar right away, they have to return your property. If they don't take any action till he sells your property and buys drugs, they get to keep the cash.

6th (rights of the accused) - How do you hire a decent lawyer after the government confiscates all your assets or spends you into bankruptcy defending yourself in audits and the like?

7th (trial by jury in civil cases) - Routinely denied in case after case that I see nowadays.

8th (cruel and unusual punishment) - 10 years for smoking marijuana rather than drinking beer?

9th (rights retained by people) - Other rights? Why, even the enumerated rights have been taken away.

10th (rights reserved to states and people) - Now, clearly it has become the rights granted by government, particularly the Federal government.

11th (suits against states) - I just had a judge throw out a client's main cause of action against the local county because, by statute, the county and its minions are incapable of being negligent.

12th (election of President) - Yeah, right.   As if Bush/Gore/McCain/Bradley is really a choice.

13th (slavery) - Pretty much still intact, unless you view working for half the year to pay taxes as slavery.

14th (equal protection) - As George Orwell observed in Animal Farm, some are *"more equal than others."* They are now the judicially-enumerated "protected classes": race (*only if non-White*), sex (*female only*), religion (*state approved only*).   The parenthetical comments are those made by the judges, not me.   This is also where six guys can be involved in a drug deal, five are cops and one goes to jail. And so on...

I wanted you to read David Duke's book so as to expose you to some alternate points of view that I knew for a fact you had discarded out of hand without considering their merits.   Not because I agreed with everything he has to say; on the contrary.   He has written an excellent overview of the racial problems of the world, from the perspective of the racist.   I wanted that to serve as the basis of a dialogue between us which could lead to resolution of the growing unease you had with what you perceived me to have become.   I invoked and risked our 30-year friendship to create that dialogue, because I felt that otherwise our friendship was doomed anyway.

Can you seriously argue that I was wrong, given your current feelings?   I don't feel that I lost anything that wasn't already lost. You weren't willing to honor that request of mine, probably because our 30-year relationship had already become relatively valueless to you.   This letter is a poor substitute for that dialogue we could have had, but worth the considerable investment of time and energy I have chosen to make, nonetheless, because I do value you.

Sincerely,

I never heard from my friend again, I am sad to report.

As I said, we are all racists, whether we believe so or not. We can't help it.

Mind you, what I have outlined in this chapter goes well beyond what the average White American would define as racism. We have come to believe that merely resisting being oppressed and divided by the very racist policies of America's ruling class is, in itself, racism. Indeed, simply wishing the White race well is seen as a racist outlook.

In other words, unless we participate in our own racial genocide, we are racists. We will explore this concept further in Chapter 13, *Defensive Racism*, but my point at the moment is to show that everybody already goes well beyond that every day. Since we already choose to be racial separatists, based on the obvious results of our personal living, working and schooling choices, is it such a stretch actively to oppose being hobbled by affirmative action and its progeny?

Chapter 12

The Truth Hurts

"Congress shall make no law...abridging the freedom of speech."
--- *US Constitution*, First Amendment (1791)

"Freedom of speech means that you shall not do something to people either for the views they express, or the words they speak or write."
--- Hugo Black, US Supreme Court Justice, *"One Man's Stand for Freedom"* (1963)

"Speaking the truth in times of universal deceit is a revolutionary act."
--- George Orwell

"The trust of the innocent is the liar's most useful tool."
--- from *"Needful Things,"* a novel by Stephen King

Free speech is a funny kind of concept. Used to be, free speech was anything that didn't physically hurt others. Don't yell "Fire!" in a packed theatre, for example, unless there really *is* a fire, of course. Truth always won out then.

Then laws developed about libel and slander, designed to rein in words that could hurt one's ability to make a living or move freely about. Again, truth always won out – if someone sued you because you called them a whore and you could prove they had sex for money, you won.

Now we see speech laws morphing into bans on "hate speech."

Problem is, the further into the rhetorical woods we go, the murkier the visibility becomes. And truth no longer provides a defense.

Once upon a time in America, truth was an absolute defense to any charge of libel or slander. Indeed, the whole point of trials and open-court litigation was pursuit of the truth. No more.

Throughout my career as a trial lawyer, always I have given the following advice to my clients, be they plaintiffs or defendants: "Just tell the truth. Then you never have to worry about what to say or what you already might have said." Whenever a client then has lied during the course of a case and refused to let me tell the other side and do my best to compensate for that lie, that client has had to find a new lawyer on the spot. Admittedly, mine is a minority opinion in a profession that richly deserves all that is heaped upon it.

Nowadays, though I still insist upon the truth (call it a weakness), I tell my clients that what they say likely will be irrelevant. Of course, most of my clients these days are politically incorrect. *There is no justice for the politically incorrect in America these days*.

Increasingly, litigation simply is window dressing, especially criminal litigation. Particularly when it involves politically-incorrect defendants. Many procedural and substantive reasons exist for the loss of truth and justice, such as media vilification and prosecutorial misconduct (beginning with gross overcharging), but they serve merely to mask the true objective: silencing dissenters through the exercise of power simply because that power is available.

Hate Crimes and Hate Speech

Used to be, we considered the role of truth merely when a legal case already existed. Today, simply telling the truth can get you put in an American jail. And it is about to get worse. Much worse.

America has crossed the line into the prosecution of pure thought crimes and there will be no turning back.

Some years ago, the state of Texas was having trouble getting its hate crime law passed. Just then, coincidentally of course, it was loudly proclaimed that some nasty White supremacists had gone hog wild and painted swastikas on the side of a Dallas Black church. Not only that, but it was reported that those terrible White people did so in response to all the hate-crime legislation rhetoric extant in Texas. Suddenly, *no problemo* - the legislation sailed through the Texas legislature a week later amidst the outcry and general indignation about racism and the "hurtful nature" of such "crimes." Texas' governor signed the bill into law immediately, of course.

Teach them nasty White people a lesson, eh? Difficulty is, eyewitnesses saw a *Black* guy painting those swastikas on the church. *Of course, though this fact was reported to the police the day after the swastikas appeared, it was kept from the public until much later.*

It is not just sloppy writing on my part that blurs the distinction between hate speech and hate crimes, since they really are the same thing in the eyes of law enforcement these days and, unfortunately, the American public, as well. Currently, all American hate crime laws require some criminal *act* component. Thus, the enhanced penalty for a hate crime murder is much stiffer than mere murder. And, the penalty for painting swastikas on Black churches is far greater than for mere "tagging," which now is actually considered art in parts of Los Angeles.

Remember, though, that what is being penalized is the perp's state of mind, or thoughts, while engaged in a criminal act. Since there already is a penalty for the crime itself, what really results is a penalty for the thought. Yep...a thought crime, pure and simple. And leftists openly are chomping at the bit for the day they can decouple the thought from the act and penalize it alone. That was one of the things Clinton desperately tried to get passed before he sank from view: a pure hate speech law, similar to those now existing in

Canada, Britain, France and Germany, to name a few Western nations a bit farther down the slippery slope than America.

Leftists argue that there is no real difference between a hate crime enhancement and a hate speech law and, of course, they are right. Though leftists think that is why hate speech laws should be enacted, in reality it is why hate crime laws of every stripe should be *rescinded.*

And, of course, hate crime legislation works only in one direction, as we have seen countless times already. Remember all the Blacks rioting in both Seattle and Cincinnati in recent years? Who got charged with hate crimes? That's right, only *White* people, even though only a White man died – that, in Seattle when he tried to rescue a White woman from being gang raped by several Blacks. Talk about racial profiling!

What truly puts the lie to the establishment's motives in charging hate crimes and collecting statistics about them is the fact that Hispanics are counted as *victims* of hate crimes, but never as perpetrators. Hispanic *perpetrators*, which they so often are, of course, are considered *White,* as dictated by the FBI's Uniform Crime Reporting program, itself a product of the Hate Crimes Statistics Act passed by America's congress fourteen years ago. This artificially inflates the proportion of hate crimes attributed to Whites, of course, but the real reason is that virtually only Whites ever are charged.

In 1999, per the US Bureau of Justice Statistics, there were over 657,000 Black-on-White crimes of violence, versus about 91,000 White-on-Black crimes of a similar nature. That's a ratio of over 7 to 1. Considering that Blacks comprise about 1/7th of Americans, that means that *Blacks are fifty times more likely to commit a violent interracial crime than are Whites*. No wonder that even Blacks don't want to live in Black neighborhoods. No wonder that, when he hears footsteps approach in the night, Jesse Jackson admits relief when seeing that the person approaching is White.

190

Meanwhile, 1 out of every 45 White-on-Black crimes is called a hate crime, while a ridiculous 1 out of 1,254 of Black-on-White crimes get that classification! An astounding 80% of all Hate Crime charges are lodged against White people in America.

My eldest daughter, now 21, was taught in her high school social studies class that *only White people can be guilty of hate crimes*, owing to the past oppression of minorities! Your children are being taught this in public school, too, by inference if not directly. We now home school our two younger children.

Say the N-Word, Go to Jail

Think the foregoing is simply apocryphal? Think it doesn't translate into reality? Ask Lonny Rae. A client of mine, Lonny Rae recently faced five years in prison for slinging the N-word at a Black guy who had just mauled his wife. She was a reporter, on assignment for the local newspaper, who took a picture of one of the referees following a high school football game late in 2000. Kenneth Manley, the referee, didn't like it and grabbed her around the neck as she walked away, in an attempt to take the camera from her.

We sought and received a change in venue so that Lonny Rae didn't have to submit to the judgment of members of the small community in central Idaho (Council) where he was held in such low esteem for *"gittin' the football team in trouble,"* as so eloquently put by the town ruffian that then proceeded to break Lonny's ankle in a fistfight one cold evening after the referees' association had placed the Council High School on probation for "fan harassment."

The harassment? After Manley let go of Lonny's wife and disappeared into the red brick field house to shower and change clothes, Lonny got a good look at the injury to his wife's neck and went ballistic. He turned and shouted into the building: *"Tell that nigger to get out here, 'cuz I'm a gonna kick his butt."*

191

The referee never was charged with assault and battery (and still never has been charged with anything), yet Lonny was booked for a violation of Idaho's Malicious Harassment statute (the hate crime law). That was when the media from nearby Boise went into an orgy, covering the "racist" Lonny Rae both in print and on TV. Lonny never again got work in the area.

Even the local newspaper got in on the act, eventually referring to Lonny's wife as "the antichrist." Yes, that is the same newspaper that had assigned her to cover the football game in the first place. And that is the same newspaper that let her go when advertisers threatened to pull their ads if she remained on staff.

"Welcome to Council," says the sign at the town outskirts, *"The community that cares."*

The local authorities claimed it was just coincidental that Lonny was charged only a day or so after the referees' association placed the Council High School football program on probation.

Following a quick two-day jury trial, Lonny Rae was acquitted of the hate crime charge (a five-year prison term could have resulted from a conviction). However, just before jury deliberations, and over my strenuous objection (we already had rested Lonny's defense), the judge added assault and disturbing the peace as lesser-included offenses for the jury's consideration. The jury convicted Lonny of assault. A month later, the judge sentenced him to seven days in the county jail, suspended pending appeal.

In a rare win for the politically incorrect, I took the case up on appeal and prevailed, albeit upon what I would call a technicality.

The Idaho Court of Appeals stated: *"Because we have concluded that assault is not a lesser included offense of malicious harassment in this case, Rae's judgment of conviction for assault is vacated."*

The Court of Appeals seized upon the *"does some act which creates a well-founded fear in the other person"* language of Idaho's assault statute in holding that assault is not a logical subset of the hate crime law. Go figure. Of course, on the stand, the Black guy confessed that he never was afraid of Lonny Rae, so the distinction is valid in this case. I simply figured there were better reasons for distinguishing the two statutes, but, then, nobody except Lonny Rae ever did care what I thought.

Go here for the full text of the judicial decision published:

> *Idaho v. Rae*, Docket No. 28229, 2004 Opinion No. 8 (http://www.isc.idaho.gov/opinions/rae.pdf).

So what was the technicality? The trial judge did not require the jury to enter a finding on Disturbing the Peace if it convicted Lonny of Assault, which is why a judgment of acquittal on all charges finally had to be entered, despite the appellate court also ruling that Disturbing the Peace *is* a lesser-included offense of the Idaho Hate Crime statute.

What I found most ironic about the decision issued by the appellate court in the Rae case is the language quoted from another case by the judges, used to justify the trial judge's adding a lesser-included offense to the charges after the defense had rested and with no prior notice to our side: *"Our courts are not gambling halls but forums for the discovery of truth...neither the prosecution nor the defense should be allowed, based on their trial strategy, to preclude the jury from considering guilt of a lesser offense included in the crime charged."* (*State v. Watts*, 131 Idaho 782, 784-785, Ct App, 1998)

The appellate court's statement seems ironic in light of prosecutors never suffering any penalty for overloading charge sheets in order to guarantee convictions and heavy penalties, which in turn forces defendants to plea bargain more readily. But, what I find most curious is that this "forum for the discovery of truth" didn't care about the fact that the only person who actually did commit assault, as well as battery, and who physically injured another person, *never was charged with anything!* Who? Why, the Black guy, of course.

Remember, he attacked and injured Lonny Rae's wife. That's what got Lonny Rae so mad in the first place.

If the courtroom is a "forum for the discovery of truth," then somebody please explain to me why that Black guy sat there in front of the judge, walked away and, to this day, never has been charged with a thing.

Yet, Lonny Rae and his wife both lost their jobs, his foot was broken by the town ruffian, then they lost their home and many possessions when they ran out of money and had to move away. Because he did the right thing and stood up for his wife's honor. Because he objected to the brutalizing inflicted upon her by the Black guy who never was charged with anything.

Already, we have seen that "the truth" is nothing but an accidental byproduct of our courts today. Now, it should be clear to the most casual observer that justice, real justice, often is absent as well.

By the way, in case you were wondering, I handled the Lonny Rae case, including the appeal, *pro bono*, because I thought the principles involved were important. The court didn't even award us costs for our successful appeal. Your tax dollars paid for the considerable sum it took to bring Lonny Rae to trial and to fight his appeal, though.

Symbolic Speech

It isn't just verbal speech that is coming in for one-sided application in America today. There is a time-honored tradition of what is known as "symbolic speech," flag burning being the most notable example.

However, in mid 2003, the US Supreme Court dealt free speech yet another mortal blow when it ruled, in *Virginia vs. Black*, that states may outlaw cross burning. This ruling flies directly in the face of a long line of flag desecration rulings, which hold that flag burning is symbolic speech, thus deserving of First Amendment protection. So, too, is cross burning a form of symbolic speech, of course. Why else would one burn a cross, save to make a statement? Maybe not one with which you agree, but a statement, nonetheless.

Speaking for the Supremes, Justice Clarence Thomas, the only Black member of the bench, said, *"Just as one cannot burn down someone's house to make a political point and then seek refuge in the First Amendment, those who hate cannot terrorize and intimidate to make their point."* Thus the court advances the frontier of American thought crime yet another notch. Now, if the perps in this case had burned down another person's cross, I might cede Justice Thomas his point, but the leap of faith required to bridge the logical gap in his statement is simply too terrifying for me to contemplate.

If I don't "hate," can I still burn a cross? How does one divine my secret thought while performing my symbolic speech? Is this like saying the N-word, which is okay if you're Black, but now a hate crime if you're White? Can the new law properly be called "Burning while White?" Talk about racial profiling!

Can I still burn a menorah with evil intent and not expect a trip to slamland? Since what is being punished is the evil intent, what if I harbor the evilest of intents and burn, say, a lawn chair? Do I go to jail?

Is that swooshing sound we hear that of Justice Thomas and the other Supremes sliding downslope?

I signed an *"amicus"* brief which was filed with the Supreme Court in *Virginia vs. Black*, arguing against the position they now have adopted. It was another's writing, which I approved, and which had been hired out by a conservative group, a group which has been noticeably silent since the ruling came out. They asked me to submit the brief because I am admitted to practice before the U.S. Supreme Court. A nationally-known columnist, in all seriousness, suggested that I be disbarred for having dared submit this brief.

An ardent supporter of free speech, it was an easy call for me to agree to sign my name to a brief supporting cross burning. And, I would do it again, even though it was apparent at the outset just what the result was going to be. You see, the court had consolidated two different cases: in one, Whites burned a cross in a Black family's back yard and, in the other, Whites burned a cross on their own private property. Clearly, the court was not going to approve the former. By putting the two cases together, the court signaled its intent to outlaw the latter.

Few will argue that cross burning is anything but ugly behavior. But, it is just the sort of ugliness in which true beauty resides - the beauty of free speech. Too bad that, as a society, we have yet to mature to the point where we see real beauty regardless of the context.

I like to remind others that it is only the most reviled among us, usually reviled precisely because of what they have to say, that come in for legal lynching in the name of tolerance. None are more intolerant than those who preach tolerance. For the rest of us, of course, tolerance is a nonissue, as it should be for all. And the purveyors of tolerance are among the more admired members of society, too, like beauty queens who get by in life without trying.

I often say that the First Amendment is the only one left with any life; even so, it is lying prone and breathing shallowly.

Who Controls America?

In 2003, when Malaysian Prime Minister Mahathir said the world is run by Jews by proxy (that is, through their *goyim* puppets), he was roundly condemned. And what he said was called a lie by Israel, where a furor erupted. Recall that Israeli Prime Minister Sharon has said, *"We, the Jewish people, control America, and the Americans know it."* (Sharon to his cabinet on October 3, 2001, as reported by

Al Jazeerah.)

Why do you suppose it was necessary for the American President, of all people, to denounce Mahathir? If not acting at Jewish direction, why would the President even care? Mahathir told the truth, after all. Problem is, the truth involved Jews.

America makes it illegal to boycott the products of only one country in the world: Israel. And that law is enforced, as Cook Composites and Polymers Company recently found out. Cook was fined $6,000 merely for responding *"to a request from a customer in Bahrain...stating that the goods being shipped were not of Israeli origin and did not contain Israeli materials."* (*North Kansas City Company Settles Charge Related to Boycott of Israel*, Kansas City Star, June 25, 2003). Again, merely telling the truth runs afoul of the law. And, as this boycott ban law blatantly shows, it is the truth about only a single ethnic group that counts: *Jews.*

Historical Revisionism

Enter Historical Revisionism, the quest to set the record straight. During war, governments issue some of the most ridiculous statements and push them as fact, in order to get their citizens on board with their current war effort. The American claim during the first Gulf war that Iraqi soldiers stole a Kuwait hospital's incubators, leaving babies to die on the cold tile floors, is a particularly egregious recent example. It could have been a scene from *"Wag the Dog,"* it was so outlandishly false, as since admitted by officials. The idea was to get Americans behind the effort to intercede in the Middle East. It worked. Problem is, the story still occasionally surfaces and gets passed around.

Historical Revisionists endeavor to get history written correctly. Currently, their main effort concerns World War II and the propaganda pushed, first, to get America into the war and, later, to

197

keep it there until its bloody end. That propaganda has endured and grown, in fact, turning into a major industry, the main purpose of which is to advance Zionist interests.

Even though the stories about lampshades made from human skin and soap rendered from the fat of Jewish victims have been as thoroughly debunked as the Kuwaiti baby incubator fable, they still occasionally bubble to the surface.

The lies about the gas chambers and the ovens have only partially been revealed. Similarly, though Jewish historians themselves admit that far fewer perished, the myth that 6,000,000 Jews perished in German concentration camps persists and is actively promoted at all levels of society.

A side note: outlandish claims of Jewish casualties is nothing new. They claimed 6,000,000 in WWI, too, believe it or not. And, as historian/journalist Michael Hoffman has pointed out: *"There are two early 'Holocaust' tales from the Talmud. Gittin 57b. claims that four billion Jews were killed by the Romans in the city of Bethar. Gittin 58a claims that 16 million Jewish children were wrapped in scrolls and burned alive by the Romans."* (*Judaism's Strange Gods,* Michael Hoffman, Independent History, 2000).

Publicly challenging Jewish "Holocaust" claims will lead to a prison sentence in most Western countries. And truth is no defense. In fact, *telling the truth is the problem*, since revealing the lies is deemed anti-Semitic, in and of itself. In fact, attempting to defend oneself against these charges in court, once one is charged in some countries, such as Germany, will result in fresh charges being filed. Yes, you read that last sentence correctly. Repeating the offensive statements in court is a separate offense!

ADL Tyranny

The Jewish ADL (AntiDefamation League) has been

instrumental in getting hate crime laws passed in most of America's states. Now they endeavor to convert those laws into pure hate speech laws, as now exist in Canada and most of Western Europe. Already, the American laws are perverted and misapplied in order to punish mere speech, but that is not enough. Once speech itself, with no accompanying crime, becomes formally illegal in America, then eradication of truth as a defense will follow, as it has in Canada and Western Europe. And it will be the truth concerning a single ethnic group that will be most disallowed, of course: *Jews.*

You needn't believe just me that Jews are special when it comes to suppressing the truth. Listen to none other than America's Attorney General, John Ashcroft, as he prostrates himself before the ADL: *"Ninety years ago, the founders of the Anti-Defamation League dedicated themselves to the noblest ideals. They vowed to use their time, their energy, and their earnings to stand against intolerance and to stand for freedom...This administration believes that acts of anti-Semitism must be confronted, condemned, and denounced...As history shows, verbal attacks on the Jewish people are portends (sic) of more savage criminality to come...The ADL has proven time and again its ability to warn of the dangers to the innocent when the good and truehearted do not band together to oppose hate."* (*Prepared Remarks to the ADL of Attorney General John Ashcroft*, New York, New York, November 7, 2003, http://www.usdoj.gov/ag/speeches/2003/aganti-defamation.htm)

And Ashcroft's is not a lone voice in the Administration, either. FBI Director Mueller pandered to the ADL at its 24th Annual National Leadership Conference in May of 2002: *"I have long admired and respected the work of the ADL, and I appreciate your longstanding support of the FBI. I know that under my predecessor, Louis Freeh, this partnership reached new heights...I am absolutely committed to building on that relationship."* (http://www.fbi.gov/pressrel/speeches/speech050702.htm)

This is the same ADL, by the way, that has been adjudged guilty of massive theft and illegality in assembling a computerized database of Americans it dislikes. And this is the same FBI that busted the ADL in 1993, a bust which led to a judicial ruling that the ADL violated a number of state and Federal laws when it stole data from a variety of government offices, *including the FBI itself.* (http://www. impactnet.org/html/adl_spying.html)

They steal from the government, yet that same government then turns around and praises the ADL and the partnership it has with one of the very agencies from which it stole! Meanwhile, it is just business as usual for the ADL and the Jewish interests it advances.

Zionist Rule

It should not go unnoticed, either, that the guy responsible for the ridiculous prosecutions of so many White American dissidents lately, Michael Chertoff, is a Zionist Jew who, as Director of the US Justice Department's Criminal Division, directed the efforts of the FBI for Ashcroft.

Clearly, the Jews are getting their way in America, as they have in Canada and Western Europe and just as they did in Russia early last century. Today, of all Western Countries, only in America can I get away with writing this book. However, even in America I get roundly condemned and widely censored...for telling the truth...about Jews.

President Bush proved himself to be nothing but a water carrier for Zionism. With the eight original 2004 Democrat Presidential candidates each being either Jewish or married to a Jew, the Democrat outcome was a foregone conclusion. The debacle that the "War on Terror" turned into is what sealed Bush's fate. Making President Bush a one-term President (inevitable as of this writing, I believe) merely provides the illusion of "throwing the rascals out." The real problem with the two-party system in America is that only one side loses at a time.

Tomorrow

Tomorrow I will be unable to bring these truths to you in America. Tomorrow I will be imprisoned, or worse, for even trying to do so. So will a great many others. Already, tomorrow has come to Canada and Western Europe.

What's more, today's hate crime laws protect only certain groups of people: Blacks, Jews, homosexuals, women and certain minorities. After all, it is still ok to tell the most reprehensible jokes about lawyers (I'm one), rednecks (I'm one), Whites (I'm one) and men (I'm one), but when was the last time you heard a Rastus and Liza joke?

Like today's hate crime laws, tomorrow's hate speech laws also will protect only certain groups of people, Jews in particular.

Tomorrow already is here in Canada, Germany, England, Italy and so many other Western countries. It almost is here in America. It soon will be, if the ADL has its way.

A Shift in Focus

Today we focus on one's intent with the current breed of American hate crime laws. For example, Blacks who say "nigger" are just funnin' around with their homies. Whites who say "nigger" are racist bigot crackers and put in jail.

Just as the truth of one's comments no longer matters, mere intent no longer is the core issue. Pure hate speech laws focus upon the *effect* one's comments have, regardless of one's intent.

Hate speech is hurt speech. The truth hurts, in other words. And, like a sword, it can hurt in both directions.

Just ask Nusrat Hussein, a Canadian resident who publishes a small newspaper for his local Muslim community.

You see, in 2003 Mr. Hussain had the temerity to reprint my essay, *"It Wasn't Arabs"* in his paper, *"The Miracle,"* which has a circulation of about 2,500 in and around Vancouver, British Columbia.

The Canadian Jewish Council (CJC) wanted to have Mr. Hussain imprisoned just for printing my little diatribe. In fact, this became a huge affair in Canada, with radio, TV and the press converging on poor Mr. Hussain. Imagine what they would like to have done to me. Mr. Hussain finally extricated himself from the brewing legal troubles by publishing a profuse apology.

"It Wasn't Arabs" developed a life of its own. It began as a personal rant, then developed into a laundry list of complaints to be laid at the doorsteps of Jews. Here is an excerpt:

> *It wasn't Arabs who sued to remove "under God" from the Pledge of Allegiance - it was Jews.*
>
> *It wasn't Arabs who sued to remove the Ten Commandments from that Alabama courthouse, had Judge Moore removed from the bench and now seek to disbar him - it is Jews.*
>
> *It isn't Arabs who sue to remove nativity scenes from public venues - it is Jews.*
>
> *It isn't Arabs who erect menorahs in public venues in place of crosses - it is Jews.*
>
> *It wasn't Arabs who sued to remove group prayer from public schools - it was Jews.*
>
> *It wasn't Arabs suing to remove decorative lights from schools at Christmas - it was Jews.*
>
> *It isn't Arabs who refuse to allow children to say grace over their school lunches - it is Jews.*

Nearly ninety points like these, delivered just like these. And it has gone around the world again and again. Glad to see I am making a difference in the fight against tyranny and injustice.

Never mind that everything in it has been proven true, time and again. What matters is that some Jewish feelings got hurt. The truth hurts. But it shouldn't hurt the truth teller. Unless the truth being told is about Jews, goes the new/old conventional wisdom, then the rules are different, just as we see around the world, day after day.

That essay of mine, *"It Wasn't Arabs,"* had some Canadian Jews in high places hyperventilating. *"Free speech does not mean hate speech, and I think this article clearly is hate speech,"* said Nisson Goldman of the CJC. That is CJC, as in the Canadian Jewish Congress. They were the very guys demanding that Mr. Hussain be prosecuted.

What is so ironic, though not generally known, was that *"It Wasn't Arabs"* actually was inspired by the CJC itself! It began with an email exchange I had with CJC's Executive Director, Bernie Farber late in 2003, wherein I played off his relegating clearly-provable truths to the category of rumors by prefacing them with the phrase *"I'm not going to believe."* The piece knocked around in my mind for a month or so before I actually wrote it. Here's the reply I sent to Mr. Farber which actually served as the genesis for *"It Wasn't Arabs"*:

> *"Ah, it's always great to hear from you, Bernie!*
> *"You know, I've given this considerable thought and decided that you are absolutely correct. In fact, henceforth, I intend to adopt your way of thinking:*
> *"I'm not going to believe any of the stupid rumors I hear about Jews being gassed during WWII.*
> *"I'm not going to believe any of the stupid rumors I*

hear about Jews being burned in ovens during WWII.

"I'm not going to believe any of the stupid rumors I hear about 6 million Jews dying during WWII, especially since the total European Jewish population actually increased.

"I'm not going to believe any of the stupid rumors I hear about Jews being just like everybody else, just with a different religion.

"I'm not going to believe any of the stupid rumors I hear about Jews being members of a religion or culture, rather than a distinct race.

"I'm not going to believe any of the stupid rumors I hear about Jews being friends of Christians.

"I'm not going to believe any of the stupid rumors I hear about Jews not having disproportionate sway in America's government.

"Finally, I'm certainly not going to believe any of the stupid rumors I hear about Israel being America's best friend.

"BTW (by the way), Bernie, how is it that "your type" gets away with your brand of hate speech, directed at my "type" from up there in the land of tolerance? Especially, considering you are the high muckety muck of the "Canadian Jewish Congress?" There are none so intolerant as those who preach tolerance..."

Showing a rare measure of restraint, Bernie had no further response for me.

We have seen how free speech in the world has been whittled away, bit by bit, going from prohibiting harm to punishing mere intent, then intent regarding only certain people. We see the next iteration in America being hate speech bans, the touchstone for which is the effect one's speech has on another's feelings. That's for tomorrow. What about the day after that?

Remember who is pushing all this censorship. Jews like Bernie Farber, of the CJC, hot on the trail of poor Mr. Hussain, whose crime was printing an essay that told the truth. *Because Jewish feelings were hurt.*

The Russian Experience

Let's not forget who took over Russia early last century. American Jews went to Russia and overthrew the Tsar, using American Jewish banker money. One of the first things they did was to outlaw anti-Semitism, the very thing being attempted in America today. Before they were done, over 20 million White Russian Christians were slaughtered (over 40 million, if you believe Alexander Solzhenitsyn) by the Russian communist Jews, people who started out by seeking to stop expressions of anti-Semitism *because Jewish feelings were getting hurt.*

US President Harry Truman, who presided over the end of WWII and its aftermath, thereby possessed of a critical viewpoint on Jewish behavior: *"The Jews, I find, are very, very selfish. They care not how many Estonians, Latvians, Finns, Poles, Yugoslavs or Greeks get murdered or mistreated as D[isplaced] P[ersons] as long as the Jews get special treatment. Yet when they have power, physical, financial or political neither Hitler nor Stalin has anything on them for cruelty or mistreatment to the under dog."* (*Harry Truman's personal diary,* 1947.)

Lest you think Russia's to be an isolated experience, consider the following chilling quotation from Jewish Talmudic scripture: *"Extermination of the Christians is a necessary sacrifice."* (*Zohar, Shemoth*).

The European Experience

Look to Europe for America's future speech laws. Already, it is impossible to say the things I say in virtually all European countries and in Canada. Yes, even England, France, Italy and Germany, our erstwhile allies. *Especially* those countries, in fact.

In Hungary, the democratically-elected Parliament in early 2003 passed a law stipulating a two-year prison term for *"someone who publicly insults a Jew."* (http://www.fpp.co.uk/online/03/12/Hungary FreeSpeech.html) What's more, if the insult amounted to an expression of "hatred," the sentence went up to three years! At the last moment, Hungary's President declined to sign the bill. It will be back, just like the American Federal hate-crime legislation kept coming back until it was passed.

Think about it for a moment: two years in prison for publicly insulting a Jew in Hungary! Regardless of intent. They just have to have their little Jew feelings hurt. Add a year if you mean it!

I couldn't make stuff like this up, folks.

Ernö Lazarovits, of the Federation of Jewish Communities in Hungary, said, *"I am very disappointed. I will tell you, very frankly, I hope that people who practice and promote anti-Semitism will not only be told, 'don't do that in the future,' but that they will be put in jail."* There was no report as to whether Lazarovits was giggling when he issued his statement.

The article cited just above concludes with a notation that underscores why Jews eventually attain all that they seek: *"Despite the setbacks, the Jewish community has vowed to press ahead with its goals for strict laws against all political opposition, similar to the ones already on the books in Germany, France and Austria."*

In early 2004, a French court fined French comedian Dieudonne M'Bala $10,000 and convicted him of inciting ethnic hatred for a comedy sketch he performed which was deemed to be critical of

Israeli policies. M'Bala's actual crime? He dressed up as a rabbi and, in a televised comedy sketch, exhorted Parisian youths to join the "US-Zionist axis of good," in a spoof of America's having named Iraq, Iran and North Korea the "axis of evil." What really did in M'Bala was capping off his skit with a "Heil Israel" Nazi-like salute.

Meanwhile, Back in Canada

Meanwhile back in Canada, where my writing almost got somebody else sent to prison, we clearly see tomorrow's America. Very recently, a man was arrested in Toronto for spray painting graffiti which consisted of a Star of David, an equals sign and a Swastika. The charge? Hate Speech. Not littering. Not vandalism. Hate Speech. Political criticism of Israel has become hate speech in Canada.

Pending in Canada's parliament as of this writing is House of Commons Bill C-2, which will make it illegal for anybody in Canada to watch any Arabic-language television channel. The punishment for daring to tune in Al Jazeera from a satellite: a $25,000 fine and one year in prison. They pretend the law is to discourage signal piracy, but why make it illegal to intercept a signal not otherwise available anywhere in Canada?

Many Americans and most Canadians fail to distinguish between their two cultures, a reality which makes the future of free speech in America a particularly dicey proposition.

We're not talking about crimes here, people. We're talking about the Jewish equivalent of blonde, redneck or lawyer jokes. (Notice again that Whites are the only people about whom it still is politically correct to tell jokes.)

It's coming.

Tell a joke, go to jail.

Coming to America

Already in America, and as of this writing, a bill pends before the US Senate which sets up a federal tribunal to investigate and monitor criticism of Israel on American college campuses. What's at stake, of course, is federal funding, without which any public college immediately would have to close its doors. Incidentally, only two colleges in all of America do not presently accept government subsidies. Presumably, even the private colleges could be reached through the various tax exemptions they are granted. Bills come and go, you might say, so what's so special about this one? What's so special is that it already has passed the House of Representatives, and it passed *unanimously*, under the title *"International Studies in Higher Education Act"* (HR3077). I expect this bill to be signed into law by the time this book is published.

Simultaneously, the American House Committee on International Relations has introduced a bill, *HR 4230*, which charges the US State Department with the duty to "monitor and combat anti-Semitism" *everywhere in the world*. This will formalize what already has become reality: America will become the world cop for Israel's interests – indeed, Jewish interests of any sort, wherever they might be found. Talk about a recipe for neverending war!

Maybe the "America, cop of the Jews" bill will not pass this time around. Frankly, I will be surprised if it does. But, it will be back. Eventually, it *will* be passed.

Hate speech laws in action. They are coming to America next.

Already, the imprisonments have begun, even in America, albeit by twisting and subverting other laws. Some people have died, too, but their deaths falsely are attributed to other causes.

Truly, hate speech simply means anything that Jews hate to hear. That's why we have to have Jews to identify it for us.

This is just the beginning. The beginning of what could well become wholesale slaughter. How many will lose all that they have? How many will be sent to the new American gulags? How many will be murdered and "disappeared" in America before we rise up and throw off this tyranny, just as Russia's most recent generation finally is doing?

How many, before we say no to the new laws being pressed upon us?

How many?

It's coming.

Tell a joke, die.

Time is Running Out

Time is running out. Most have yet to figure out who the bad guys really are.

Most Americans have yet to tumble to the fact that a long, slow rolling coup has taken place in America, with the result that most of us now are on the outside, looking in. We pretend that we still are at the party and that the pane of glass separating it from us does not exist. TV has accustomed us to being mere observers.

"Well, gawrsh...the football games are still on TV and there's beer in the fridge!" Yes. All true. Like a Penn and Teller sketch gone horribly wrong, we have focused on the wrong hand while the magician did the deed with the other.

So far, most of us have yet to feel the boot of government directly upon our necks. But, some have.

For now, America seems tyrannical only to those it tyrannizes.

For now.

Already, simply because of these internet writings, I dare not travel to most Western countries, including Canada. The best reception I could hope for would be to be placed upon the next returning flight, you see. Of course, if I were not American, America would be on that list, too.

Yes, I have been audited by the IRS. Yes, my property has been reappraised upwards. Yes, they mess with me as much as they can. Court TV repeatedly has broadcast the Christine trial, wherein I defended the politically-incorrect parents wrongfully accused of abusing their own children, whom they loved deeply. I caught bits of the broadcast, each time becoming disgusted with the incredibly-biased editing job and the biased commentary of most of the anchors about the defense we erected. (Against the Jewish prosecutor and the Jewish social worker/accuser...reported upon by the Court TV Jewish anchor.)

It must drive them crazy, trying to figure out how to disbar me. Of course, the only thing that keeps me quiet about so much that I have seen in the American legal system (names, dates, places) is the certainty of my disbarment if I were to talk openly. For now, my bar ticket is important enough to me to keep me from spilling the beans. Pity. See how it works? And I am among the most outspoken in America today, as recently certified by the Southern Poverty Law Center!

But not much longer. The American clampdown is coming. Fast.

All the other stuff is just symptoms of the fundamental problem. There simply is nothing else even close to being this important. *You have to wake up!* Credibility be damned. You have to realize who is doing this, and why.

You have to realize that they are in charge of America now: Wolfowitz, Perle, Kissinger, Fieth, Abrams, Grossman, Haass, Schlessinger, Zoellick, Sembler, Fleischer, Bolten, Goldsmith, Goldman, Gildenhorn, Gersten, Golden, Weinberger, Bodman, Cohen, Davis, Bloomfield, Lefkowitz, Frum, Greenspan, Bremer, Berman *et al.*, *ad nauseum*. Just a few of the top names from the second Bush Administration, which far outstripped Clinton's for

Jewish sycophantism. But most Americans won't wake up to the growing peril, not until it is too late.

Until they get the laws passed which allow them to jail people like me, they use blatant censorship to keep so many like myself from contaminating your mind.

The Jews bought up all the media outlets and have controlled them with a vengeance. Now comes the Internet, allowing a free flow of ideas and, especially, the truth concerning Jewish machinations throughout the world.

Prior to the 2004 major political party conventions, the Jewish Anti-Defamation League (ADL) sent the platform committees of both the Republican and the Democrat political parties written demands that they include language which would allow direct regulation of all Internet content: *"Hate on the Internet cannot be entirely unregulated. Law enforcement officials... should actively police the web, preventing and punishing online... libel and defamation."*

"Hate" and *"libel and defamation"* are the code words used by the ADL when it speaks of the content of newsletters like the one that I disseminate containing information like that in this book. If the ADL has its way, as it eventually will, I will be shut down and imprisoned for my irregular mutterings and you will hear nothing but the unadulterated party line and outright lies now fed you by the mainstream media and your "elected" representatives. This is the very sort of thing that people like I have been fighting for years now. It is the silence of most Americans that makes it possible for such an exceedingly small minority to be regimenting us in this fashion.

Direct regulation of the Internet is their goal. Meanwhile, there are other methods which prove nearly as effective.

In Defense of Spam

The single thorniest problem for the cabal astride America today is the Internet. Indeed, it is a worldwide problem for them, since they fancy themselves the rulers of the world now.

I and others in the Patriot community come in for unbelievable assaults upon our web sites, in every manner conceivable, as well as viruses and email "spoofing," whereby our domain names and email addresses are forged onto offensive emails, usually containing viruses, which then are broadcast to so many. I personally have traced many of these to sources in Tel Aviv, Lebanon and New York's upper East Side. Guess who is responsible?

Ultimately, though, the Internet will have to be brought to heel and people such as I shut down altogether. We simply present too great a threat to them by putting the truth out there. And spam, I think, is their answer.

Many think that Internet spam derives its name from the square meatball in a can. Not so.

The term actually comes from the old Monty Python comedy sketch in which a restaurant's customers are presented with an extensive menu of dishes, each of which is composed almost entirely of Spam. Thus, *it is the sense of unavoidability, even inevitability, of email spam that prompts usage of the word*, not any physical characteristics of the product itself.

The strict definition of email spam is *unsolicited, unwanted, bulk email of a commercial nature*. It is the ulterior profit motive that truly distinguishes spam and thereby lessens availability of a First Amendment defense. A long line of US Supreme Court cases have held that commercial speech is to be afforded much less free rein, thus the restrictions we see on liquor and tobacco ads, not to mention pornography. The Supremes always have based their decisions on the intrusively manipulative profit-seeking motive underlying such communications.

In the case of pornography, the justification also is protection of children, though the Supremes pretend that pornographic communication isn't speech, at all, therefore undeserving of constitutional protection.

We lawyers are not supposed to solicit clients directly. The profit motive is what entitles the Supremes to prohibit us (supposedly) from trolling hospital corridors for personal injury clients. The sole exception occurs if we are offering to represent a client *pro bono* (for free). Then, anything goes. After all, you didn't think all those nuts wander into the ACLU's offices on their own, did you?

Often, the term spam is used to refer to any unwanted email, even that invited by oneself in the first place by some sort of outbound communication.

So - why am I defending spam? Because I'm a free-speech nut, for one thing. The real reason, however, is that I believe spam to be the vehicle by which the Internet will come under total government control and censorship, thereby taking away our last semblance of a free press. In fact, I believe it is a conspiracy by those who run things, *designed to get us to demand that the government intervene and control the Internet.*

For example, California's recalled Governor Gray Davis signed a law before he left office that prohibits sending most commercial email messages to anyone in California who has not explicitly requested them. This law, which also prohibits companies inside the state from sending unsolicited commercial email to anyone outside California, imposes fines of $1,000 for each message, up to $1 million for each campaign, and gives people the right to file private lawsuits. This is how it starts.

I get more spam - and more truly offensive spam - than anybody I know. A lot of it is in retaliation for my political views, which are pretty widely distributed over the Internet. It all began in earnest after I dared to represent a White separatist in a free speech case.

There is more, too, that you simply might not have had occasion to consider. For a while, I was automatically adding all spam senders to my email list. I admit I was doing this in retaliation, but it backfired and, in so doing, revealed something to me: all the porn spam going around is being sent by Jews. I know this because *they* started filing complaints with my Internet Service Provider (ISP) *that I was spamming them.* Imagine.

It's okay for them to send email to my children that shows naked White hookers going down on naked Black men, but my little contribution to political incorrectness is too offensive for their precious Chosen sensibilities! Caused me a bit of trouble until I figured out what was happening by tracing the complainers back to their Chosen lairs. *Jews.* Again. Seems like every time I turn over a rock in America these days, there is a Jew beneath it.

I can't believe these porn sites actually draw that many paying customers, but I could be wrong. I find it even harder to believe that enough men respond to the penile enlargement emails to justify their expense. Rather, I would give fairly long odds that this incredibly offensive material is sent around specifically to outrage people like myself. People who will then demand that the Internet be censored. Out with the bath water, of course, will go baby, and that will be the end of all emailed newsletters and alternative news sites that tout anything but the State line. That's what I think is coming and what will be the legacy of our rising up against this porn spam. Talk about tough choices.

Already, the filters employed by many spam blockers and child "protection" firewalls are hard coded to block White nationalist sites. My own newsletter has been banned from access to AOL ATT.net subscribers more often than not. The leftist organizational types (marching to a kosher tune) slipped that in while you weren't looking. Kids can get detailed "fisting" instructions on the internet but are protected from learning about the mettle of our founding fathers or how the current American regime runs roughshod over the Constitution.

Even now, I am hard pressed to defend porn spam. Rather, we should enforce existing laws against such pornography being made available to children. But Federal Prosecutor Chertoff (now Federal Judge Chertoff, his reward for locking up *real* American patriots who dared to criticize Zionists) and the rest of his Chosen fellow travelers wouldn't do that, of course. Much easier to go after those nasty White separatists for disagreeing with affirmative action and illegal immigration. And, of course, then they wouldn't be able to use porn spam as the excuse, finally, to shut us all up.

At best, ignoring how one is governed leads to government of, by and for the ignorant. At worst, it leads to death and revolution. But, even then, there will be hope.

Only by losing all that we have, will we finally be free.

Consider what the day after tomorrow might bring. Are you getting mad yet? I am, and I'm not alone.

It is time. Time for a change.

I recollect having read somewhere that it was Lucifer, the Dark Angel, who urged God to deny free will to mankind. However, God thought it important that man have the ability to make unfettered choices about all things. Today, that same Dark Angel speaks through governmental authorities via hate speech laws. We have forgotten how important it is for man to learn to choose the right things for the right reasons. However, *to choose right, one first must be free to choose wrong.*

Chapter 13

Defensive Racism

"I have given my life to alleviate the sufferings of Africa...whenever a White man seeks to live among them as their equals, they will destroy and devour him, and they will destroy all his work...Never fraternize with them as equals. Never accept them as your social equals or they will devour you. They will destroy you."
-- Dr. Albert Schweitzer (1952 Nobel Peace Prize winner), *From My African Notebook* (1961)

"No one may be indifferent to the racial principle, the racial question. It is the key to world history. History is often confusing because it is written by people who did not understand the racial question and the aspects relevant to it... Race is everything, and every race that does not keep its blood from being mixed will perish. . . Language and religion do not determine a race--blood determines it."
-- British Prime Minister Benjamin Disraeli

"Civil rights laws were not passed to protect the rights of White men and do not apply to them."
-- Mary Berry, Chairman, US Civil Rights Commission

Of the many ethnic groups now occupying America, only White Americans actively must practice and demand a form of reverse racism, on pain of being branded "racist" by all, including their own brethren.

Affirmative Action

Affirmative action began as a "hand up" to a single generation of American Blacks and was to disappear thereafter. The assumption: because of pervasive racism, Blacks had been held back. Given true equality, Blacks could hold their own. Just a single "catch up" boost would be sufficient to reach the achievement levels necessary to match those of Whites. Thereafter, the natural abilities of Blacks would be enough to maintain parity. That's the theory.

The implicit assumption was that Blacks and Whites are equal in all respects. Blacks were deemed by the leftist intelligentsia of fifty years ago as being, essentially, White people with really dark tans. Quite aside from inherent racial differences which defy the best intent of any social program, the leftist program required that Black people *become* White people, in fact, reflecting the very real racist bias of the left, a bias which persists to this day. It never occurred to anybody, least of all the civil rights activists of the time, that they just might not wish to become White.

The assumption that Blacks could hold their own in all venues was wrong. Designed to last but a single generation, affirmative action now is being institutionalized as a permanent form of handicapping Whites to produce equal outcomes for all American races. What was to have been a hand up has become a handout. What was to have created equal opportunity ended up producing equal outcomes, the lynchpin of socialism.

Blacks, of course, cannot be expected voluntarily to yield up an advantage to which they have grown accustomed to viewing as their birthright. Persuaded by both the White establishment and their own opportunistic leaders that their circumstance in life is the result of rampant White racism, Black resentment grows. But, then, so does White resentment, albeit for different reasons.

As a consequence, Whites must hobble themselves and their

children with affirmative action, else be called "White supremacists."

Whites must embrace diversity, to the point of importing ignorant savages from deepest Africa into the midst of America's cities, else Whites are deemed insensitive.

Whites must surrender their European-derived culture and birthright in the name of multiculturalism, else be viewed as intolerant and kin to the Ku Klux Klan.

The constitutional right to assemble and freely associate no longer entails the right to exclude those who wish to mingle among any and all others. First, this meant society in general, then residential neighborhoods, then public organizations, then private businesses, then private associations.

Next we can expect the hordes that have overrun America to have the right to move into our homes with us. If you think this is farfetched, then look at what happened in Zimbabwe and South Africa at the turn of the century.

Resisting illegal immigration now is seen as being racist. So is objecting to affirmative action, quotas, diversity and multiculturalism.

Used to be, racism meant wanting to control other races, including their exclusion from neighborhoods and workplaces. No longer. Then, racism became equated with hate. Today, it is considered hateful simply *not* to embrace other races with open arms. Of course, this standard is applied solely to White America, whereas all other races are encouraged to maintain their individual identity, culture and customs, up to and including the point of exclusion of others.

Defensive Racism

Defensive racism, as used in this book, really is not racism at all when measured against the yardstick of hatred, but merely an attempt at survival and self determination. The difference is in orientation.

Again, regrettably, this is true only for those of White European extraction.

Consider the difference between offensive racism, such as seeking to expel Blacks, and defensive racism, as exemplified by opposing affirmative action.

Offensive racism implies superiority - defensive racism assumes equality.

Offensive racism seeks genocide - defensive racism seeks self survival.

Offensive racism would be lynching a Black man for spitting on the sidewalk. Defensive racism is moving where no Blacks live.

Offensive racism might seek to exterminate Jews - defensive racism merely opposes the Jewish incursion into White society and its desire to eradicate Christianity.

Offensive racism might seek to conquer Mexico and subjugate its citizens - defensive racism merely opposes the flood of illegal immigration into America.

Zionists, and all neoconservatives most recently, like to say: *"You're either with us or against us."* In other words, if you are not a Zionist, then you are anti-Semitic. There is no middle ground.

The same is true for charges of racism. If a White man does not actively debase himself and seek destruction of the White race, then he is a racist, by definition.

It is *not* racist to seek physical safety for oneself and one's family from anybody who is violent or from groups which have proven themselves disproportionately violent. Such groups might be exemplified by violent-offender ex-convicts, for example. Blacks, for another example. Some Pacific Islanders (Tongan and Samoan, in particular). Mexicans.

Disease is another excellent reason for racial separation for the sake of physical protection. Some disease seems endemic to certain races by virtue of cultural practices and mores. For example, though

Blacks comprise only 12% of America's population, they account for well over 50% of all HIV infections. The risk of becoming HIV infected is staggeringly higher as a consequence of sexual relations with Black people, versus other races.

It might be argued that a cultural lack of hygiene accounts for a good deal of the spread of diseases like Hepatitis and Chagas' disease, both of which are legion among illegal immigrants from south of America's border with Mexico. That does not explain away the racial nature of the origin of disease. On the contrary, it merely buttresses the argument. So it's more "nurture" than "nature." So what? It's still racial in origin.

To expose oneself or one's children to such groups significantly heightens the possibility of physical harm.

It is not racist to want to live.

It is not racist to want a productive future, safe from unnecessary risk of harm, for one's children.

It is this definition of racist alone that I am willing to accept for myself, thus the name of this book. It is this form of "racism" that I defend.

Consider the following phrase, first coined by David Lane, now serving prison time for his membership in The Order, a violent White separatist organization: *"We must secure the existence of our people and a future for White children."* This is known as the "Fourteen Words," repeated throughout the ranks of White separatists and supremacists in America. It is held up as being a particularly virulent expression of White racism. However, let's read it again...together... *slowly*:

"We must secure the existence of our people and a future for White children."

Now, read it again.

We want to live. We want our kids to have a future. That's all it says.

It doesn't smack of White separatism, even, unless you believe it necessary to live apart from other races for the White race to survive.

"Racist" is exactly how this fourteen-word phrase is characterized, virtually by all who discuss it.

However, even assuming, *arguendo*, the prevailing interpretation, let's turn it around and make it into a clearly non-racist statement. This can be done simply by restating it in the negative, thereby highlighting just how ludicrous is the prevailing interpretation: *"Our people need not survive and White children don't need a future."*

Only by making the meaning destructive of and by the White race can one remove the racist implication of the phrase, as currently construed by an overly politically-correct society.

To that, I say *"Bunk."*

There is nothing wrong with wanting to live and wanting one's line of descendants to live safely. There is nothing wrong with seeking to perpetuate the White race. After all, every other race gets to seek its own perpetuation and aggrandizement without a peep from anybody.

If it is racist to want to live and to see one's own race survive, then I plead guilty, and proudly so.

Why is it okay to ask *"When are you going to meet a nice Jewish girl and settle down?"* yet it would be racist in the extreme to ask *"When are you going to meet a nice White girl and settle down?"*

A Word About White Supremacists

Those who shout down people such as I are the very ones who most closely resemble the excessively militant on my side of the fence, the White Power guys.

I do not feel a need to join the chorus condemning White supremacists. Because White supremacists do not seek to harm my family or myself, unlike militants of other races, I refuse to condemn them, while I do condemn the supremacists of other races. After all, the day may come when the only thing standing between my family and those who seek to kill us all will be those who now are shouting *"White Power."* Nor do I need to defend them. They are big enough to take care of themselves, trust me.

Do I condemn violence if practiced by White supremacists? Sure, if it is offensive in nature, rather than simply defensive. Will I object to supremacists of any flavor if they kill or harm others? Absolutely. The book you now hold in your hands is just such an objection. Same thing if a supremacist of any stripe merely *advocates* the harming or killing of others. However, I try my best never to confuse political rhetoric with live action, as should everybody.

Far more Black and Jewish supremacists do harm to White Americans than the other way around. Indeed, the incidence of harm done by White supremacists effectively is nil.

Merely because I provide a logical rationale for and give voice to the primary concerns of those who consider themselves White supremacists, doesn't mean that I subscribe to their solutions. That is insufficient to lump me in with them and condemn me, but such niceties are lost on those who issue blanket condemnations.

I don't care if others don't like that I refuse to condemn White Supremacists. Free speech and the right to free association are firmly ensconced in the Constitution that I recognize and that I hope once again will govern America.

Conventional Views About Racism

American Blacks are pervasively poor, uneducated, ignorant and both drug and crime ridden. If, as the politically correct would have you believe, Blacks are the same as Whites, apart from skin color, then the only possible reason for the condition of American Blacks is...American Whites, of course. White racism. This line of reasoning has a certain appeal until one examines the premise.

To expect Blacks to be accountable for any or all of their own conditions is to jump squarely into the middle of a belief in racial differences other than skin color. As previously discussed, the politically correct interpret differences in terms of superior and inferior, so intellectually are incapable of going there. It is so much easier for them to see Black crime, drug addiction and dissipation as the direct results of White racism.

Of course, with thinking like theirs, it is easy to conclude that only Whites are capable of being racist. That is why a White who says *"nigger"* can be charged with a hate crime while a Black who says *"cracker"* is just venting. That also is why it no longer is acceptable to tell jokes about classes of people other than lawyers, blondes, rednecks and white men.

Non-White college organizations like Mecha, which seeks the overthrow of southwest America, and sundry Black clubs are encouraged on campus. Organizations which promote White interests are deemed racist and banned.

Note the irony of all this occurring in the name of diversity, which really means forcing everybody into thinking the same way. Studying Black culture is done in the name of diversity. Studying White culture, however, is racist.

Notice the additional irony in how all the non-White clubs and organizations seek advancement and favor at the expense of White people, while White organizations merely seek equal treatment for all. Yet, it is the White organizations that are called racist.

And Whites, most of all, play into the hands of the divisive elements in society by doing anything possible to avoid being labeled "racist," as though such implies that one thereby admits to having just strung up a Black man.

That's the problem with labels, of course, and why the real haters love to blur the lines between definitions. It facilitates their control of all of us.

I was called anti-Semitic for daring to represent the Aryan Nations in a highly-publicized trial. Even one of my best friends was unable to see past the label for such a transgression. I no longer bother to try to avoid the label. I merely respond with, *"Do you blame me, after all that the Jews have done to my family and myself?"* As an Anti-Semite, of course, I get equated with Hitler. *Sigh.*

More recently, because Jews have so overused the term "Anti-Semite" as to render it near meaningless, my response today likely is to be, *"That's Mr. Anti-Semite to you!"*

As an unabashed defender of White society against the onslaught by other races, I get branded a racist, too, as though I just got back from burning down a Black church. So be it. *Do you blame me, after all that they have done to my race?*

Practicing Defensive Racism

How does one practice defensive racism? Easy.

First of all, do not accept the label. Anybody willing to call you a racist almost certainly is the real racist then present. Pursue their reasoning and turn it back upon them.

Move to an area free of the other races apart from which you wish to live.

Speak out and denounce the double standard which marks Whites as hate criminals 80% of the time, though Blacks are 50 times more likely to commit violent interracial crimes.

Refuse to allow your children to be victimized by a racist school system. Run for your local School Board, even if you have no children in school at the time, and be vocal. Remove your child to a private school. Better yet, home school your children. Lodge complaints of reverse racism against its practitioners, regardless of their skin color.

Refuse to vote for anybody that favors extension of the current system. This means never voting Democrat or Republican again, of course. Remember: *the lesser of two evils is still evil.*

Actively and vocally condemn affirmative action and all entitlement programs of any sort.

Denounce and actively campaign against judges who practice a double standard with regard to White defendants.

Hire qualified White people for jobs. Never hire to meet racial quotas of any sort. Quit and get a new job rather than submit.

File reverse discrimination lawsuits whenever you are discriminated against because of your skin color.

Complain to advertisers and television network producers about the disproportionate representation of Blacks in commercials and programs. Object to commercials and programs that stereotype Whites as stupid, rednecks or bigots. Object to the deification of Blacks by their being cast as military Generals, Presidents and the like. Better yet, sell your TV set.

Boycott Black products and services. Refuse to allow your children to buy music products from Black artists. Refuse to allow your children to see movies starring Blacks.

Refuse to allow your children to date, even casually, members of other races. Of course, if you live someplace which is all White, this becomes virtually impossible for them, don't forget.

Boycott Jewish products and services. This necessarily means virtually all media and entertainment products, especially the bile spewing forth from your television set. However, note that it is illegal to boycott Israeli products and services.

Boycott any product carrying "kosher" markings. This, too, is going to be particularly difficult, since so many producers and manufacturers buy into the Jewish extortion scheme in order to avoid any sort of active boycotting of their products. Yes, indeed, this is a variation on the tried-and-true *Jewish* criminal "protection" racket.

Look for any of the following letters, usually in circles or ovals, on a product: COR, U, MK, K, BCK, KSA, WK, KVH. Also, the words "Parve" or "Pareve," which mean "Passover." Amazingly, you will find these words and/or symbols on a great many *non-food* items. Do not be confused by the traditional trade and copyright marks: C, R or TM.

Show pride in your race and openly speak of your heritage to others, especially your children.

Study the logical reasoning underlying the various conclusions set forth in this book so that you may intelligently deal with those who wish to show you up for being a racist fool.

Call in to radio talk shows and try out your skills, both as an orator and as an effective advocate for our point of view.

Buy a case of this book (or any other that advances the cause of White America) and distribute copies as gifts to friends, or sell them at a discount to others.

To be a defensive racist is to be no racist at all, but that distinction is lost on those who condemn us. We need to get over it and get on with the real work before us: *"We must secure the existence of our people and a future for White children."*

Chapter 14

The Future

"When I want to understand what is happening today or try to decide what will happen tomorrow, I look back."
--- Oliver Wendell Holmes, 1841-1935 American Supreme Court Justice

"I have but one lamp by which my feet are guided and that is the lamp of experience. I know of no way of judging the future but by the past."
--- Patrick Henry speech, Williamsburg, VA, March 23, 1775

"It is not the brains that matter most, but that which guides them: the character, the heart, generous qualities, progressive ideas."
--- Fyodor Dostoyevsky, 1821 – 1881, Russian novelist

"The sky is falling! The sky is falling!"
--- Chicken Little

Want to know where you are headed in life? Simple. Just turn around for a moment and take a look at where you are coming from. Piece of cake.

However, *accepting* the evidence of our own eyes in such an act of self examination is much harder than the actual perception, which is why so many of us seem surprised by the way in which our lives turn out.

The same debility applies to the manner in which we perceive our families, our schools, our businesses or *any* organization to which we belong. We simply refuse to believe that things won't turn out all right in the end. Wishful thinking. We all do it.

The Way We Were

Just fifty years ago, this simple exercise would have produced a bright outlook. America was emerging from a major war stronger than when she entered, while all those around her had weakened. Times were good.

The baby boom, reflective of America's inward turn at the time, was a harbinger of better things to come. War production was turned to consumer items. The American dream was within the grasp of every American, it seemed.

America was almost exclusively White and European by extraction. The crime rate was minuscule. There were no racial problems of which to speak. The Civil Rights Movement was several years away. Segregation was the rule. Miscegenation was illegal.

In the space of only fifty years, things have changed remarkably and in ways that simply were not foreseen during the halcyon days of the 1950s.

The Way We Are

We've covered a good deal of America's current condition already. Let's quickly overview and summarize that material:

Today, non-Whites already are the majority in America's single largest state: California. Non-Whites comprise a majority of public school students in Louisiana, Texas, Mississippi, New Mexico, Hawaii, Florida and, of course, California. Several other states will join this group in the coming generation.

Massive immigration, both legal and illegal, almost exclusively from third-world countries, has fueled this sea change in American demographics, which began with the 1965 passage of the *"Immigration Reform Act."*

America swelled from a total population of 200 million at midcentury to almost 300 million today. All of America's population increase, and more (owing to a decline in the White birthrate), is attributable to immigrants (and their children) during the latter part of the 1900s. Now, the children of those immigrants are beginning to have children.

We spend more on education today, per student, than ever before, yet our schools have become centers for underachievement, drug dealing, gangs and ethnic violence of every type imaginable. Staggering beneath the demands of the "No Child Left Behind" ideology, we have sacrificed our best young minds on the altar of political correctness.

California possessed the finest school system in America just two generations ago. Today, it is near the bottom of the list. America once produced the world's leading scholars in virtually all fields of endeavor, especially the sciences. Today, we lead only *some* third-world countries and then only in *some* areas.

The legacy of unchecked immigration, a considerable portion of which is illegal, can be seen clearly in the states bordering Mexico. Hospitals, forced by law to deliver free medical services, staggering on the edge of bankruptcy or already closed. Third-world diseases, some once eradicated in the US and others never before seen, break out in epidemic fashion with disturbing regularity: tuberculosis, Chagas, even leprosy. Schools sinking beneath the demands of multiple-language instruction. Soaring crime rates, particularly involving theft. Lower-level jobs lost to newcomers and wages dragged down due to the increased competition for work.

Racial preferences, engineered by the courts to last but a single generation so as to provide a one-time "leg up," have become institutionalized and extended to every walk of life. Originally, the

Civil Rights movement simply demanded equal rights. When equal rights didn't produce equal outcomes, American courts inferred that rampant racism must be the problem, never thinking to look to racial differences, which so much of society decided to pretend do not exist.

Racism, too, has become institutionalized, with some going so far as to accuse all White people of being racist, *per se.*

Hate crime laws were created, then broadened to include mere speech, and applied overwhelmingly against only members of the White race. Once designed merely to stiffen sentences for crimes committed under the influence of racial animus, the latest versions of these laws have decoupled the act from the intent. Moves now are afoot to dispense with the intent requirement altogether, and focus solely on the impact of speech, such that if the feelings of a minority group are hurt, one goes to jail, just as takes place in Canada, Australia, Germany and so many other European nations.

Middle-class workers pay the taxes. Not the rich, just ask ex-Enron CEO Kenneth Lay. Not the poor, just ask Je$$e Jack$on. Middle class. Taxes go in one direction only these days, despite the ballyhoo of the Bush tax cuts, the benefit of which mostly inures to the benefit of the rich.

Government is the only growth industry in America today, and it is government at all levels. Government wages and benefits keep going only in one direction. In the 1950s, government workers made significantly less than their private-industry counterparts; now it is just the reverse. While the total tax bite goes up, the size of the group shouldering it decreases (private industry workers only, because taxes deducted from government payrolls have no effect on the total tax burden), leading to even more taken from the common man.

Today, the middle class sees its bread-and-butter blue-collar jobs headed overseas due to NAFTA, GATT and the WTO. What middle-class upper-level jobs don't flow overseas with companies are sent there nevertheless, in what euphemistically is referred to as "outsourcing," or the workers merely are replaced with lower-paid foreigners imported on H-1B visas by their companies. Racial preferences provide the whipsaw effect, with middle-class White Americans the odd man out.

For the first time since the advent of the two-income family, many people who truly want and need work are unable to find it at any salary. Since two incomes now provide the same standard of living as used to be supported by a family's single breadwinner, each family now has *twice* the chance of falling into economic catastrophe. Because most live from paycheck to paycheck, it takes the interruption of only one of a family's two incomes to lead to bankruptcy, so overstretched are today's homeowners.

Families are falling into the financial abyss in record numbers, putting the lie to the apparent good economic times. Each year of this new century has marked new record levels of bankruptcy, by both individuals and small businesses.

When the job goes, so does medical care for the middle class, most of whom cannot afford the $8,000 to $14,000 per year family cost of decent health care coverage. Meanwhile, illegal immigrants get their health care for free from hospitals and clinics that are forced to send the costs back through other, *insured*, patients' claims, leading to the huge increases in health insurance premiums that now force so many Americans to do without.

White Americans are displaced from college, first by racial preferences in admissions and financial aid; second, by huge increases in tuition and fees to help pay for the preferences; and third, because what should have been the family's tuition payments have been taxed away or taken by unemployment.

Among the requirements for increased taxes are a need to support America's prison industry, yet another segment of government seeing explosive growth. Traditionally, American prisons held one out of every thousand members of society (considered a high level

233

internationally). Today's prison populations have leapt to four out of every thousand. It is no wonder that some crime has dropped slightly, aside from the fact that America has seen a full two generations of good times (crime increases significantly during bad economic times). Increases in the jail population began directly after the "Civil Rights" revolution of the 1960s, a revolution that since has fomented so much racial hatred on both sides of the American racial divide.

When crime figures are adjusted for race, true White crime falls almost to nonexistent levels, similar to the levels of White crime in those European countries which still are predominantly White. American Blacks commit seven times the total number of violent interracial crimes committed by Whites. Since Blacks comprise only one seventh of the population, simple math forces the conclusion that *the average Black is 49 times more likely to commit a violent interracial crime than the average White.* And, don't forget that Hispanic crime perps are logged in as being *White.*

The existence of disproportionate percentages of minorities in prison continually is pointed to as evidence of pervasive and pernicious White racism in America's legal system. *The truth is that the Black prison population percentages fall well short of the actual percentage of crimes committed by Blacks.* Certainly, there aren't 49 Blacks in prison for every White. Part of this disparity results from a Black population that accuses White policemen of racism at every opportunity, which all too often results in a reduction, if not the outright dropping, of charges. Occasionally, the charge gets parlayed into lottery-level civil awards, leading to official policy requiring that Blacks be given far greater latitude in all walks of life, especially when it comes to being charged with crimes.

As the ratio of White prisoners declines, the violence they experience at the hands of fellow inmates, particularly prison rape, is on the rise, reflective of the general anger of minorities who have been encouraged to blame Whitey for every problem.

Have nots always believe there should be an equal distribution of the fruits of society's productive elements. The haves always believe in distribution according to merit. This tension grows in America as the gulf between the economic classes grows, a tension that, more often than not, is drawn along racial lines. In particular, Blacks and Hispanics resent what Whites traditionally have had. Whites resent the welfare and the *"you owe me"* mentality which has evolved among both Blacks and Hispanics.

As Hispanics, who tend to be more industrious than Blacks, carve into traditionally Black turf, resentment also grows between these two groups. The media does its best to hide this animosity, as it does the animosity held by Whites toward both minority groups. No such effort is made concerning minority resentment, though, which is fed and fostered by media portrayals of Whites as predatory and undeserving, thereby legitimizing the hatred felt by Blacks, especially.

America is a like a giant steam boiler whose overflow valves have been stoppered, ready to explode at any moment into a paroxysm of racial warfare. In fact, as evidenced by the crime rates, that war began years ago and now is intensifying. *Imagine what will happen when the coming economic hard times hit.*

The Way We Will Be

Where we are is the bad news. Now for the worse news: *the future.* Remember, the recap we have been wading through was for the purpose of providing a trend line for previewing the future. Amazing things have taken place over the past 50 years. Even more amazing things await America during the next 50 years, simply by extension of the trend line.

Largely, what has taken place has been the result of an interaction among genetic racial differences and demographic change. The genetic differences will continue for as long as evolution requires, certainly hundreds, if not thousands or hundreds-of-thousands, more years. The demographic changes will worsen.

America was over 90% White fifty years ago. Today, it is about 70% White and declining rapidly. Black and Hispanic birth rates are high, much higher than White birth rates. Already, Whites have become a minority in the states of California, New Mexico, Hawaii and, most recently, Texas, according to the Census Bureau's latest figures.

At current rates, Whites will be a minority in all of America before the middle 2000s. America's total population, 200 million in the middle of the last century and nearly 300 million today, will exceed 400 million by then, with more than the total increase coming from immigrants and their offspring (due to declining White birth rates).

Internationally, there are about 600 million Whites today in a total world population of 6 billion. The world's population is expected to double to 12 billion by the end of this century. During that same period, Whites are projected to decline to a total of about 300 million, owing to current low levels of White births and high levels of White miscegenation.

In early 2004, a Gallup poll found that 87% of Americans see the coming drop in America's White population beneath the 50% level as being either *"a good thing"* or something that *"doesn't matter."* The same poll saw 70% of Whites approving of interracial marriage.

White women are considered prizes to the males of virtually all other societies and races. Women tend to pair off with those who have power, a genetic imperative designed to ensure survival of the female and her offspring. Increasingly, the power will be shifting to races other than White.

Facts are facts, regardless of your politics: already mating with non-Whites in record numbers, White women will do so in ever-increasing numbers as time goes on. The result, happily pointed to by many, even many in the White race, will be genocide, pure and simple. Eradication of the White race from the face of the earth. And, at current rates, sooner than you might think.

Today, it is considered racist to frown upon your White daughter dating a Black. How long before that same daughter is considered racist if she refuses to date Blacks?

If you think walking the streets of cities with high Black populations is dangerous today (*e.g.,* Washington, DC, Detroit, New York, Los Angeles, New Orleans), imagine what it will be like in fifty years. Especially if gun confiscation occurs by then, as is likely. My grandfather's era was one hundred years ago. Your grandchildren's will be around the turn of the next century. What kind of world are we making for them?

What on earth have we been thinking?

The American experience is being replicated throughout Western Europe, birthplace of White civilization.

The Good News...sort of

The good news, if you want to call it that, is that *America's natural resources simply cannot support this sort of growth*, therefore will force at least a partial solution of some sort. The same is true to an even greater extent throughout the world.

Water, already a problem in many areas, will be a disaster in the face of future demand. Oil effectively will run out much sooner than generally believed: when economically-inelastic demand factions (the ones who simply *must* have oil at any price) outstrip supply, not when the last oil is pumped to the surface.

Gasoline is a largely elastic demand for the average American, since we simply drive less in the face of higher gas prices, but there is a core demand for gasoline that must be met at any price. I see bicycles in the future of a great many, even most, Americans.

Farms have been plowed under to make way for the suburbs. Once breadbasket to the world, America will be unable to feed her own before long.

Air pollution will increase, then subside as oil supplies dwindle.

The AIDS pandemic is just a harbinger of things to come, I fear.

We have seen how American jobs have been flooding to foreign countries with the factories that require them, together with outsourcing by companies that stay in America. We have seen how the low-level American jobs increasingly are being taken by immigrants, largely illegal immigrants. The future will see an uptick in a trend begun today with what is known as H-1B and L-1 visas, whereby trained and educated workers are imported to America to displace American high tech workers.

Responding to a temporary bubble which now has disappeared, companies have developed a taste for these imported foreign workers who are satisfied with far less in wages and benefits than the American workers they replace. And, as we have seen, the workers that get replaced overwhelmingly are White.

The Coming Economic Pandemic

Touted by the one worlders as the natural evolution of humanity, a world without borders is a world with no economic safety net. Previously, when one or more countries fell under sway of serious economic recessions or depressions, borders tended to confine the damage. With today's retrenchment and redistribution of industry, no safety net is possible. When any significant country catches a cold, the rest of the world will sneeze. God forbid a fatal economic disease should rise up anywhere.

Fact is, however, that fatal disease already exists and has swept the globe. It is called fiat money. Simply put, fiat money is any money, the value of which changes based upon actions of the government responsible for it, not due to economic underpinnings. The American dollar is the perfect example, with our government running the printing presses nonstop, just to keep the doors open.

Unlike what many people call "real money," such as gold and silver, all down through history fiat money always has been watered, diluted and abused by its issuing government, until it soars into hyperinflation and becomes worthless. In times past, even real money was weakened as the result of people and government shaving off the edges, leading to the grooved edges which now are minted into coins to discourage shaving.

There are only limited quantities of gold and silver available and only a limited amount which can be mined each year, with each year seeing decreasing amounts of ore hauled from less productive mines all the time. The very fact of the rarity of precious metals is what keeps them from being abused. That is why governments hate to use gold and silver as money. They cannot steal from the population through inflation merely by printing more.

Those of a more conspiratorial bent of mind believe the current decline in the value of all fiat currencies throughout the world is intentional. How better to implement a single currency for use throughout the world than by making all currencies fail at once? And governments get a huge bonanza in the process by paying off their debts with ever-more-worthless currency that they simply print for pennies on the dollar. How better to pave the way for a single world central bank?

Death of the West

Pat Buchanan, in his best seller, *Death of the West* (2002), opines: *"So it may be that the time of the West has come, as it does for every civilization, that the Death of the West is ordained, and that*

239

there is no sense prescribing new drugs or recommending painful new treatments, for the patient is dying and nothing can be done. Absent a revival of faith or a great awakening, Western men and women may simply live out their lives until they are so few they do not matter."

Maybe. If so, who is to blame?

Already, the truths revealed in this book make it virtually unpublishable, which is why you probably are reading it courtesy of some no-name printing house, distributed furtively at patriot conferences and via small ads in odd journals. Therefore, it won't hurt to include the following two quotes from Jews themselves:

"I can state with assurance that the last generation of White children is now being born. Our control commission will, in the interests of peace and wiping out interracial tensions, forbid the Whites to mate with Whites...Thus the White race will disappear, for mixing the dark with the White means the end of the White man, and our most dangerous enemy will become only a memory. We shall embark upon an era of ten thousand years of peace and plenty, the Pax Judaica, and our race will rule undisputed over the world. Our superior intelligence will enable us to retain mastery over a world of dark peoples." Rabbi Rabinovich, in an address delivered in Budapest, Hungary (January 12, 1952).

"We must realize that our party's most powerful weapon is racial tensions...While inflaming the Negro minority against the Whites, we will endeavor to instill in the Whites a guilt complex for their exploitation of the Negroes. We will aid the Negroes to rise in prominence in every walk of life, in the professions and in the world of sports and

240

entertainment. With this prestige, the Negro will be able to intermarry with the Whites and begin a process which will deliver America to our cause." Israel Cohen, *A Racial Program for the Twentieth Century* (1912).

Look at the dates of these last two quotes again. Amazing, isn't it? Who says there is no conspiracy afoot? What is even more amazing is that I will be called racist merely for including these two quotes, with the most strident cries coming from Jews. Put that thought aside for a moment, though, and consider the racist timbre of the Jewish remarks just quoted, which call for no less than murder on a grand scale: genocide of the White race.

The Advantage of Perspective

Chicken Little was right. In fact, Chicken Little was a piker.

The primary advantage of getting older is the perspective one gains. Partly due to experience – gotten the old-fashioned way, with pain. Partly due to hormonal changes. Both tend to moderate one's outlook on things.

I got an early taste of it several years ago, when I first was treated for prostate cancer (now in remission for many years, thank you, and almost certainly a total cure). I don't remember the drug, just that it was terribly expensive, administered by shot into my abdomen and good for six months. It killed testosterone production (testosterone, you see, is the fuel that drives prostate cancer at first).

Part of a chemo treatment program, later to be joined to radiation, the drug totally changed my outlook. For the first time in my life, I could see any pretty girl and have no desire for her. Intellectually, I could appreciate her beauty and I could interact with her with none of my body language or subterranean communication, about which we know so little, communicating sexual tension. Women related to me

241

differently – more comfortably. I learned to distinguish the sexual from the other aspects in relationships which always end up so confusingly, often so terminally, intertwined.

Like Billy Crystal explains to Meg Ryan in the movie *"When Harry Met Sally,"* about ugly girls, in explaining why men and women can never be just friends: *"You pretty much want to jump them, too."* Well, men *can* be friends with women; we just need a little perspective, which means a period without being driven by our hormones. Otherwise, Harry was absolutely correct.

With advancing age comes a significant decline in testosterone production. Thus a modest version (lust light?) of the perspective I gained is imparted to all men in their late fifties and beyond. Even they, however, still are at effect – they still "pretty much want to jump them, too." Otherwise, there would be no old fools, of which there always is a bumper crop. Guys who deny this are lying, ladies. And not a single one of them has a clue about that which I have been describing, unless they have been freed somehow, either temporarily or permanently, from the grip of their hormones. They haven't the perspective from which to appreciate or understand. They hear the words, but they simply don't *get* them at a visceral level.

By analogy, if you are a parent, try to explain the value of having children to someone who hasn't any. It can't be done. As mentioned before, the closest I have managed to come is, *"For the first time, you learn that it is possible to love someone else more than you love yourself."*

I honestly believe that the injection I received should be mandatory for all men at about age 25. One time only, of course. It would last only six months, yet it would yield a perspective on relationships that most men never attain.

Here's another brief vignette, more on point, about the value of gaining perspective. I recall working with equipment leases at my first accounting job, leases which had been written in the early 1950's using interest rates of 2% and 3%, about the same as they are today. They were the "old stuff" to be worked through because nobody would give them up in the face of the prime rate then going through the roof, hitting the mid-teens before finally cooling off. I remember hearing my boss, who should have known better, remark that, never again, would we see interest rates that low, because the business world had changed. I'm sure he is dead now, so he was right, in a sense. Of course, he was literally dead wrong, too.

Night of the Living Debt

Today, I hear younger people, who never saw the prime rate hit 17% thirty years ago, talking as though interest rates always will be low. Certainly, government is acting that way, not to mention the millions of Americans recently opting for Adjustable Rate Mortgages for their homes. From my perspective, I know better. Interest rates go up, and they go down. It takes a long time to see the entire cycle at work. You can bank on the fact that interest rates will increase again – probably quite soon. And, they likely will go through the roof again. This time, however, things are *very* different from what they were back in the 60's and 70's. In fact, things are far worse than they were prior to the 1930's.

Today, astronomical levels of debt are carried by government, business and individuals. Already, even in this low-interest-rate climate, we see record levels of bankruptcy, both personal and corporate. Even state and local governments are starting to go bust. That debt will crush the American economy when rates rise. Even a one- or two-percent increase in interest rates will send us into the serious economic depression that we merely have been deferring. *Imagine what adding 15 points to the rates will do!*

Rising interest rates will mean the death of a great many Americans. *Literally.* When they rise, the sky will fall. The grand

American experiment will shudder to a halt. Other nations know this. That is why they do all they can to prop up the dollar.

When the dollar goes, so does the whole house of cards, because America still is the engine of the world economy, albeit now as the consumer of last resort, not the producer, as in the past. That is why corporate insiders are selling stock at a record pace. That is why many foreigners are bidding up the price of gold. That is why so many, like myself, have fled the cities for the relative safety of the countryside.

It will happen. It will happen soon. The perspective I have gained from a lifetime of observing the economy, business and government absolutely guarantees it. Those who think otherwise and do not prepare are young fools. No fool like an old fool – hormonally. *No fool like a young fool – economically.*

When rates rise and the dollar dies, government will be unable to meet its obligations and will at last be forced to make some hard choices, the likes of which have not been seen by hardly any American now alive. The American underclass brought up to rely upon the welfare and social infrastructure built up since the last Depression will take to the streets. The racial warfare that exists already in the streets of American cities, the news of which actively is suppressed, will explode. Next time, Beverly Hills will be sacked, along with every tony suburb of every city in America, because every city possesses the raw materials: a sullen and angry horde of Blacks and Mexicans, many of them illegals, all of them conditioned to feel entitled. *All of them conditioned to believe that Whitey is the problem* due to pervasive and pernicious racial discrimination.

When rates go up, the dollar will evaporate into hyperinflation. Wheelbarrows full of dollars will be required to buy bread. Overnight, millions of Americans will join the record numbers of those now living in poverty in America. Though home mortgages will seem cheap in the face of inflation, we will not have even the

244

small purchasing power then required to retire them. The banks will take our homes from us in droves, 1930's style.

More on this fiscal and monetary disaster, and how to prepare for it, in Chapter 17, *Money's End Game: Depression II.*

The Debt Bomb

When the debt bomb goes off, government at all levels will go bust, meaning their tax revenues will be used entirely in the servicing of existing debt. Unable to borrow more, government services will evaporate and government workers will be laid off in droves. Unlike last century, when government was comparatively small, the ranks of the unemployed will be increased as a result of a shift in government policies, not decreased due to public works projects.

Don't forget that a much higher percentage of America's workers today are government employees, which translates into an even faster nosedive when the private (tax paying) sector crashes and burns. Just prior to the Great Depression, government absorbed only about 10% of the nation's total output. Today, that figure approaches 50% when the country's spending deficit is included, as it must be.

The U.S. government tells us that unemployment today is no more than 5 or 6%. Casual observation suggests a true rate approximately double that level. In the first Depression, unemployment peaked at about 25%, meaning about 13 million out of work, with a great many of those who had jobs being woefully underemployed. A similar level of unemployment today would mean about 45 million out of work (those two-earner families which have replaced the previous single-earner standard have ballooned the percentage of Americans employed, don't forget), with a huge number of those still employed actually *under*employed in terms of hours, salaries or both.

Poverty beyond anything ever before experienced by Americans, well beyond the capacity of American institutions to handle, will result.

Young adults unable to find work will return to live with their parents, often bringing their own young families along with them. Older folks, their pensions and Social Security benefits rendered meaningless by the hyperinflation engendered by a crashing dollar, will be taken in by their own children, often from the confines of nursing and rest homes that have become too expensive to underwrite. Households will bulge at the seams with extended families, just as we see in many immigrant homes today.

With the concentration of families and record foreclosures, many houses will sit unoccupied and for sale, some for years on end. In the meanwhile, many will be vandalized and broken into, with squatters taking up residence. The value of housing, America's final investment resource, will plummet, perhaps even to levels experienced in the 1930s: 10% of their former value. Of course, this contemplates adjustment for purchasing power. Particularly keep in mind that, because of hyperinflation, *such an extreme loss of home values could occur in the context of housing prices higher than those that exist today!*

Local crime, already a problem in even the smallest towns and cities, will skyrocket in the face of declining state and local tax revenues and the concomitant decrease in police forces.

The infrastructure will crumble well beyond that seen in some of the poorest urban centers today, with streets going unrepaired and outside lighting curtailed.

With essential services like trash pickup going by the wayside, all cities and towns will begin to look like today's third-world slums.

Payback Time

Already angry with government at all levels due to its intrusion into our personal lives, most Americans will sit by and refuse to help.

246

Some will see it as a time to exact retribution. That is when the "lone wolves" that the Southern Poverty Law Center and the ADL so fear will go into action. They know this. That is why they and their counterparts in government (can you say *"Patriot Act?"*) are striving mightily to crack down on all of America, especially the political dissidents, record numbers of whom now occupy the cells of federal prisons. That is why so many federal employees, even National Park workers, have been armed. That is why local police departments have been turned into military outposts.

Southwest America will become a no-go zone for all but the Mestizos who already have renamed it Aztlan. A flood of have-nots from the cities will be met with hostility at the borders by well-armed country folk.

In the coming hard times, your skin color will be your uniform. Regardless of how touchy-feely politically correct you might wish to continue to be, Blacks and mexicans will not be impressed. There will be a great many bleeding hearts literally bleeding in the streets.

Blacks will take over entire cities and concentrate in the South, where their greatest numbers already dwell, for their mutual protection.

The military response that government will feel compelled to employ merely will escalate things to full and open warfare throughout the country. Besides, military power arises from economic power, not the other way around. The Federal government will have all it can do merely to pay the interest on the national debt held by the owners of central banks and other foreigners.

America will become a living hell for most. *The sky will fall,* in other words.

We have seen this scenario during our lifetimes played out overseas, albeit on a smaller scale. Foreigners possess little of the naiveté that is so rampant throughout America. They know what is coming. Bush has seen to it that they feel we deserve it, too, so they

247

will not lift a finger to help when it comes.

When the sort of war that America has grown accustomed to inflicting upon small, defenseless countries finally comes to America, then Americans will understand the pain, degradation and hopelessness that real war can inflict. Just ask the Iraqis, Afghanis or Palestinians what life is like for them. That is what can and will happen here. There *will* be American suicide bombers.

Interest rates. That's the key. A lifetime of perspective tells me they will rise – substantially.

It may start with a concerted program of terrorist attacks by outsiders. If so, that merely will serve to tip the first domino over. Eventually, the domino labeled "interest rates" will fall and, from there, things will spiral totally out of control. There needn't even be a trigger event, as the dominoes already are rolling over, as if in slow motion, and there is no setting them aright again.

You can bet the central and international bankers know all this. Indeed, they were accused by many of pushing the world into economic chaos in the 1930's. They went from being fabulously wealthy to being scandalously wealthy as the Great Depression (soon to be renamed The First Depression) segued into world war, giving them a fresh profit opportunity. Now they are outlandishly wealthy and seemingly bent upon making this the last lap around the Monopoly board, since they already own almost everything. It's that "almost" that seems to stick in their craw. So long as there is the least little bit of truly free enterprise, private property and economic independence out here, their personal safety cannot be guaranteed.

Why? Because they can. Because it's there. Because they are terrified that we might figure out this shell game and come for them where they live. Well, they are right. Enough of us *have* figured it out. And we know where they live. This time, they *should* be nervous.

As we all seem to do, they have created the very reality they most fear. *They forgot that pigs get fat, but hogs get slaughtered.* This time, they have gone too far. Their lackeys, the Bushes, the Kerrys, the Rumsfelds, the Ashcrofts, *et al.*, will offer us little diversion when it comes time to root them out.

Modern Nuremberg trials of visible leaders will not suffice this time.

There's another cycle, a view of which perspective born of age affords, something that I like to call the Cycle of Strife. *Tyranny breeds freedom and freedom fosters tyranny,* regardless of the type of economic or political systems employed. I happen to recall what America once was like, back in the early 50's. Younger citizens lack that perspective. Things are quickening now, so that the relative freedom of the 80's will seem far distant, too. Trust me, there is a much bigger gulf between the 50's and the 80's than grew during the last 25 years. Nevertheless, President Bush was intent upon setting a new land speed record for American tyranny, so that even children have noticed the difference.

Parallel Universes

Like the theme for a second-rate science fiction movie, I see a possible alternate future for America, one even uglier than the vision just conjured: The rise of what can only be described as *The Fourth Reich.* The parallels between pre-WWII Germany and America today are chilling. All that is missing is the economic despair that will enable a charismatic dictator to gather all the reins of power into his hands, just as Hitler did then.

The *Patriot Act* alone, not to mention its intended successor and various pieces of enabling legislation, is an eerie echo of Nazi Germany's *"Decree for the Protection of Nation and State."* Sounding superficially reasonable and supposedly invocable only in times of extreme crisis, Germany later was to realize the horrible truth. So, too, has America yet to learn the awful truth about what is possible under a fully-implemented *Patriot Act.* Every single provision of Nazi Germany's *Decree* can be found mirrored in the *Patriot Act.*

Just as in Nazi Germany, throughout today's America we see unquestioning masses accepting the pronouncements of the authorities without a whimper, glad to be giving up their liberties, deemed necessary to gain a little (false) security. Chilling is the only way I can describe the spectacle of our citizens cheering on America's brutal adventures in the Middle East.

This alternate future could well become the Orwellian state described in the novel *1984.* Is this really worse? *Yes.* At least with the previous poverty scenario, a high degree of freedom was one of the results, with eventual recovery a certainty.

Hope Springs Eternal

Pandora's Box is an old Greek fable about the world's first woman, Pandora, who could not resist having a look in a box left in her keeping by the Gods. Once opened, evil entered into a previously perfect world along with all manner of vice, trouble, pain, suffering and discomfort. As the box emptied, however, one small remaining gift emerged: Hope, which went forth to sooth the pain and injuries then being inflicted upon the world's inhabitants. When all else fails you, goes the moral, you still have hope.

Patriots like to ask, *"Is it time yet?"*

Almost, my friend. Almost. I can all but smell the cordite in the air. Remember, though, that the first American patriots shot *back*; they didn't shoot first.

Bide your time a while longer. When the time is right, our leaders will emerge from our ranks and we will begin to pick up the pieces. America worked once as a constitutional republic. It can work again.

And, yes, Chicken Little was right. But, so was Dostoyevsky: *"It is not the brains that matter most, but that which guides them: the character, the heart, generous qualities, progressive ideas."*

We *can* do it. We *will* prevail. We did it before. What more proof do you need, in order to know that it is in our genetic predisposition? Because of that, we can do nothing else. Breeding shows.

Character, above all else, counts. That is the true legacy of our forefathers, a legacy which cannot be legislated away by Congress, judicially usurped by the courts or summarily seized by the Executive Branch. All that other stuff that has so incensed us at the moment is just words, just things, just stuff.

Let those who favor unchecked immigration from the third world and racial intermarriage fall by the wayside, as miscegenation takes its toll among their ranks. The European-American White gene pool thereby will be strengthened and purified by their departure.

We and our children and the strength that lies within us, stretching in an unbroken line from our distant European ancestors – that is what truly counts and what, in the end, will make the difference.

Be proud of who and what you are – it really is all you have. *It is more than enough.*

Chapter 15

Treading Water

"America is at that awkward stage. It's too late to work within the system, but too early to shoot the bastards."
-- Claire Wolfe, *"101 Things to Do 'Til the Revolution"* (1999)

Pretty grim so far, isn't it? The most common question I get from readers is, "Okay, I'm convinced of how bad it is. So what do we do about things right now?"

In fact, there is a great deal to be done right now.

Personal Preparedness

Ensure that you personally prepare for the coming hard times. That is a book in itself, but involves ensuring the safety of yourself and your loved ones. Some will resist. Some will think you nuts. But, there are things you can do quietly and covertly, even in that context.

Most importantly, you must plan now and be ready to implement that plan the moment the wheels come off.

If you live in a city, you need to plan how to get out in the event of a catastrophe. Immediately. Not the next day. Not that night. Immediately. Remember what South Central LA looked like just hours after the Rodney King verdict was handed down. That's how quickly it will degenerate.

No freeways. They will be death traps. You need an escape route that takes you through neighborhoods you know will be safe for a time. Being among the first to leave will help to ensure that roads are not blocked.

You must have a plan in place for assembling your family for the trip, regardless of the time of day that it becomes necessary.

Assemble a "bug-out" kit and keep it in your trunk.

Store enough gasoline in cans in your garage to get you to wherever you already have planned will be your retreat. Recycle the contents through your car every six months, because gasoline degenerates fairly rapidly. Keep your escape vehicle gassed up and well-serviced at all times.

Make a list of the things you can grab while the family is being assembled. Keep the list in the bug-out kit. Make a copy and keep it in your sock drawer, in case the car is busy picking up kids. Think apocalyptically today. If and when the time comes, it will be far too late to think at all.

You won't be capable of rational thought when the need arises, but you will be able to follow your list. Include any gold and silver you might be keeping stashed away (if you don't have any, then shame on you). Include weapons - you will need them, rest assured.

Get permission in advance, even if you treat it as a big joke, to arrive on the doorstep of friends or family in the country, if that is what you must do. Otherwise, they will not be happy to see you. Arrive with enough of something or other that makes you a valuable and welcome addition to their enclave. Food. Gasoline. Bullets. Gold. That sort of thing.

If nothing ever happens, which I consider exceedingly unlikely (that is, bad times are inevitable, in my humble opinion), then you will have wasted nearly nothing. In fact, you will make money on the appreciation in gold and silver that has taken place and will continue for several years. If something happens, a few hours' preparation today may spell the difference between life and death. *Yours*.

Moving Day

If you've a mind to, now would be an excellent time to move your family to an area likely to be among the safer in the country, regardless of what may happen. That will not include either the Southwest or the Deep South. Nor will it include any city of any serious size. Nor should it include areas within 100 miles of any coast (can you say, "nuke-induced Tsunami?"). The more paranoid will want to stay at least 400 miles away from Yellowstone Park.

As you will learn in the last chapter, *"New America,"* I expect that whatever survives of White America to be carved from the Northwest and the heartland.

Given America's recent predilection for invading small, defenseless countries, it is not at all unthinkable that we could be nuked in retaliation by somebody. Remember that nuclear fallout would be carried hundreds of miles by prevailing winds, which generally flow east by southeast. This consideration alone eliminates all of America except NE Washington state, N Idaho, NW Montana, bits of northern N Dakota and Minnesota and a few rural West Coast areas. Get on the internet and track down some projected fallout maps from an all-out nuclear strike against the US and you will be amazed.

Why not move to another country altogether? Because, given America's current ambitions for empire, there is no place that really is safe *from* America.

Only three areas could hold their own against America: Europe, China and Russia. Europe has become as multicultural as America and worse regarding civil liberties. The latter consideration makes Canada equally undesirable, quite aside from the weather. Australia is as bad as Canada. China simply isn't going to allow you to immigrate and assimilate. That leaves Russia.

How ironic that the country we grew up hating and fearing, the one we saw as being the epitome of repression and poverty, now shows signs of being the last great hope for White freedom. Russia is throwing out the last of the communists and learning how to prosper with true private enterprise. America dares not attack or invade Russia, don't forget.

I don't normally traffic in things supernatural, which I like to call "that woo-woo stuff." However, in researching aspects of this book, I kept stumbling across a prediction made by Edgar Cayce, sometimes known as "the sleeping prophet" because he made uncannily accurate medical diagnoses and a number of future predictions while in a trance-like light sleep. Shortly before he died at the end of 1944, while Russia was firmly in the grip of totalitarianism and expanding its reach, Cayce gave the following reading: *"[Through Russia], comes the hope of the world. Not in respect to what is sometimes termed Communism or Bolshevism -- no! But freedom -- freedom! That each man will live for his fellow man. The principle has been born there. It will take years for it to be crystallized; yet out of Russia comes again the hope of the world."* I include this quote for what it might be worth, since it seems to be coming true, particularly in view of the fall of Russian Communism.

A move into the far-western reaches of Russia, around Moscow and St. Petersburg, might well be a good investment in your future. I expect practically nobody reading these words to move to Russia, but you might make sure you and your family members have your passports up to date...just in case. The day may come when you will be able to secure passports only with great difficulty, if at all. Wait until you need them and I guarantee you won't have enough time to get them. Yet another cheap investment in a possible future.

Our Job for Today

With our personal plans in place, what can we do?

Vote? A total waste of time to vote for either Republicans or Democrats. All leading candidates are vetted by the ruling elite in advance, at all levels of government. And voting for the lesser of two evils is what gave America George W. Bush (that is, if you don't count the Supreme Court's role, of course). Remember: *the lesser of two evils is still evil.* Never vote for a Democrat or a Republican again.

Sign petitions? Don't bother - nobody who counts will consider them.

Write our congressmen and demand action? Useless. Like teaching pigs to dance, it is a waste of your time and merely annoys them. They don't need us in order to continue in office and they know it.

Outside of personal and family preparations and positioning, we who are awake have just one job until events come together to allow the creation of a New America: *we must awaken the others.*

Imagine a neighbor, friend or family member awakened by events, too late to prepare, confronted with your obvious advance preparations: *"Why didn't you tell me? What on earth were you thinking, not to demand that I wake up? You knew! Why didn't you think enough of me to make me aware?"* Is that a memory you want to carry with you for the rest of your life, especially if they end up not making it?

Yes, you might lose some friends who decide you have gone over the edge. This is the single consideration that prevents all of middle America from rising up *en masse* today to end racial preferences, removing politicians at every level of government and taking back America.

"Maybe it won't get worse." "Maybe it will get better." "Maybe I'll have plenty of warning." "The government would never actively hurt me." In the immortal words of Wayne, from the movie "Wayne's World": *"Yah, sure. When monkeys fly out my butt!"*

257

Already, there is a loose coalition of groups doing just that - trying to awaken America, that is. We are called members of the "Patriot Movement" or, as the feds derisively like to refer to us: "Patriots." Who would have thought that the word patriot would ever become a dirty word in America?

The Patriot Movement is the only serious domestic obstacle confronting the cabal now astride America.

For the Hard-Core Patriot

For the balance of this chapter, let me address what commonly is thought of as being the more radical, right-wing element in the Patriot Movement.

I am aware that a significant majority of those reading these words have not yet fully awakened. It is your hearts and minds I most wish to reach and bring on board with the problems confronting all Americans. It is you for whom I have written this book.

Nevertheless, the choir could stand with a little tuning, and I am hopeful that a good number of them also are reading this. Bear with me, as what I have to say to my more radical friends ultimately concerns you, your friends and your family.

Splintered, disorganized, fraught with infighting and jealous squabbles, denizens of the Patriot community truly make up the Gang that Couldn't Shoot Straight. Even so, we represent America's best, possibly last, hope for redemption from the bottomless pit into which our warmongering, capitalist/exploitive, fascist rulers seem bent upon flinging all of America.

If only we could get on the same page. If only we could agree upon what it is that we want. Freedom, to be sure, but you don't just go out and get freedom; first you must do or get something from which freedom results. And there may well be a number of intervening steps. Or many different paths to the same objective.

258

One thing that unites us is our dissatisfaction with America's current regime and a belief that our liberty and freedom already have been eroded beyond the point of no return. In other words, the system now is out of the people's hands and cannot be used to effect change. Witness the "choice" presented at each Presidential election. Consider the meat grinder that America's justice system has become.

Besides, recent immigration alone has guaranteed that, never again, will America be as we remember, let alone as our forefathers dreamt it could be. It was all that, and more, for a time. That was then. *This is now.*

Many have been calling for revolution. I cannot join in that call for two reasons:

First, I would get myself disbarred, then thrown in jail. I would be of no use to anybody, least of all my family, were that to happen.

Second, the time is not yet right because the majority of common folk, including large essential elements of organizations like the military, the FBI and local law enforcement, have yet to accumulate enough dissatisfaction to join in, once the lines are drawn. We must be drawn further into the abyss, with the pain of unemployment, poverty and imprisonment inflicted upon a great many more of us, before America will be ready to rise up and throw off the tyrants in control.

Instead, we must determine just what it is that we should be doing. *Awakening others* seems the only logical answer, because there simply is nothing else that *can* be done at this time, other than preparing for hard economic times.

I firmly believe that we needn't worry about leadership. Events will cause our true leaders to step forward when the time comes, just as events propelled the character played by Mel Gibson in "The Patriot" to assume his mantle of leadership, finally. He paid dearly for that conversion, however, just as did America's founding fathers in real life. So shall we.

Awakening Others

How to awaken our countrymen, while we wait for events to catch up to us?

Much of what we do is a waste of time, such as all the meetings of which we have grown so fond, the Internet chat forums in which we lurk, the newsletters we send one another. We need to stop preening for our fellow choir members, get out there and make new converts. We must awaken America to the menace which has befallen her.

The media won't do it; indeed, the media is a large part of the problem. Without the media, already the entire government would be behind bars simply for existing revelations about 9-11. Forget about the media doing anything except hindering legitimate efforts to advance the cause of the people.

Mostly, we seem to seek approval from those already on board. When we run afoul of the system, often we scream loudly and make outlandish statements which serve only to alienate those who might be sympathetic to our plight, yet fear the appearance of supporting radical behavior.

Those who secretly applaud us already are ours, in any event, and will come around in their own time. Already, they have experienced their trigger event or have otherwise been awakened secretly, therefore they should not be our primary concern.

I submit that what we should want is results. Little else matters. And the results we should want? Awakening those still in thrall to the establishment.

To be effective, we must keep our eye on the ball and focus on the tactics and strategies calculated to get the results we need. Focus on the objective and be single minded.

If putting on a clown costume and urinating on the White House rose bushes will get a result that we need, then that is what we should do. Nothing should be deemed too outlandish. Not even something as outrageous as getting a normal haircut, eschewing tattoos and buying a decent suit. No sacrifice should seem too great, even if it entails moderating our rhetoric, getting a normal job, living in a normal neighborhood, driving a normal car and acting normal at all times. We must make sacrifices in pursuit of our objective.

Face it: people relax and become much more receptive when they are comfortable. People are comfortable when those around them are predictable. Nothing is more predictable than a nice suit, white shirt, conservative tie and polished shoes. For many, this is asking far too much, I realize. Pity. They are the ones among us who simply don't mean what they say, else they would be willing to do what it takes to get results.

Insecurity is the basic human condition. We all possess it in spades. We would rather adopt our attitudes from those we respect and like - those we aspire to be like. Trust me, this does not magically end when we graduate from high school; it is a condition we carry to the grave.

Manage By Objective

Consider what our objective is. Who our target audience is. Who will they respect and want to be like? A skinhead mouthing obscenities and threatening all within earshot? Or someone that seems like all the other authority figures in their lives? You know the answer. You don't want it to be the answer? Too bad. *That's the way things are.*

Further, we must act within the parameters of what is legal, as it is self defeating to get arrested - no results, you see.

Similarly, it is not productive to be attacking others in the movement, for whatever reason - again, no results.

261

First step in the analysis: results. What, exactly and realistically, do we want? If your answer is 14 words (David Lane's memorable *"We must secure the existence of our people and a future for White children"*), then you have gone too abstract - focus a level or two beneath that.

Once the clear, specific and attainable results are comprehensively catalogued, defined and articulated, then the means to attain them becomes a relevant inquiry.

For example, getting people of European ancestry to move to the American Northwest might be a rational result to be desired. Merely calling for it or demanding it, however, does not get the job done. View it in Sales terms: what are the objections and considerations raised by the prospect and how do we overcome them? How do we engage the prospect in the first place? Hell, how do we even identify potential prospects? Better, how do we *create* prospects?

This analysis requires feedback loops. Once we identify potential prospects, it may be necessary to alter our presentation in order to transform them into bona fide prospects.

Wanting to move to the Northwest and live in an all-White republic modeled on the US Constitution is one thing. That objective dictates pretty easily-identifiable tasks: quit job, sell house, rent trailer, *etc.* Getting others to want it is something else altogether, though implicit to the goal as stated, and is the much tougher task, with a host of as-yet-undefined subtasks.

Another result, the one I most wish to focus on herein: awakening others so that they will prepare for the troubled times ahead and be ready to shoulder their share of responsibility for rebuilding America once the wheels come off completely, as I firmly believe must and will happen. Trying to make the wheels come off is not a legitimate result, aside from the fact that any such activity doubtless would be illegal, thus outside the parameters of our analysis.

Hidden Effects

Many complain of the constant rejection by the unawakened. Yes, that will happen. In fact, it will be the rule, rather than the exception. Keep in mind, however, that everything you say and all that you do goes into their minds. You may not see the effect, but it takes place, I assure you.

Here's an analogy: When I was younger and stupider, I smoked cigarettes - two to three packs a day. I had tried a couple of times, with only limited success, to quit. Yet, the need was building within me on a daily basis. The smell, the holes in my clothing from dropped embers, the dirty ashes all over everything, the ostracizing by friends; all this and more added to my mounting dissatisfaction and disgust with my habit. All went into the hopper. Then, one day, while fumbling with a lit cigarette and trying simultaneously to change gears at an intersection, I had had enough. I stubbed it out in the ashtray and have not had even the desire for a cigarette for over thirty years.

My point? To the casual observer, I continued for a time just as before, a committed smoker. Then, suddenly, I was a nonsmoker. *"What caused the change?"* many asked me. I was hard pressed to answer, as the critical mass for the change had been building for years. That cigarette fumble in the car simply was the last straw.

Consider others to be like the smoker building up to a decision to quit. They will go along, seemingly as before, but your words and actions will fester within them, unseen by you. The more they respect you, the more influential will have been what you had to say. More will be added by others...then something will happen, what I like to call a "trigger event," and they will blossom before your eyes. Maybe they will get mugged by a Black. Or pushed around in a bar by some drunk Mexicans. Or, God forbid, raped. Or lose their job to a less-qualified beneficiary of affirmative action.

Effective Activism

Unfortunately, a good deal of what we do is counterproductive, leaving us in worse shape than before, with our countrymen looking even more askance at us. This results from our total unwillingness to consider what our goal should be, to manage by objective, as Peter Drucker, the world's foremost pioneer of management theory, would put it.

Here is a sampling of quotes from Drucker that I think we, in particular, would do well to memorize:

"Efficiency is doing things right; effectiveness is doing the right things."

"Effective leadership is not about making speeches or being liked; leadership is defined by results, not attributes."

"Management by objective works - if you know the objectives. Ninety percent of the time you don't."

"Rank does not confer privilege or give power. It imposes responsibility."

"The best way to predict the future is to create it."

The Elegance of Simplicity

It doesn't have to be complicated. In fact, simple is better. Truly effective managers recognize the elegance of simplicity, as that is what allows them to keep their eye on the ball, to keep the objective always firmly in view.

Not that complicated things cannot be elegant. Witness the Sistine Chapel. Or a pretty girl.

Computer programmers and system designers immediately know

what I mean when I speak of the elegance, the beauty, that arises from a solution to a problem that achieves its objective with a small percentage of the effort that might previously have been required. Aside from getting the same job done effectively, it is the very simplicity of a new, more efficient approach that draws true appreciation.

Henry Ford revolutionized manufacturing with a simplistically elegant new approach: the assembly line.

Always, elegance is accompanied by a form of gracefulness, a grace born of effortless movement which is simplicity personified.

Consider skiing. Elegant skiing always is the most effortless.

The beginner clatters down the slope, bending, leaning too far, correcting, correcting too much, recorrecting, muscles continually at odds and tensed against one another, falling down, getting up...you get the idea...exhausted and ready for lunch after two runs.

The expert skier elegantly and effortlessly glides in and out of the little hillocks called moguls, skis always together, moving fast and decisively, upper body stationary and perfectly balanced, finally stopping at the bottom without breathing hard.

None can dispute the lack of grace attendant to the actions of so many in the Movement. Gracelessness bespeaks inefficiency and ineffectiveness. Focus on the objective and drive relentlessly toward it, along the simplest and most direct path. Form follows function. Grace is a consequence of effective and efficient action.

Being Truly Accountable

Remember that the objective is outside ourselves. We must come to the realization that we are accountable, not just for our intent, but also for how we affect others. Indeed, those effects are the most important aspect of that which we profess to do.

When we speak out or act in a manner calculated to affect our countrymen, we must be aware of the responsibilities we have toward them and to one another. This is one of the responsibilities of leadership, because we appoint ourselves as leaders whenever we act or speak out.

We must appear to the unawakened to be rational and supporting a just cause. We must show how we are just like them, but for one or more injustices to which they have yet to fall prey. This is the simple truth, you know.

I deal with a broad spectrum of people in my travels, ranging from tattooed skinheads to the most liberal of bleeding hearts. Always, I am struck by how similar we all are, but for an exceedingly small percentage of our outlooks. We all are concerned about work, bills, kids, the future. We all pretty much have the same values. Yet, we allow ourselves to be divided by others and some within our own ranks, using labels in a blatantly propagandistic fashion.

"Racist" and "anti-Semite" are the most common labels thrown about. Refuse to accept them until you include the throwers in their definition, which always is easy to do. Based upon my experience, and despite appearances, there is very little difference between the hard-core skinhead and the liberal bothered by the unfairness of racial preferences.

We forget that, in reality, everybody is a racist, by one definition or another in common use. Yes, it is strange that someone who objects to being displaced as a result of affirmative action gets tagged with the same label as genuine supremacists (whatever the flavor, supremacists are the true racists, in my book).

Incidentally, anti-Semite now is losing its currency, since Jews ceaselessly fling it at virtually everybody, even some of their own brethren.

We bear a responsibility to our contemporaries in "The Movement" to reflect favorably upon them, else we dishonor ourselves because the public lumps us all together in its view. This is a reality denied only by the dishonest and disingenuous among us.

If we, with our common beliefs, can't work together, reason the great bulk of our countrymen, how could they ever hope to work with us?

If we can't bother to look and act like them, how will they ever be comfortable with us?

We preach how racial awareness causes one to want to be with one's own kind, then we go out of our way to drive a wedge between ourselves and the very people we claim to wish to reach, what with tattoos, haircuts, boots, weird clothing, outlandish remarks and violent behavior.

If we mean what we say about creating racial unity, we should be wearing suits, conventional haircuts and speaking in measured tones about things that realistically are attainable.

It's a simple matter of defining objectives and clearly seeing the means of attaining them.

Solutions

Many complain that the leaflets, booklets and screeds that those in "The Movement" pass out serve only to polarize opposition from those whom we seek to awaken. Because there is such obvious merit to these concerns, we must be particularly mindful of our target audience and tailor our presentations appropriately. This goes back to what I said earlier concerning sales theory and the development of prospects. Push too hard and you lose them; indeed, you may create a voice to be added to the chorus of the opposition. Push too softly and you produce few, if any, results.

Imagine simply handing someone a pamphlet which blames all the ills of Western Civilization upon the Jewish race (not far off the mark, just between you and me, by the way). The typical unwashed reaction will be to reject both you and the meritorious points which might therein be contained. While our intent is laudable, we ignore the effect we have upon others by demanding that they see things from our perspective. That is inefficient, ungraceful and scarcely facilitates our objective of awakening them. It isn't even an inelegant solution. At best, it simply is no solution. At worst, it becomes part of the problem.

Wearing Nazi regalia, sporting a buzz haircut and/or displaying tattoos often has the same effect of "backing up" those we hope to influence positively. We become our own worst enemy in such a situation, because the White Race would have been better off had we stayed home and watched Saturday morning cartoons.

Just as the war against free speech now is shifting its focus from the intent of the speaker to the effect upon the listener, so do we need to shift our focus. Results, don't forget - that's what it's all about.

If you disagree with me so far, then I submit that you simply are after results different from awakening others. In fact, you are bent upon self destruction. If you still disagree with me, then look around yourself and ask what results "The Movement" has to show for its efforts in recent years. If you still disagree with me, please mark this page, set this book down and go do something else for a while. Come back after you have perked on things a bit more.

Often, adroitly using an opponent's weight and movements against himself will procure the best results, just as taught in oriental fighting disciplines. Consider the huge Jewish outcry over the alleged anti-Semitism of the movie, *"The Passion of the Christ."* Now consider how badly that backfired for Abe Foxman, chairman of the ADL, and his fellow travelers. Mel Gibson's movie is a marvelous fulcrum for discussion and ax grinding, provided it is not overdone and one concentrates on the Jewish overreaction.

Simply asking someone if they have seen *"The Passion"* and then inquiring about their feelings concerning so many Jews calling it anti-Semitic and seeking its suppression will yield a gold mine of results. As people discuss this topic and express their opinions (which only rarely will be contrary to our own), they actually develop their opinions on the spot. Having voiced their opinions, our prospects become invested in them. They then feel psychologically compelled to defend the opinions they have just voiced to you. From prospect to convert to acolyte, all in one easy step.

Can it be this easy? Yes. Remember the simple elegance of graceful movement, at once effective and efficient. This is the conversational equivalent of expert skiing and is within the grasp of all beginners because it simply requires listening. You set aside your own ego and needs while you nudge someone toward a foregone conclusion. And there are several other key topics that can be employed in this form of awakening others, as discussed below.

Jump Starting the Process

Even so, some form of media which shocks the average American is necessary, in order to jump start the awakening process. In particular, the National Alliance (NA) lately has struck upon a two-pronged strategy that is delivering results: leaflets and billboards. But, there is a difference from past leaflets and billboards in today's NA strategy. The leaflet simply says, *"Love Your Race"* and carries a picture of a lovely blond woman. The billboard says, *"Who Rules America?"* and gives the NA Internet web address. Initially, people have a strong reaction to these media but, upon honest reflection, are unable to identify anything wrong, thereby highlighting the very thing that really is wrong with race relations in America today: the grotesque double standard whereby White Americans always come up the loser.

Average Americans are not yet ready to abandon the guilt they believe they must shoulder if they stand up for their own race the way that every other race in America stands up for itself. We must get them ready to make that transition.

What the NA leaflets and billboards do, Mel Gibson's movie does with a vengeance, albeit with a healthy assist from that predictable Jewish overreaction.

We aren't talking supremacy here, folks. We are talking about how to bring people from a self-defeating mode of thinking to one of true equality. They want to go there, believe me, because they see the unfairness of racial preferences.

The alternatives are so simple. We have them ready to hand, just begging to be used to awaken others. Two things that cause even the most liberal American to see red are affirmative action and illegal immigration. Suggest Black slave reparations and watch even the hardened liberal squirm in discomfort. Here is where we can make progress and awaken others. Here is where we must concentrate our efforts.

Chosen Gifts

Count on the ADL regularly to drop a gift in our laps, too, such as the overreaction to *"The Passion."*

The debacles in Afghanistan and Iraq, now clearly seen to have been for Israel's benefit, are another ripe area to be mined...particularly when you mention how prominent American Administration Zionist Jews such as Richard Perle and Paul Wolfowitz have agitated for widening the battlefront to include the rest of the Middle East.

Or the call for torture of American enemies by Alan Dershowitz, prominent Jewish attorney and Harvard law professor, a call which has been echoed by Canadian Jewish attorney and law professor Alan Young, who advocates expanding the application of torture to American political dissidents. Dissidents like you and me. To "kick start" our brains, to borrow Mr. Young's phrase, into thinking the "right" way...his way...the Jewish way. This is the sort of outrageous Jewish overreaching that takes place every day and which effortlessly can be used against them, like a mystical oriental judo maneuver.

Exploiting Outrage

Talking up patent injustice visited upon particular individuals in society, as I try to do with some legal cases, is another productive approach. The Zionists make this so easy, what with their gross overreaching and ridiculous attempts to stifle free speech.

Rather than complaining about Blacks taking our White daughters, we should be railing against racial preferences and quotas that steal our jobs and unfairly relegate us to poverty. Racial miscegenation will be dealt with in its own time, as events unfold.. Indeed, it will cease to be a problem.

Rather than espousing our own questionable racial superiority, we should be demonstrating against illegal immigration and the toll that it takes on the social welfare net we have erected for our children and those legally among us who fall by the wayside.

Face it, Whites aren't superior, just different. Races have differences. Differences have nothing to do with being superior or inferior. Get used to it. If you haven't gotten this message by this point in this book, I despair of your ever getting it.

Not that differences don't count, mind you - they do. Some differences count so much as to require strict racial separation simply to ensure the physical safety of one race from another's hostility. This is another problem that will solve itself in time, though not without severe discomfort to all involved.

Rather than marching with Confederate battle flags and shouting "White Power," we should be protesting America's use of military force abroad. The South lost the War of Northern Aggression. Get over it. Worry more about the current American aggression abroad that is killing our sons and daughters and increasing the likelihood of America being nuked by somebody.

An emerging issue of major importance to the average American is the increasing migration of our jobs overseas, as factories move abroad and existing jobs get "outsourced" by companies that maintain only a token presence in America. Protesting NAFTA, GATT and the World Trade Organization wherever it meets are things that unawakened and unemployed Americans can understand and respect.

We are being whipsawed by the loss of our low-paying jobs to illegal immigrants and our higher-paying jobs to foreign countries. Many of the better jobs that aren't leaving America are going to better-educated foreigners, willing to work cheaply, brought here under H-1B visas by the multinational corporations whose loyalty is only to their own bottom line.

Everybody can relate to job losses as an issue, especially those who are out of work. In particular, America's growing legions of unemployed are a hotbed of potential racial awakening. Most of them already have had their trigger event by virtue of being unemployed while those less deserving continue to earn an income - and, after all, they no longer need fear losing their jobs for expressing politically-incorrect points of view.

Using the System Against Itself

Run for office and use the platform to speak out. Who cares if you win? Jim Condit understands this perfectly and was the first to make me aware of the value of running for office. No, Jim has yet to be elected to anything, but by filing for office, he gets access to a number of opportunities to awaken others. These opportunities are all the more important now that criticism of candidates by the rest of us during the 60 days prior to each election has been outlawed. Oh, you didn't know that? Thank Congressmen John McCain and Russ

Feingold for that little statutory gem which was passed so recently.

Jim Condit, whom I have met a couple of times and who regularly chides me for not pushing this more, makes an excellent point: Run for office at any level, for any job, and use the platform to speak out - you get coverage, credibility (of sorts) and a freedom to speak that exists in very few other forums. Plus, if you become newsworthy, then the media actually carries your message further than the sound of your voice.

If your candidacy is for a *federal* office, all FCC-licensed radio and TV stations *have* to sell you local time at the lowest rates provided to any other candidate and provide equal access to all media.

Jim is right. This potentially is a hugely effective weapon that we simply have not used.

Of course, you must abandon all hope of being elected and simply use it as an opportunity to speak out. This has value merely for the effect of helping to awaken our countrymen. And, a most effective device it can be if we avoid the temptation to speak to the mainstream and, instead, hew to the path charted by our convictions.

The Effectiveness of Simplicity

These are obvious things to be done. Simple. Elegant in their simplicity because they directly reach the hearts and minds of the unawakened American. Easy because they go with the flow that already has begun. Effective because they work. Efficient because they don't involve a lot of wasted motion.

These are things that any of us can do and do well without much practice. Will it be easy? No. All of us will come in for more than our share of negative feedback. One of the greatest minds ever produced by the human race, Aristotle, said, *"Criticism is something that easily can be avoided by saying nothing, doing nothing and being nothing."* Criticism comes with the territory. Learn to shrug it off

273

without overreaction, just as Jews seem incapable of doing, thereby affording us some of our richest opportunities.

Think you, a lone individual, can do nothing? You're wrong. Most of the foregoing suggestions are well within the grasp of the poorest and lest educated among us. Even if you are not convinced, at least stand aside and let others try without adding your voice to the cacophony they must endure. A Chinese proverb says it best: *"Man who say it cannot be done should not interrupt man doing it."*

Liberal and conservative are terms that are losing their meaning, as a direct result of the *de facto* merger of the Republican and Democrat political parties in America. Indeed, both are becoming dirty words with the average American, who proved ready to listen to alternate party viewpoints during Ross Perot's abortive run for President.

Vote. Vote against all Democrat and Republican candidates (save only Ron Paul and Tom Tancredo). Write in people if you need to. Help the third-party vote count to accumulate until it challenges the Democrat/Republican monolith.

When the rest of America sees us protesting and speaking out about the very things gnawing at them right now, we will have earned its trust and established our credibility. Then, and only then, can we hope to move our White countrymen along to demanding true equality with other races and true accountability from our government.

As our economy starts to implode, due to the massive fiscal and trade deficits, coupled with the unprecedented levels of debt and corruption at all levels of American society, Americans will be ready to take to the streets and listen to more drastic suggestions. That is when the government will move against us. Then we will come into our own. Then will our leaders emerge and begin to fashion the solutions to the problems of an America gone bad.

That is when our real work will begin. Until then, let us keep our eye on the ball before us and see just how gracefully we can manage to define and accomplish our current objectives.

Making a Difference

Meanwhile, don't think that you can't make a difference. Especially in this fight, which is to the death, the death of the White race, every single individual must be made to count.

Francis Parker Yockey wrote of the power of individuals by virtue of and as a part of a greater racial spirit, or destiny, in his masterwork *Imperium*: *"This destiny does not tire, nor can it be broken, and its mantle of strength descends upon those in its service."* This concept has been echoed by many others in many other races, from time to time.

Tom Brown, Jr. wrote a series of books recounting stories of his Grandfather, an Apache wise man who grew up outside White influence. In *The Quest* (unfortunately, now out of print, but you can reach Tom Brown, Jr. on the Internet through his website, www.trackerschool.com), Grandfather sagely observed to Tom:

> "If a man could make the right choices," he said, "then he could significantly alter the course of the possible future. No man, then, should feel insignificant, for it only takes one man to alter the consciousness of mankind through the Spirit-that-moves-in-all-things. In essence, one thought influences another, then another, until the thought is made manifest throughout all of Creation. It is the same thought, the same force, that causes an entire flock of birds to change course, as the flock then has one mind...*I suspect that it is but one bird that creates the thought that turns the flock, and the one thought becomes immediately manifested in all the others.* The individual then transcends self and becomes one

275

with the whole. Thus, at once, the bird moves within the flock and the flock moves within the bird. So, then, do not ask what you can do to affect the life force in a positive way, for the same Spirit that moves within the birds also moves within you. *One person, one idea, one thought can turn the flock of society away from the destructive path of modern times.* It is not a question as to whether we make a difference, for we all make a difference, each of us in our own way. It is the difference we make that is important." (emphasis supplied)

This, from a society that our forebears thought so little of that they were all but eradicated from the earth. What a pity.

Chapter 16

World War III

"From the days of Spartacus-Weishaupt to those of Karl Marx, to those of Trotsky...this world-wide conspiracy for the overthrow of civilization...has been steadily growing...(A)t last this band of extraordinary personalities from the underworld of the great cities of Europe and America have gripped the Russian people by the hair of their heads and have become practically the undisputed masters of that enormous empire."
--- Winston Churchill, *"Zionism versus Bolshevism,"* Illustrated Sunday Herald, February 1920

"Of all the enemies to public liberty, war is, perhaps, the most to be dreaded because it comprises and develops the germ of every other... No nation could preserve its freedom in the midst of continual warfare."
--- James Madison, April 20, 1795

"Everything has been said before, but since nobody listens we have to keep going back and beginning all over again."
--- Andre Gide, *Le Traite du Narcisee (Analysis of the Self)* (1891)

What is occurring in the Middle East as this is being written (early 2004) is precisely what took place in Europe twice in the last century: Jewish interests are being pursued and vindicated, with America used as the bully boy.

Last century, it was Germany and her people that said, *"Enough,"* then strove to throw off Jewish control of their country and drive out the Jewish Communist menace growing and committing genocide in Russia. Judea literally declared war on Germany before the first shots ever were fired in World War II, then quickly enlisted Western

277

Europe, already in thrall to Jewish banking and mercantile interests.

Think not? The term "Final Solution" actually was coined by Jews and applied to Germans prior to the start of WWII. After the war had begun, in his 1941 book, *Germany Must Perish*, Theodore Kaufman called for the forced sterilization of all Germans. The American Jewish Committee immediately endorsed this call for genocide against the Germans. Predictably, the Nazis were enraged.

Having already lost Germany well before the war got under way, European Jews became desperate to drag America aboard, just as had been done in World War I.

World War I

Here's the party line on World War I:

Austrian Archduke Francis Ferdinand, heir to the Austrian throne, was assassinated in Bosnia on June 28, 1914, by Serbian nationalist Gavrilo Princip. One month later, having failed to extract sufficient concessions from Serbia, and with the full support of Germany, Austria-Hungary (a single political unit at the time) declared war on Serbia.

Britain, France, Russia and Belgium came to Serbia's defense (the Allied Powers), with the Ottoman Empire (Turkey's precursor) joining the aggressors, the Central Powers, late in 1914. The following year saw Bulgaria join the Central Powers, with Italy coming to the aid of the Allied Powers.

America was drawn in when a German submarine sank the American ocean liner *Lusitania*, killing all 195 Americans aboard at the time.

The Central Powers lost and saw their homeland

boundary lines drastically redrawn, together with being required to pay staggering war reparations to the victors.

Before the "Great War," as it was then known, ended, 32 countries, including the United States, became involved, with over 65 million men mobilized, nearly half of whom became casualties, including more than 10 million dead.

To the victors go the spoils, as they say. Of course, it also is said that history is written by those selfsame victors. Now, here are a few things that you never learned in your high school history class, but which nevertheless are true:

Logic alone dictates that America did not enter the war because of the *Lusitania*, which was sunk on May 7, 1915. It was not until *two years later*, on April 2, 1917, that President Wilson asked Congress for a Declaration of War, which almost immediately was granted. Nevertheless, the *Lusitania* played a key role which deserves extended discussion here.

Unbeknownst to its 1,200 passengers, 195 of whom were Americans, the British ocean liner *Lusitania,* bound for England, was carrying 6 million American-made rounds of ammunition, in direct violation of the protocols of war then observed by neutral powers. That made her a legitimate military target. The ammunition was owned by American banking powerhouse J.P. Morgan and Company, merely one of a number of major Zionist banking houses slavering for war because of the profit potential. More than a year earlier, the French Jewish Rothschild banking house had sent J.P. Morgan a note suggesting a $100 million loan to pay for French arms purchases.

Somehow, the Germans knew of the illegal cargo carried by the *Lusitania*, most likely through disinformation fed to them, possibly through the infamous Mata Hari. Incredibly, the German government took the extraordinary step of prepaying for advertisements in fifty American newspapers, including all those located in New York, the

279

Lusitania's port of departure, warning Americans not to travel aboard the *Lusitania*. Only one of those newspapers carried the ad, in remote Des Moines, Iowa, because they all had been warned of dire consequences if they published German-sourced material without clearance from the US State Department. Though requested, that clearance never came.

Despite entering a war zone, the *Lusitania* was sent without an escort and left adrift in the English Channel, awaiting a pilot boat (used to guide liners ashore through shoals), the *Juno*, that never came because it was recalled by order of then First Lord of the Admiralty, Winston Churchill. Having cracked the German war code five months earlier, Britain was able to track all German submarines. Churchill knew full well that three U-Boats were in the vicinity of the *Lusitania* at the time the liner was abandoned to them.

The *Lusitania* was bait, pure and simple, jointly offered by the British and the Americans, in an attempt to drive a reluctant American public into backing America's entry into the war on the side of the Allied Powers. The *Lusitania's* significance derives from the fact that virtually every American conflict thereafter has required a similar sacrifice of innocent lives in order to line up an unsuspecting public behind a government already bent upon war (*e.g.*, Pearl Harbor, The Gulf of Tonkin Incident, 9-11).

Confounding both American and British officials, America's citizenry was not outraged sufficiently by the *Lusitania's* sinking to demand entry to the war then raging in Europe, as had been planned. Instead, popular sentiment in the US against the war merely declined to about 5 to 1, down from 10 to 1 prior to the liner's sinking.

Besides, the very next year, 1916, was an election year and President Woodrow Wilson's main slogan for his re-election campaign already had been selected: "He kept us out of the war." Once re-elected, it took Wilson less than three months to make his demand upon Congress for a Declaration of War. History since has shown that, eight months prior to his re-election, Wilson approved a memorandum given the British by Wilson's primary advisor, Edward House, which pledged American intervention if Germany would not promptly come to heel by year's end.

Wilson fancied himself ruler of the world and saw American involvement in the war as his ticket to that position atop an organization yet to be organized. In the midst of his campaign for re-election, President Wilson delivered a major speech wherein he urged a single world government in order to prevent recurrence of another war like the one then being waged in Europe. In that speech, delivered on May 27, 1916, Wilson proposed adoption of a League of Nations.

Over two years later, simultaneous with the victor nations signing the Treaty of Versailles, marking the end of the war on November 11, 1918, a Charter for The League of Nations also was adopted. President Wilson signed that Charter, then was stymied by an American Senate that denied him ratification. It was a poorly-kept secret that Wilson envisioned himself the first "President of the World," as so aptly put by then-Senator Henry Cabot Lodge.

At about the time of the sinking of the *Lusitania* in 1915, the war efforts of both Britain and France were going poorly. Both clearly saw a very real danger of losing the war to the Central Powers. Russia itself was in turmoil and about to plunge into revolutionary chaos, thus of no real help.

Even so, Germany offered to end the war in a manner favorable to Britain, but was rebuffed. The reason? *The Balfour Declaration*, which memorialized a deal between an increasingly-desperate British Prime Minister Arthur Balfour and international Zionist leaders, represented by Lord Rothschild. In exchange for the Zionists guaranteeing entry of America into the war, a flailing Britain pledged to turn over Palestine to the Zionists, who wanted it, and nothing else, as a homeland for Jews. Problem is, Palestine was not Britain's to offer. The Turks held Palestine at that time.

Signed in March 1916, though agreed to in principle earlier, *The Balfour Declaration* was not made public until the end of the following year, long after America's entry into the war. Meanwhile, the Jewish-controlled press in America shifted into high gear with vilification of the Germans and demands that America "make the world safe for democracy." It took two years to overcome the reluctance of an American public, through the joint efforts of the Wilson Administration and a unified media propaganda campaign, but it was done, just in time for Wilson to be re-elected for "keeping America out of the war."

It would take another thirty years for Britain to make good on its side of the bargain, which required that it first obtain control of Palestine.

Meanwhile, Zionist bankers on both sides of the Atlantic Ocean reaped gargantuan sums in war profits. The Rockefellers alone made well in excess of $200 million from the war.

In what simply is a coincidence to many, the US Congress passed the Federal Reserve Act in 1914, at the behest of the international Zionist banking families and just prior to America's entry into the war, creating the very mechanism by which the American people could be assessed the cost of the then-impending war, not to mention every war since that time.

World War II

Most historians concede that the seeds of World War II were planted in the very document that ended The Great War: The Treaty of Versailles. The British delegate to the Versailles Conference, Lord Curzon, was quoted as saying, *"This is no peace; this is only a truce for twenty years."* His words proved prescient, owing specifically to the draconian nature of the peace terms imposed upon the German representatives. Twenty years, exactly, were to pass before the start of the war that caused The Great War to be renamed.

Provisions of the Treaty of Versailles, crafted in large part by Zionist bankers attending the Versailles Conference in 1918, proved so onerous as to bring about the economic destruction of Germany, thereby laying the foundation for the rise of a dictator who could offer salvation to a beleaguered German population.

Germans resented the Zionist role which had turned the course of the first world war around and led to their defeat at the hands of the Allied Powers. The outrageous war reparations payments impressed upon them by Zionist bankers rankled no less, resulting in the collapse of the German economy and the impoverishment of so many. The Jewish takeover of postwar Germany was simply too much for its citizens to bear. Once again, Jewish overreaching was to backfire.

To obtain a flavor of the times, consider the following extended passage from British historian Sir Arthur Bryant's *Unfinished Victory* (1940):

> "It was the Jews with their international affiliations and their hereditary flair for finance who were best able to seize such opportunities...
>
> "They did so with such effect that, even in November 1938, after five years of anti-Semitic legislation and persecution, they still owned, according to the Times correspondent in Berlin, something like a third of the real property in the Reich. Most of it came into their hands during the inflation. But to those who had lost their all, this bewildering transfer seemed a monstrous injustice. After prolonged sufferings they had now been deprived of their last possessions. They saw them pass into the hands of strangers, many of whom had not shared their sacrifices and who cared little or nothing for their national standards and

traditions...

"The Jews obtained a wonderful ascendancy in politics, business and the learned professions (in spite of constituting) less than one percent of the population...

"The banks, including the Reichsbank and the big private banks, were practically controlled by them. So were the publishing trade, the cinema, the theatres and a large part of the press - all the normal means, in fact, by which public opinion in a civilized country is formed...

"The largest newspaper combine in the country with a daily circulation of four millions was a Jewish monopoly...

"Every year it became harder and harder for a gentile to gain or keep a foothold in any privileged occupation...

"At this time it was not the 'Aryans' who exercised racial discrimination. It was a discrimination that operated without violence. It was exercised by a minority against a majority. There was no persecution, only elimination...

"It was the contrast between the wealth enjoyed - and lavishly displayed - by aliens of cosmopolitan tastes, and the poverty and misery of native Germans, that has made anti-Semitism so dangerous and ugly a force in the new Europe. Beggars on horseback are seldom popular, least of all with those whom they have just thrown out of the saddle." (pp. 136-144)

Now read the foregoing quote again, and, in a foretaste of this book's later discussion of World War III, this time consider how appropriate this passage might be in describing present-day Western life, especially in America. All that is left is a bout of true hyperinflation to set the stage as completely as was Germany's just prior to the rise of Hitler.

In 1932, fully a year before Hitler came to power, and six years before a single shot was fired in the coming war, the World Jewish League, in the person of its President, Bernard Lecache, openly declared: *"Germany is our public enemy number one. It is our object to declare war without mercy against her."*

Hitler was the *response* to Jewish overreaching throughout Germany, contrary to the impression given by establishment historians, who would have you believe that Jewish hatred of things German devolved only from persecution at the hands of the Nazis. A clearer example cannot be found of the disconnect between Jews who cry "anti-Semite" and the motivations of those against whom the epithet is hurled.

A powerful and charismatic leader, Adolph Hitler deftly guided his National Socialist Party's rise to power, gaining a majority of seats in the Reichstag, Germany's governing Parliament, in early 1933. Shortly thereafter, Hitler was appointed Chancellor of the Reich by then-President Von Hindenburg. Only one month later, on March 24, 1933, Hitler was given full emergency powers in response to a fire that destroyed the Reichstag's own building, a fire that modern historians have linked to Hitler's followers, though blamed at the time on Jewish communists. Indeed, *"Reichstag Fire"* has come to be a euphemism for false-flag operations, wherein a terrible act is done by one party in the guise of another it seeks to vilify and/or for the purpose of gaining some advantage.

On the very day that Hitler was given dictatorial power, the following headline appeared atop the front page of The Daily Express of England: *"Judea Declares War on Germany. Jews of All the World Unite in Action."* Remember, this was a full year after the World Jewish League openly had declared war against Germany in a move that marked the beginning of a worldwide boycott of Germany, not to mention a full six years before Germany moved to recover the territory it lost to Poland.

After yet another year had passed, in 1934, Zionist leader

Vladimir Jabotinsky declared, *"The fight against Germany has now been waged for months by every Jewish community, on every continent...We shall start a spiritual and material war of the world against Germany. Our Jewish interests call for the complete destruction of Germany."*

Blaming Jews for all that ailed Germany, and not without good cause in the eyes of the German public, due in no small part to the bellicosity of Jews around the world, Hitler proceeded to take back control of the German media, colleges and banks from the Jews then in charge throughout Germany. Jews around the world demanded that America and Britain retaliate against Germany for its having divested German Jews of their accoutrements of power and control.

For the next several years, Hitler was to preside over what increasingly seemed an economic miracle, as he put all of Germany to work on monumental public works projects and, more importantly, resurrected Germany's war-making capability.

How did he pay for all this after Germany had been pauperized by the Allies several years earlier? In short, he didn't. Not in the conventional sense of the word, anyway, which was part of the problem that International bankers had with Hitler. With no money, he struck upon a scheme of barter and exchange at the national level. For example, Hitler agreed with Argentina upon a reasonable exchange rate, then simply traded German locomotives for Argentine beef, thereby cutting the banking system out of the transaction altogether.

"Hitler's 'Exchange' system became a major problem and danger for the International Bankers. No wonder the World's major Banks demanded action and intervention by their different Governments. Many serious Scientists are convinced the Boycott of German Goods by the USA and Great Britain were the start of economic war with Germany." Gestapo Chief: The 1948 Interrogation of Heinrich Müller, Gregory Douglas (R. James Bender,

1995, p. 156)

Hitler had help, too, in large measure from America and other Western countries, who poured capital and resources into a rapidly-recovering Germany, despite ongoing wails of caution from Jews around the world. Ironically, some of the most prominent Zionist bankers of the day were instrumental in financing Germany's resurrection, proving the maxim that profit rules above all loyalties.

On September 1, 1939, Germany invaded Poland, bent upon recapturing the territory carved from itself by the Treaty of Versailles. It is crucial to remember that Poland was a totally new country, pieced together by WWI's victors from territory sliced from both Germany and Russia. Two weeks later, by prearrangement, the Russians also entered Poland, from the East, neatly dividing the now-helpless country between the two resurgent powers and retaking the portions divested at Versailles.

Britain and France, both driven nearly insane by Zionist media and banking pressures, finally declared war on Germany because of its invasion of Poland. *Russia was ignored, though it, too, had invaded Poland.* Of course, Russia by then was in the firm grip of the Bolsheviks, Jewish Communists all. Professional courtesy, one might cynically remark, ruled the day.

One thing must not go unsaid: After Russia's Communist Zionist Jews took control of the eastern portion of Poland, they marched 10,000 Polish military officers, the very cream of Poland's manhood at the time, into the Katyn Forest near the Russian town of Smolensk and slaughtered them to a man. For years, this atrocity was blamed by world Jewry upon the Nazis, but documents surfacing after the Soviet Union's breakup made clear that the real culprits were Russian Jews.

Contrary to the conventional wisdom that paints Hitler as bent upon world domination, in reality he was after only two things, at least in the very beginning: reversal of the territorial losses imposed upon Germany by the Versailles Treaty and stopping Communism dead in its tracks. Hitler's hatred of Communism and perception that it was a singularly Jewish invention would lead him to invade Russia itself, though it served Germany's purposes to treat them as allies early in the war.

As the war got underway, however, Hitler saw weaknesses where none previously were perceived, such that the balance of power began to shift. If nothing else, Hitler *was* an opportunist, as he had proven in his rise to power within Germany, thus his territorial ambitions grew. (See, generally, *The Origins of the Second World War*, AJP Taylor)

In fact, as noted previously, Hitler offered Britain a favorable peace treaty that was to be rebuffed.

In early 1940, amidst a massive buildup on its western flank by both British and French forces, Germany pre-emptively attacked the Allied combine by invading Norway, Holland and Belgium. The Allied (British and French) forces were driven to the Belgian shoreline.

At Dunkirk, near the Belgian shore, Germany was poised to capture the entire British Army, yet inexplicably stopped short. Later, German General von Blumentritt would relate that the following had taken place:

> "(Hitler) then astonished us by speaking with admiration of the British Empire, of the necessity for its existence, and of the civilisation that Britain had brought into the world. He remarked, with a shrug of the shoulders, that the creation of its Empire had been achieved by means that were often harsh, but 'where there is planing, there are shavings flying.' He compared the British Empire with the Catholic Church - saying they were both essential elements of stability in the world. He said that all he wanted from Britain was that she

should acknowledge Germany's position on the Continent. The return of Germany's colonies would be desirable but not essential, and he would even offer to support Britain with troops if she should be involved in difficulties anywhere.." (Basil Liddell Hart, *The Other Side of the Hill*, 1948, Pan Books, 1983, p. 200)

Hitler quite simply did not desire the conquest of England, though it lay prostrate before him, available simply for the taking. Within a matter of days, Hitler literally could have driven through London as its new master. After demonstrating Germany's obvious superiority to the hapless would-be British and French invaders, he simply stopped and readied Germany for the upcoming Russian invasion. (Hart, *Ibid*, p. 140)

At the time, British Prime Minister Churchill called the subsequent English evacuation a miracle. To this day, Brits occasionally reference "that Dunkirk spirit," in alluding to a triumph over adversity. Some also refer to the Dunkirk encounter as evidence of Hitler's military incompetence. Little did they know at the time just how close they actually had come to an ignominious defeat, a defeat prevented only through the largesse of a Hitler obsessed with the specter of Communism.

Hitler's obsession derived from years of watching countries throughout Eastern Europe fall like dominos to Communism, once WWI ground to a close:

> "(M)ost of the leading revolutionaries who convulsed Europe in the final decades of the (1800s) and the first decades of (the 1900s), stemmed from prosperous Jewish families...typified by the father of revolution, Karl Marx...after the chaos of World War I, revolutions broke out all over Europe, Jews were everywhere at the helm; Trotsky,

Sverdlov, Kamenev and Zinoviev in Russia, Bela Kun in Hungary, Kurt Eisner in Bavaria, and, most improbable of all, Rosa Luxemburg in Berlin...The Russian revolution looked like a Jewish conspiracy, especially when it was followed by Jewish-led revolutionary outbreaks in much of central Europe. The leadership of the Bolshevik Party had a preponderance of Jews...Of the seven members of the Politburo, the inner cabinet of the country, four, Trotsky (Bronstein), Zinoviev (Radomsky), Kamenev (Rosenfeld) and Sverdlov, were Jews." (*The Jews*, Bermant, 1977, chapter 8)

In an eerie replay of the events preceding World War I, then-President Franklin Roosevelt faced re-election in 1940. Like Wilson before him, Roosevelt campaigned on a promise to keep America out of the burgeoning European war. A familiar refrain of Roosevelt's: "Your boys will not be fighting in any foreign wars." However, as was also true in Wilson's time, most at the higher levels of America's government knew better, as they watched Zionist Jews like Baruch, Morgenthau and Ickes apply leverage to Roosevelt, himself partially of Jewish extraction.

Once re-elected, Roosevelt and his Zionist handlers found it impossible to rally the American public behind yet another war involving the interests of other countries. Seeing Germany turn from Britain and focus, instead, on Russia, Roosevelt despaired of a sufficient provocation arising from the European war theatre.

However, Japan had invaded China as part of a regional war that had raged since 1937. Late in 1940, Japan, Italy and Germany signed a mutual-defense treaty, requiring assistance by the others, should any one of them be attacked by any Allied nation. Sort of a mini NATO for the Axis. Japan was to provide the key to America's entry into the European war.

Many Americans saw the impending danger and spoke out prior to America's entry into World War II. Some, like Henry Ford and Charles A. Lindbergh, were well known, even revered like today's sports stars, by the American public and afforded a substantial platform from which to rail against American involvement in what they saw as a war between Zionist Jews and Germany. Just two months before America became embroiled in the war, in a speech delivered in Des Moines, Iowa on September 11, 1941, Lindbergh explained: *"I am not attacking the Jewish people. But I am saying that the leaders of both the British and the Jewish races, for reasons which are as understandable from their viewpoint as they are inadvisable from ours, for reasons which are not American, wish to involve us in the war."*

Note the date of Lindbergh's speech: 9-11. Do you believe in coincidence? Just asking.

Though people like Lindbergh and Ford are vilified today as having been anti-Semitic for daring to claim that the Jews of their day were responsible for the war that America was about to enter, it must be noted that Jews at the time refused to mince words:

"When the National Socialists and their friends cry or whisper that this (the war) is brought about by Jews, they are perfectly right...The Second World War is being fought for the defense of the fundamentals of Judaism." (*The Sentinel*, a Chicago Jewish magazine, Oct. 8, 1940)

"The millions of Jews living in America, England, France, North Africa and South, not forgetting Palestine, have decided to carry on the war in Germany to the very end. It is to be a war of extermination." (*Central Blad Voor Israeliten,* a Jewish newspaper published in The Netherlands, September 13, 1939)

291

The mutual defense pact signed by Germany and Japan late in 1940, just prior to Roosevelt's re-election, allowed America to turn to the years-old armed conflict between Japan and China in pursuit of the provocation necessary to galvanize an American public set against entering the European war.

As 1941 progressed, Roosevelt and his Zionist handlers prevailed upon both British and Dutch petroleum suppliers to embargo oil shipments which had, until then, been flowing steadily to Japan. Bereft of any other source of oil, Japan faced the sudden prospect of falling to the much-weaker China which it had invaded three years earlier. Reluctantly, Japan turned its attention to America.

American cryptographers cracked Japan's naval codes long before the attack on Pearl Harbor took place. On December 6, 1941, Roosevelt was handed deciphered Japanese communiqués which clearly showed their intent to attack the fleet then ensconced in Pearl Harbor *the very next day.* Roosevelt's administration also was warned in advance by a British double agent who filtered Germany's communiqués. Furthermore, Australia's intelligence service had passed to Washington word that the Japanese fleet had been seen steaming toward Hawaii, just three days prior to the attack. All this and more has been disclosed by a man who, in the mid-1990s, was the first to see naval documents hidden from public view since 1941: Robert Stinnett, who authored *Day of Deceit: The Truth About FDR and Pearl Harbor on December 7* (Simon & Schuster/The Free Press, 1999). Since the inadvertent disclosure of those documents during a storage transfer, they have been reclassified by the US government, thereby continuing a coverup that now is over 60 years old.

Clearly, Roosevelt knew of the impending attack, yet kept it a secret from Admiral Kimmel, the man commanding the fleet then anchored in Pearl Harbor, who eventually took the fall for America being unprepared, along with General Short, who commanded Pearl

Harbor's land-based forces. Though both officers demanded courts martial in order to clear their names, they were denied hearings through the artifice of official findings that America's unpreparedness resulted from "errors of judgment," not "dereliction of duty." Only the latter charge would have allowed the commanders the full evidentiary public hearing entailed in courts martial.

What goes unnoticed by many is that, in the weeks leading up to December 7, all of America's aircraft carriers and their entourage ships had been removed to various islands around the Pacific, leaving only the pre-WWI battleships and sundry other older vessels behind, ships that essentially already were obsolete. In retrospect, it is clear that a trap had been baited, in much the manner that the *Lusitania* had been used to create an excuse for America's entry to WWI.

180 planes were lost, many because they had been ordered to be formed in circles, with their tails pointing out, ostensibly to protect them from ground-based sabotage. Oddly (at the time), this order came directly from the Oval Office. Planes, of course, have no reverse gear. The time it took to pull them out of formation by hand so that they then could taxi to an airstrip was critical in terms of the ultimate losses sustained at the hands of the Japanese Zeros strafing from overhead.

In terms of ships and planes, America's Pacific Fleet lost little of strategic value at Pearl Harbor. The cost in human life for America's excuse to declare war against Germany was staggering, however: 3,600 men. But, then, *a staggering loss was just what was required in order to galvanize America's citizens out of their anti-war stance.* Roosevelt had not forgotten the lesson of the *Lusitania,* which had not by itself forced a public demand for America's entry into the last war.

The rest is conventional history. Roosevelt demanded and received a Declaration of War against Japan the following day, December 8, 1941. Pursuant to its agreement with Japan, Germany declared war against America on December 11. America was in it, at last.

By the time the war ground to a halt on both fronts over three years later, more than 75 million people on all sides had lost their lives as a direct result of hostilities.

The United Nations resulted from World War II, as did the State of Israel, albeit at the expense of the Palestinians, in fulfillment of the pledge made by Britain in *The Balfour Declaration* so many years earlier.

Another legacy of World War II, perhaps the most important to world Jewry, was the so-called "Holocaust," which has been used to advance the cause of Jews everywhere ever since, providing the drop-dead label of "anti-Semite" to be used against anybody who might dare criticize anything Jewish.

No, 6 million Jews did not die. Yes, a great many did die, generally from Typhus, which was epidemic in all prisoner camps - anywhere from 260,000 to nearly 2.5 million, depending upon whom you might choose to believe. Even the Jews have given up on the 6 million figure officially. No, there were no gas chambers. No, there were no ovens. No, there were no lamp shades made of human skin or soap rendered from human fat. It is well beyond the scope of this book to discuss or document any of the foregoing, but there are references aplenty on bookshelves and over the Internet.

However, logic alone disproves the conventional Holocaust story. Consider why Germany, fighting a war on two fronts and already short of fuel and all war materiel, would load millions of Jews on rail cars and ship them all over Eastern Europe to camps specifically built to house them, then feed them, clothe them, tattoo them in order to keep track of them...*just so they could be killed* in gas chambers and have their bodies burned in ovens using even more scarce fuel, the existence of neither of which ever has been documented.

Germans were nothing, if not efficient. If extermination of Jews was what they were after, they would have killed them the same way that the Russian Jews killed from 20 to 80 million (again, depending upon whom you choose to believe) Russian Christians earlier in the century: *a bullet to the base of the skull wherever they might be found.*

The fact is, the total European population of Jews actually increased slightly from the beginning to the end of the war, according to census figures of the time. The same cannot be said for so many others who did the fighting and dying in World War II, all for the greater good of Zionism. *75 million people died in WWII, yet the only ones that we are supposed to remember are 6 million Jews, most of whom never existed in the first place.* What is wrong with this picture?

Well after World War II was over, America's first Secretary of Defense, James Forrestal, was to quote Joseph Kennedy, American Ambassador to England prior to the war (and father to a future US President), as saying British Prime Minister *"Chamberlain stated that America and the world Jews had forced England into the war."* (*The Forrestal Diaries*, ed. Millis, Cassell, 1952, p129).

Like World War I, the second World War was started by Jews and fought to advance Jewish interests. America had no interest of her own involved in either war. In both wars, America's entry was contrived by incidents that were planned by America's own leaders, in concert with Zionist leaders of the time, all of whom allowed thousands of lives to be lost in pursuit of merely an excuse to declare war outright. This tried-and-true formula has been invoked once again and will as surely lead to World War III.

This may seem a lot of ground to cover for a book entitled *In Defense of Racism,* but it assuredly is ground that must be covered. The very race that has cost America so dearly in the past is at it again. It is no crime to oppose one's own destruction, even if we must suffer the sobriquet "anti-Semite" for doing so. Ultimately, this is the very form of racism that must be defended at any cost.

World War III

This time, the Middle East is to come under Jewish hegemony. Genocide is being committed by Israel in Palestine and, through Israel's surrogate, America, in Iraq, as well, with all other Middle Eastern regimes scheduled for submission in the coming years.

WWIII is desired by both sides to the Middle Eastern conflict, which can be characterized only as Judea against Islam. Jewish interests believe it will play out as before, with America's awesome military machine making possible the subjugation of their enemies; the Muslims, in this case. Muslims want it because they have been left no other option, as evidenced by a seemingly endless stream of suicide bombers and *Arab children shot dead for throwing rocks at Israeli tanks*.

Very likely, history will record that WWIII began on September 11, 2001, with the World Trade Center disaster. In fact, in the fullness of time, historians may come to stretch the timeline all the way back to the first Gulf War in 1991.

This time, America has been used to *lead* the fight, much as Britain was used in the past, while Zionists once again idly stand by, risking nothing. Interestingly, though American Jews have been leading an assault against Christianity since its inception (some would argue it began before the advent of Christianity, on the day that Jesus Christ was crucified), today's American hard-core Christian fundamentalists have been conned into advancing Jewish interests.

Meanwhile, and just as before, an economic crisis of world-class proportions has been created by the international banking cartel through manipulation of the money supply, creating an artificial period of general prosperity.

As before, monetary inflation has translated into price inflation, first in the equities markets, then the bond markets, then the real

296

estate market and, finally, in the supermarkets.

As before, rampant price inflation will create an upward spike in interest rates, which will, in turn, force a tightening of the money supply. Like a pendulum set in motion, that tightening will force massive corrections throughout the world's economies, in order to compensate for the previous artificial prosperity. Once again, as true economic depression takes hold, *"there is no such thing as a free lunch,"* will become conventional wisdom.

As before, war will be required to distract the population and to pull the world's economies out of the pit of depression into which they have been thrust.

As before, the countries involved will require huge amounts of funding to manufacture the weapons of war, funding which readily will be provided by the international Zionist banking families, to whom the countries involved will become even more deeply indebted, as in last century's major wars.

As before, those same banking families will enjoy staggering profits by funding all sides of the impending conflict, both directly from investment in the manufacture of munitions and indirectly, from the interest to be collected in perpetuity on the debt.

As before, that interest, as we will see in the very next chapter, *"Money's End Game: Depression II,"* will come from heavy taxes levied upon the civilian populations of the combatants and their descendants. We also will see that there will be other serious profit opportunities in the offing for the already obscenely wealthy.

Quite literally, there is nothing new under the sun.

Dubya is Divinely Selected

Throughout 2003, George W. Bush repeatedly claimed that God had chosen him to lead America. Glad he cleared that up. For the longest time, I wondered how he got the job.

President Bush has been on a Mission From God, you know. To kill. Must be an Old Testament thing, because I don't recall Jesus having exhorted his Disciples to kill in God's name.

As of this writing, it appears that Bush's reluctance to undergo another Afghanistan or Iraq prior to the 2004 election might somehow have been overcome. Seems he has learned nothing from his plummeting poll numbers. Or, like the chronic gambler, perhaps he is thinking, *"Just one more roll of the dice...then my number will come up...then I'll be a winner...just one more roll..."*

Of course, the more cynical might argue that his poll numbers are manipulated by the Zionist-controlled press and being used to force his hand in a desperate bid for re-election.

Sometimes, it seems that I am the only one who remembers that, in 1999, Bush came from nowhere, virtually overnight, to become the Republican frontrunner - and in possession of a record-breaking war chest. I recall saying at the time, "George *who?"*

Recent revelations concerning computerized vote machine rigging provide part of the answer. Winning the key electoral state, which just happened to be governed by his own brother, albeit by judicial edict, yields more of the solution. President Bush's appointment of Zionists, especially Zionist Jews, to virtually all key government power positions provides still more. Bush's crusade (carefully chosen word there) against all things Arab completes the puzzle.

On a Mission from God

President Bush *is* on a Mission From God. The Old Testament God, at that. The *Jewish* God. Written by Jews, the Old Testament is known as the Tanakh to the Chosen. The Tanakh consists of three parts, one of which is the Torah, encompassing the first five books of Moses. The Talmud consists of all Jewish religious teachings, including the Tanakh.

Christian fundamentalists (think President Bush - think John Ashcroft) believe the Old Testament to be the *literal* word of God, to be followed to the letter. They believe the Muslim mosque sitting atop Jerusalem's Dome of the Rock must be destroyed, so that a Biblically-foreseen Jewish temple can be constructed in its place. Never mind that this mosque is one of the holiest shrines to more than a billion Muslims around the world. Incredibly, many Christian fundamentalist sects *actually have amassed substantial building funds to assist with raising that Jewish temple.*

And don't forget Armageddon, which is to be fought nearby - and won by the Jews, with the full support of Christians, of course. Else, no Rapture. No Second Coming, either. The real problem with all this is that America's government is being run by people who don't seem to care about peace at all, at any cost...not until the Rapture, anyway. America's Jewish pro-Israel lobby might well wish to reconsider its alliance with Christian fundamentalists, simply for purposes of its own survival in the long term. Clearly, American fundamentalists, including Bush and Ashcroft, cannot be reasoned with regarding Israel.

Jerry Falwell clearly enunciates the fundamentalist posture in his book, *The Fundamentalist Phenomenon:* *"To stand against Israel is to stand against God."*

Are you understanding fundamentalist President Bush's claim to be on a Mission From God, not to mention America's unflinching support of Israel, a little better now? I think it sounded better coming from Dan Ackroyd in *The Blues Brothers.*

Onward, Christian Soldiers

This is all why American Christian fundamentalists have become so cozy with Israel, the star of Biblical/Talmudic events and

299

prophecy.

Don't forget, there is the issue about whether modern-day Israel is the same as the Biblical Israel. Or, whether modern-day Jews are descended from the Biblical tribe of Judah, or merely are some Eastern European interlopers wearing the name, like the human skin worn by the demented killer in *Silence of the Lambs*. But those are distinctions that never cross the unfurrowed brows of American fundamentalists.

Nor do Christian fundamentalists worry much about the New Testament requirement that all Jews get religion in the old-time sense and accept Jesus Christ as their personal savior. Or that American Jews are bent upon eradicating Christianity altogether.

Of course, Israel primarily is an atheistic country, so it has no problem with subverting American religious naiveté to its own political ends. And subversion is something that the Chosen do *so well*. In fact, the official motto of the Mossad, Israel's secret service, is *"By way of Deception, Thou Shalt Do War."* Consider the *USS Liberty*, for example. 9-11, for another.

Deception raised to a racial art form. That is why American Jews, historically the most left-wing element of our society, have been able to recast themselves as Neoconservatives and seize control of the Republican party.

In the single most interesting aspect of this entire spectacle, while the Chosen use their fellow travelers in America to strike Christianity from all public venues, they simultaneously use American Christians to advance their own plans for world domination. I still find this odd couple pairing to be nothing short of incredible.

America as Victim

America will become the textbook case study for nationwide Stockholm Syndrome, whereby the abused becomes bonded to the abuser as a means to endure pain, privation and violence. Incidentally, the condition was named in memory of four Swedes who, in 1973, were held hostage for six days in a bank vault and became psychologically attached to their captors.

Very recently, America provided nuclear missiles that Israel can deploy on its fleet of German-provided submarines. This, in addition to several hundred homemade nukes already resting in Israel's bunkers. Israel now possesses the means to make Biblical prophecy seem to come true, so as to drag America along for the ride and do Israel's dirty work, enroute to *Judaica Uber Alle*.

Somehow, I cannot help but think that, this time, things might not go as planned. Indeed, as developed later in this book, I believe that this coming war will result in the destruction of Israel and a breakup of the United States, similar to the manner in which the former Soviet Union fragmented. However, due to the racial tensions that exist in America today, breaking up will not be nearly so as easy as the Russians found it to be. More on this racial aspect in the last chapter, *New America.*

The Fourth Reich

The more things change, as they say, the more they remain the same. The very conditions which led to the rise of fascism and the creation of an anti-Jewish fervor in pre-WWII Germany are coalescing in America today.

Peruse the following quotations from three different books which discuss the Jewish component of German society between world Wars I and II and consider just how like today's America they sound:

> "Jews were never a large percentage of the total German population; at no time did they exceed 1% of the population during the years 1871-1933...

"But, Jews were overrepresented in business, commerce, and public and private service...

"They were especially visible in private banking in Berlin, which in 1923 had 150 private Jewish banks, as opposed to only 11 private non-Jewish banks...

"They owned 41% of iron and scrap iron firms and 57% of other metal businesses...

"Jews were very active in the stock market, particularly in Berlin, where in 1928 they comprised 80% of the leading members of the stock exchange. By 1933, when the Nazis began eliminating Jews from prominent positions, 85% of the brokers on the Berlin Stock exchange were dismissed because of their 'race'...

"At least a quarter of full professors and instructors (at German universities) had Jewish origins...

"In 1925-6 Jewish students comprised 25% of the law and medical students...

"In 1931, 50% of the 234 theatre directors in Germany were Jewish, and in Berlin the number was 80%...

"In 1929 it was estimated that the per capita income of Jews in Berlin was twice that of other Berlin residents." (*Hitler, Germans and the "Jewish Question,"* Sarah Gordon, Princeton University Press, 1984)

"In (pre-Hitler) Berlin, most of the theatres were Jewish-owned or Jewish-leased, most of the leading film and stage actors were Jews, the plays performed were often by German, Austrian or Hungarian Jews and were staged by Jewish film producers, applauded by Jewish dramatic critics in Jewish newspapers...

"The Jews are not cleverer than the Gentiles, if by clever you mean good at their jobs. They ruthlessly exploit the common feeling of Jews, first to get a foothold in a particular trade or calling, then to squeeze the non-Jews out of it...

"It is not true that Jews are better journalists than Gentiles. They held all the posts on those Berlin papers because the proprietors and editors were Jewish." (*Disgrace Abounding*, Douglas Reed, 1939, pp. 238-9)

"(I)n Berlin alone, about 75% of the attorneys and nearly as many of the doctors were Jewish." (*The Transfer Agreement*, Edwin Black, 1984, p. 58)

Jews describe their ascendancy in cultures as being like cream rising to the top of the barrel. I see it more akin to the parasite getting atop its host and sinking its hooks too deeply. Just as so many Jews have explained to me in endless detail, I think it likely to be cultural. Jewish mothers, and all that. Well, genetic, too, but that is just culture gone to seed. It is as irresistible a compulsion for them as it is for Salmon to swim upstream in order to spawn. They can't help themselves. They get control of a society and take and take and take...until they are ejected, just as they have been ejected from so many societies down through the years.

False Flags

Just as before World Wars I and II, there is a significant majority of the American public that opposes any further involvement of American troops in affairs beyond American shores. 9-11 appears to have been a "false flag" operation, designed to foment public fervor for war abroad. False, because of all the unanswerable questions, such as the following:

Out of a total work population of about 40,000 people

normally in the WTC at 8 am on any given workday, less than 13,000 were present at the time of the catastrophe. Over 4,000 Israeli employees were absent.

Though the four planes involved usually were packed for the particular flights, on this particular morning, each was only one-fourth full. 4 times one-fourth equals one full plane. One plane, the *"Let's Roll"* jet, was shot down, as evidenced by eyewitnesses and the several-miles-long trail of debris over Pennsylvania.

The unverifiable telephone calls reportedly from passengers and crew members were all reported by only government employees or telephone company operators.

Cell phones do not operate in moving jet planes, as the cell towers, even if in range, are unable to acquire the signals before the next tower in line must attempt acquisition.

The transponders, electronic devices which transmit each plane's identity, all were switched off simultaneously. Coincidentally, each of the planes involved was capable of being controlled remotely via radio signals *passed over the transponder channels*.

Employees of the Jewish company Odigo have admitted to being given advance warning.

Willie Brown, Mayor of San Francisco, was warned by none other than Condoleeza Rice not to fly on September 11.

Massively unusual stock market positions were taken in and against companies involved in the disaster, just days beforehand. The identities of those making the trades (and billions of dollars) have been kept a closely-guarded secret.

Several Israeli "moving company employees" were observed filming the disaster in progress from a nearby rooftop, where they were celebrating and high-fiving one another repeatedly.

Numerous experts have concluded that neither building could have collapsed without extensive demolition charges, the very charges that firemen on the scene reported hearing and seeing.

Pictures exist of firemen peering out from WTC II, where most of the jet fuel exploded outside the building, due to the very near miss, thereby proving that the fires were out early on.

The jets could have gotten through America's civil and military defense systems only if those systems had been told to stand down previously.

Names of the hijackers were released almost immediately. In the following weeks, almost all of them were found to be alive and well, in various parts of the world.

No Arabs turned up on the autopsy slabs once all the bodies were recovered.

The "plane" which crashed into the Pentagon was filmed and clearly is either a missile or small jet, painted to resemble a commercial jet.

A bulbous appendage to the fuselage of one of the WTC jets was photographed, with what appears to be a missile being launched from it in the split second prior to impact.

Larry Silverstein, Jewish real estate tycoon, acquired the lease on both WTC towers just three months prior to 9-11. The terms made him not responsible to the owners for "acts of God," though he is the sole beneficiary of the $7.2 billion insurance proceeds. Lucky Larry.

Many, many more anomalies exist concerning 9-11, the total weight of which inexorably leads to the conclusion that Arabs had nothing to do with the disaster. Instead, indicia implicate Israel's

Mossad, in league with rogue elements of America's military and governmental security branches.

Other highly suspicious acts have taken place since 9-11, all pointing to the same crew as that which actually pulled off the WTC disaster:

Israelis have been arrested in Mexico City in recent years, carrying explosives sufficient to crater a government building.

Mysterious bombings have taken place in diverse parts of the world, including Indonesia, employing sophisticated explosives and triggering mechanisms not normally found in the hands of terrorists but consistent with Israeli covert operations.

A massive series of train bombs shook Spain to the core and led to a change of government early in 2004. Conveniently, some of the same sort of markers were turned up at train stations as have been found in connection with other Mossad operations. Two of the men arrested by Spanish authorities were described as being "of Middle Eastern descent" and "with Indian passports." So what? In early 2000, eleven Zionist agents "of Middle Eastern descent" were arrested on a Bangladesh flight. Each had an Indian passport. Subsequently, they were accused and charged with plotting terrorist acts. "Of Middle Eastern descent" has become the standard media phrase used in lieu of "Israeli." Non-Jews invariably are referred to as Arabic, Islamic or Muslim.

Repeatedly in America during the period following 9-11, Israeli teams were arrested by local authorities, always with very suspicious items and acting in suspicious manners, often near strategic installations, such as Naval air stations or nuclear power plants. Always, the locals thought they had nabbed Arab terrorists. Always, it turned out that they were Israeli "students" or "moving company employees." The feds stepped in every time, pursuant to orders from the Justice Department, assumed jurisdiction and deported the Israelis back to Israel, with their mission never again questioned by any governmental authority and all investigations closed.

Like Pearl Harbor, the loss of life in 9-11 prompted the American public to back President Bush's call to arms and demand for war against the "evildoers." The subsequent loss of life and poor progress of America's war against both Afghanistan and Iraq, however, have sapped that same public of much of its blood fever.

More calamitous events, to be laid at the doorstep of Arab terrorists, can be expected, designed to galvanize both Europeans and Americans into supporting further military intervention, this time into Syria, Lebanon and Iran. As of this writing, Saudi Arabia's rulers seem destined to be toppled and replaced with an Islamic fundamentalist government. Since Saudi Arabia possesses the single largest oil deposits in the world, America would feel compelled to intervene, just as she did in Iraq.

Israel will claim it simply is coincidental that it is the sole beneficiary of fallout from such attacks, while it continues to demand that the West subjugate its enemies in the Middle East.

The Economics of War

There are too many ways in which a world-wide shooting war could escape the cauldron that the Middle East has become for me to say with any certainty how it will evolve. I suspect, however, that North Korea and China simultaneously will move on South Korea and Taiwan, respectively, at some point when America has become overcommited to and overstretched within the Middle East, which will provide the tipping point.

Given the deadly state of economics in America, however, it is a safe bet, nay, a certainty, that a major war will result.

Franklin Roosevelt's New Deal social programs are credited with extricating America from the Great Depression. That simply isn't true. If anything, Roosevelt's fiscal policies actually deepened the depression which had spread worldwide. For example, between 1933 and 1938, unemployment actually *increased* - 19.5%. World War II is what did the job of pulling America out of the depression, as is well known to both the central bankers and to America's current policy makers. They now have painted themselves into a corner, economically speaking, far worse than that in which America found itself in the 1930's. The tried-and-true solution, world war, remains to be used. It will be used, rest assured, as it is all that is left to them.

The certainty of war can be seen in the manner in which the US government blithely continued to overspend its receipts, thereby pushing both the National Deficit and America's International Balance of Trade Deficit to new record levels each and every month of 2004.

The unprecedented expansion of the American money supply (the official definition of the word "inflation") by the Federal Reserve Bank under Alan Greenspan's guidance is another clear sign. Money is being spent like there is no tomorrow or, at least, as if those in the know believe there will be no tomorrow. The only way out of the massive debt now atop America at every level is massive price inflation, which will fuel interest rate spikes, which then will lead to a global depression of such severity that we will begin to number them, much as WWII caused us to rename The Great War. That brings us to *Money's End Game: Depression II.*

Chapter 17

Money's End Game: Depression II

"The few who understand the system, will either be so interested from its profits or so dependant on its favors, that there will be no opposition from that class."
--- Rothschild Brothers of London, in a letter to fellow members of the establishment (June 25, 1863)

"By this means (fractional reserve banking) government may secretly and unobserved, confiscate the wealth of the people, and not one man in a million will detect the theft."
---*The Economic Consequences of the Peace*, John Maynard Keynes (the father of Keynesian Economics) (1920)

"It is well that the people of the nation do not understand our banking and monetary system, for if they did, I believe there would be a revolution before tomorrow morning."
--- Henry Ford, Ford Motor Company founder

"Yer already dead. Yer jist too stoopid to know it."
--- Old codger in wheelchair, *Texas Chainsaw Massacre* (2003)

So, what's a chapter on money and economic depression doing in a book about racism? Well, as we will see, it is key. Earlier, we developed the rationale for protection from physical harm by other races inordinately predisposed to hurt us. However, as we also have seen, the racial discord is merely a means to an end for the Zionists pulling the strings.

Money is Power

Recall I mentioned freedom from "fiscal harm," as well as from physical harm. Money, as they say, is power. Power is what it is all about to some people – control of others. Notice who has gathered the reins of power into their hands? How have they been doing it? With money, of course. Where do they get their money? From the workers, of course. People like you and me. How do they get it? Well, they sure don't *earn* it. Nobody ever got rich by working for wages, as most of us know all too well. There are lots of ways they get our money away from us, only a few of which we truly notice or understand.

Yes, they charge interest, which is a story in itself once you realize that you pay upwards of 24% annualized interest on your credit card balance.

And they tax us. Do they ever. Taxes at every level and for everything. And anything that isn't taxed requires a license fee. To illustrate the boundless avarice of burgeoning government, cities particularly like to tax facilitators of the tourist trade, such as hotels and taxis, employing the dubious rationale that the ones paying those particular taxes don't vote locally anyway. That's why a hotel room can be quoted as being $49.95, yet end up costing $67.75. Of course, tourists carry their resentments home to their own local governments, which engage in the same sort of avarice.

Increasingly, the attitude of government is that all income belongs to it and it "allows" us to have some of it for ourselves. Tax cuts are spoken of in our nation's capitol as "expenditures," which says it all. Tax cuts are spoken of in our nation's capitol as being

310

"expenditures," in a telling outlook. It is a singularly *Communist* outlook, by the way...a *Jewish* outlook.

But there are other, more profitable ways to take our money away from us, and without most of us even noticing. Primary among the hidden ways is inflation, which involves the government simply printing more paper money with no corresponding increase in goods or other assets. Thus, you end up with more dollars chasing the same number of goods and the price of the goods gets bid up until all the money available is used. And, yes, that is exactly how it works in practice on a national scale (macroeconomically, as the fuzzbrains would call it).

The Central Bank Racket

Money also can be acquired by a government from a central bank, which is a private corporation. In exchange for money, the government gives its IOU to the central bank in the form of notes and bonds, bearing interest paid to the central bank as time goes by. In an ever-expanding economy, the interest paid to the central bank only goes up. Of course, if the economy contracts, the interest still must be paid.

Where did the central bank get the money for which it collects so much interest in the first place? Why, it simply printed it. And that, gentle reader, is why gold and silver as a medium of exchange is so disfavored. As we will see in a moment, gold and silver is *real money*, since it carries its own inherent value. Yes, you can charge interest upon the loan of real money, but first you have to *give* something in order to get it. Getting paper money simply requires turning the crank of a printing press. Getting non-paper money is even easier: one need only create credits in a ledger, and this is a *one-legged entry*, the bane of bookkeepers everywhere. The entry? Debit receivables, of course.

311

Throughout the following discussion, I use "currency" and "paper money" for ease of visualization only. In reality, most money is created via one-legged bookkeeping entries.

Only with paper, or *fiat money*, does the general banking system effortlessly get to slice off a piece of each dollar each time it makes the rounds.

Only with fiat money does a central bank get something for the nothing it expended, in the form of interest on the note signed in its favor by the government to which it lends its "money," the stuff it simply printed, don't forget. In order for an economy to have enough money to pay the interest, both it and the money supply must be increasing nonstop. Think about it for a moment and you will see why, since the interest payments to the central bankers are taken out of the system. Yes, it is just like a Ponzi scheme, where the pyramid crashes if ever it stops growing. Not "just like," either. It *is* a Ponzi scheme. *Talk about usury.*

There is nothing new about this system, which is why there are such strong proscriptions against usury scattered throughout the Bible. One of the things America's founders fled was the Bank of England, owned by the usual (Jewish) suspects and running a classic central bank scheme.

The difference in a central bank scheme from most pyramid scams can be seen when growth does stop, with the result that the money supply contracts in response to the effect of fractional reserve banking running in reverse. The government then hands fiat money back to the central bank to retire some of its indebtedness, which the central bankers then can use to buy goods and services. This is still more money for nothing, don't forget, since at the beginning the central bankers simply printed up the paper money and ascribed value to it.

The central bankers get this massive infusion of money with which to buy things just when the prices of things are plummeting, thus they are able to buy foreclosed homes, farms and factories for pennies on the dollar, just as they did in Depression I. An extra bonus: with all that extra cash, the bankers can afford to lend to both sides in the widespread war that inevitably accompanies severe economic hardship...just as they always have done, as we saw in Chapter 16, *World War III.*

When the war is over, the governments find themselves more indebted than ever and the citizens must start all over again to accumulate equity in homes, farms and businesses, purchased at re-normalized prices with loans once again available from a banking system fed by its central bankers.

Where does the government interest paid to the central bank go? Into the pockets of those owning the central bank. Rockefeller, Rothschild and a few others, in the case of America's Federal Reserve Bank, which is Federal in name only. The same names, plus a handful of still others, in the case of all other Western central banks.

Where does government get the money to pay the interest? From taxes, of course. So, for the privilege of having the convenience of paper money that costs perhaps two pennies to print, you and I pay dearly in annual interest to people who never risked a single cent of their own.

Remember how Hitler's system of barter at the national level (German locomotives traded for Argentinean beef) so infuriated the international bankers prior to World War II? They weren't getting the cut of the transaction that would have been guaranteed if he had been using debt-based fiat money as a medium of exchange.

Periodic economic depressions lead to massive deflation in the value of things backed by debt, such as real estate, due to the shortage of money created by a spike in interest rates. That's when the bankers really clean up, by stepping in and buying everything in sight for pennies on the dollar. That's one of the main things that got Jews kicked out of Germany by the Third Reich, remember. That is

313

exactly what happened in America during Depression I.

In the 3 or 4 generations since Depression I, folks have managed to reacquire a good deal of the real estate their families owned but then lost to bankruptcy and foreclosure back then, although today it is mortgaged to the hilt. It is time for another shearing of the American sheep. Depression II will provide that shearing.

People won't have enough money for the things they simply must have, and so will sell the things they don't really need for whatever they can get. And they won't get much. Whatever property isn't taken in foreclosure, then put on the market to further depress prices, will decline in value along with the property that nobody will buy...until it is cheap enough, that is. And that will be at about 10% of current prices, if history repeats itself. And it always does, you know.

No, you aren't missing a thing. On the contrary, for the first time, probably, some reading this actually *are getting* it. This is just the way things work. And who are the central bankers? Aha. *See?*

Why do ordinary banks put up with all this? First, they must, in order to receive a license to engage in banking. Second, because of the allure of fractional-reserve banking. Deposit a dollar and the bank immediately loans it out to a borrower. Imagine that borrower then depositing that same dollar into his own account, which just happens to be at the same bank. The bank gets to lend that dollar out yet again! How? Because only a *fraction* of total deposits at a bank must be maintained in *reserve* to cover anticipated withdrawal demands – a *fractional reserve.*

Now imagine the entire banking system, save only the central banks, as one large bank and the analogy is complete. After nominal reserve requirements, each dollar deposited results in a net addition to the money supply of nine other dollars these days. Nine dollars on which member banks are paid interest while they pay out far less interest, if any, on the deposits. All from the deposit of a single dollar. What a deal, huh? No wonder they stand still for the central bank Ponzi scheme. Economists call this the *multiplier effect*.

The central bank stands ready to lend member banks any sum necessary to make up shortfalls, of course. After all, they print the stuff for next to nothing. How did the central bankers get the government to go along with this? The old-fashioned way: *they bribed those in power.*

National leaders always have been well aware of this scam. Andrew Jackson even managed to throw out America's first central bank in 1836. For the next 75 years, America operated without a central bank, 75 years which saw absolutely no price inflation and no erosion in the purchasing power of its money, save only the transient effects of the Civil War. An ounce of gold varied in price from $18.93 to $18.94 throughout the 1800s and well into the early 1900s. Then, Woodrow Wilson, with the prospect of becoming the first President of the World (see Chapter 16, *World War III*) dangled before his eyes, knuckled under and allowed the current central banking system to be established. In the nearly one hundred years since that fateful decision, the purchasing power of the dollar has fallen to 1% of what it was then. Yes, today's dollar is worth exactly *one* 1910 penny. Guess where the other 99 cents went. Ah, see....*now you are catching on.*

No Free Lunch

There is nothing new under the sun. An economic meltdown is coming. It cannot be avoided, so overleveraged has everybody in America become. With that meltdown, as surely as night follows day, will come war. Just like last century. *Just like always.* Exactly. Precisely.

Repeat after me: *There is no such thing as a free lunch.* Say it again. You'll be hearing it a lot in years to come. It was particularly popular during America's first Depression. It will become popular again, because the wisdom thereby expressed is timeless. America has had an extended, even gargantuan lunch, never suspecting that a bill ever would be presented. Well, it has come due. I can see the Zionist waiter approaching now, with the bill firmly in his grasp.

And that is why a chapter on money is in a book on defensive racism. Because fiat money and its consequences are the means of controlling and shearing us and the control is being done along racial lines. We deserve fiscal protection and we haven't been getting it. Indeed, scarcely anybody seems to realize we even need protection or that we are, in essence, being systematically and repeatedly harvested.

Among themselves, Jews like to refer to goyim as "cattle," and not simply as a pejorative. The label is a commentary upon our perceived function as a resource to be used by them.

Fiat Money

Recently, I traded a horse for a pickup truck. Then, I traded the pickup for an excavator's bill. Here's the riddle: What was the money in the series of transactions - the horse, the truck or the abstract notion of the value of either in terms of dollars? BZZT! Time's up. Answer: all the above (it was a trick question, as are most that involve money).

Many years ago, I was single and made enough money to ski somewhat regularly (actually, each and every weekend during ski season, plus every holiday and for the full extent of my annual vacation from work). I measured my disposable income in terms of lift tickets (then about $16 at California's Squaw Valley, if purchased at the Safeway in Truckee on the way to the mountain). I evaluated most of my purchases in terms of how many lift tickets the money I might have to give up would otherwise yield.

Being single then, the type of date I would spring for depended upon a great many things, but always was expressed in terms of lift tickets. There was a cheap Italian restaurant near the industrial part of town where you could get triple shots for a dollar. If my date was young enough, she could be persuaded the place had atmosphere, though it's main attraction to me was that dinner and an evening's drinks for two cost me one lift ticket. You could always sell an extra lift ticket in the parking lot. *Lift tickets were money* because they were liquid.

Here's the punch line: *anything* can be money. You just need to be able to negotiate (trade) it for something of value, whether or not the thing traded has intrinsic value.

Paper money has an intrinsic value of 2 cents per bill, if you accept the amount the U.S. Treasury actually receives for each Federal Reserve Note it prints:

> "The Federal Reserve system pays the U.S. Treasury 020.60 per thousand notes - a little over 2 cents each - without regard to the face value of the note. Federal Reserve Notes, incidentally, are the only type of currency now produced for circulation. They are printed exclusively by the Treasury's Bureau of Engraving and Printing, and the $20.60 per thousand price reflects the Bureau's full cost of production. Federal Reserve Notes are printed in 01, 02, 05, 10, 20, 50, and 100 dollar denominations only; notes of 500, 1000, 5000, and 10,000 denominations were last printed in 1945." (Donald J. Winn, Assistant to the Board of Governors of the Federal Reserve system)

Even so, we act as though these pieces of paper have as much value as a corresponding amount of anything which fetches the store of value represented by the numbers on a particular Federal Reserve Note.

As of this writing in early 2004, the Zimbabwean dollar actually is worth less than an equivalent physical quantity of toilet paper, leading some actually to use money in its place.

Sometimes, virtually nothing will serve as money. Some like to say that gold is the only real money. But, to a man dying of thirst in the desert, a pile of gold is useless unless it can be negotiated for something of value (and to a thirsty man, only water has any real value). In reality, gold simply is a somewhat rare metal, but a metal, nonetheless. What "intrinsic" value does gold possess? Well, that depends. After all, you can't even eat it. In contrast, during the Roman Empire, soldiers were paid in a then-rare commodity that often was used as money: salt (origin of the phrase, *"not worth his salt"*). The modern word "salary" is derived from *Salarium*, the Latin word for salt.

Money is a concept which changes from time to time and place to place.

Anything used as money but that does not itself have inherent value is "fiat money," a dirty phrase to Patriot types. Fiat money is any money the value of which can be dictated by its issuer. Even gold can appear to be "fiat money," because it so extensively is traded by way of markers, such as stock certificates, mutual shares, hedge contracts (known as derivatives) and the like.

Gold substitutes trade as though they were the real thing, therefore have the ability to directly impact the price of real gold. As a result, even real, physical gold can be (and currently is) a form of fiat currency so long as its price is directly, albeit temporarily, manipulated through paper markers. The effect is a general depression of the price of gold due to the illusion of a much larger supply of gold in existence, well and substantially beyond anything that physically exists. Until, that is, the paper equivalents are rendered valueless. That is when gold truly shines.

Real Money's Mere Reflection

Gold deserves an extended discussion at this point, because of its particular value in times of economic strife. Historically, gold has been a particularly good means for transporting wealth from one side of an economic meltdown to the other. Silver works, too, as do platinum and backhoes and things that people can eat.

Only precious metals carry their value unimpeded, from start to finish and beyond the other side, as well. That is their special allure.

In the following discussion, I will speak only of gold. Understand, however, that I thereby refer to all precious metals with "gold" merely serving as a form of shorthand.

Many have heard of gold derivatives and how there is so much more gold out there in the form of derivatives than physically is produced each year, which keeps the price of gold artificially low (temporarily making it a form of fiat currency, as described). Few understand derivatives, though they are dreadfully simple. "Derivative" is a term that covers any security, or paper representation of value, which *derives* its value from the price of a commodity, gold in this example. Generally, derivatives refer to futures contracts and options, which theoretically exist to remove risk from the marketplace for a gold producer.

You see, a gold producer with known deposits can sell his future production on the open market at a price directly related to (derived from) the current price of gold. He gets the money now, and can then invest in mining the gold, confident of not losing money when the gold finally is dredged up and refined. It is called hedging and is what farmers, ranchers, and lumbermen - indeed, all commodity producers - do to remove risk from the market for their product. They give up the chance for unforeseen extraordinary profits in order to gain the peace of mind afforded by avoiding unforeseen extraordinary losses. It is a form of insurance – for the price only, of course, as they

319

still must bring their product to market.

Problem is, anybody can sell a hedging contract. And a lot more anybodies sell them these days than do the actual producers of the commodity. Mainstream banks, acting as surrogates for the central banks, have been particularly active in selling contracts for the future delivery of gold.

If people suddenly demanded delivery of even a fraction of the outstanding "futures" contracts, the price of gold would go up a thousandfold because there is so much more gold sold for future delivery than ever will be produced or could be delivered. Futures contracts almost never are fulfilled by delivery; rather, they settle in cash - electronic fiat currency - thus proving that this form of investing is nothing more than pure gambling. Most futures contracts have nothing to do with the commodity; they are bets made about what the price of a commodity will be in the future. There is no difference between futures trading and what any bookie does every Thursday with his customers in anticipation of Game Day, except that only *some* of the college and pro games are rigged.

The sale of futures contracts impacts the price of gold just as surely as if physical gold changed hands. Thus, gold becomes a fiat currency when the derivatives markets are manipulated, as they have been lately, to hold the price of gold down (and the value of the dollar up, which is why the central banks need surrogates to make the derivative sales in the first place, since technically it is illegal for them to rig the market).

The Gold Lease Scam

Gold leasing by central banks is another exercise which causes gold to act like a fiat currency. For example, the German Bundesbank announced its intent to sell 400 to 600 tons of gold between 2005 and 2009 as part of a new gold agreement, as reported by Germany's

Boersen Zeitung newspaper in early 2004. The price of gold immediately dipped by several dollars, but then climbed back up to its previous level, which represented a gain of $100 per ounce since the start of 2003. The British central bank made a similar stir in 1999 with a similar announcement, closely followed by the "Washington Agreement," whereby 15 central banks agreed to an annual cap on the sale of their gold holdings. Finally, they had the desired effect: gold was driven to its bear-market low of $252, a level from which gold only recently has extricated itself, not to mention being a level that almost certainly never again will be seen...not by the dollar, at least.

What isn't mentioned - what has been a closely-guarded secret of the central banks - is that they, greedy to squeeze out the very last drop of profit from anything that isn't nailed down, mostly already have gotten rid of their gold reserves. You see, otherwise, gold just...well...*sits* there. While the central bank gold technically is not sold, the gold is just as gone, never to return. What they did was lease it to certain close business affiliates, who then sold it in years past, with the leases costing about 1 or 2 per cent. Now, 1 or 2 per cent may sound right today, but the leases were made, by and large, during times of much higher interest rates. Who could resist that sort of deal? Pay 1 or 2 percent for something that you sell and then invest the proceeds to return 10-20 percent per year...

These announcements of central bank gold sales are genuine. *Of course* the banks have to be selling large quantities of gold. They already leased them out in arrangements whereby they never will see the gold again because it is long gone..into East Indian dowry chests, among other places. *Of course* the people to whom they leased the gold have to cover those leases. *Of course* the banks have to sell, so as to hide the fact of the leases in the first place. *Of course.* But no physical gold changes hands. It was gone long ago. It's like a corporation or public entity talking about selling its buildings and equipment to the bank and then leasing them back (thereby moving debt off the balance sheet and to footnote status as a lease). No change in the status quo, simply accounting folderol to fool the plebeians.

These sales actually are driven by the lessees. Why do the lessees want to close out their low-interest leases? Could they possibly be expecting the price of gold to be much higher later on and for an extended period of time? Closing contracts now avoids the possibility of having to cover at significantly higher prices later on, when the bank inevitably must call in the gold.

The central bank announcement has no lasting effect on the price of gold, since no actual gold changes hands. It already changed hands back when it was leased and then sold into the marketplace by the lessee, which artificially depressed the price of gold, since the market assumed the banks still had possession of the gold. The price of gold today already reflects that past change. Without more real sales to drive the price down, it is only a temporary psychological effect we see, caused by the plebeians who haven't yet figured out this shell game. Plebeians like you and me. Well, maybe not you and me anymore, but almost everybody else, to be sure.

The Not-Federal No-Reserve Non-Bank

Fiat money merely means money that can change value at the whim of its issuer. Like the dollar, which has depreciated to less than 10% the value it possessed when I was a youngster and only 1% the value the dollar possessed when my father was a kid. By whim, the government simply printed more money during that time period, one hundred times as much, in fact, as was warranted by the pile of things available for sale now, versus then.

"Not too bad," you might think, since the government gets the value for the overprinting of money ("money" is a term that I use, because everybody else does the same thing, but which includes the

322

creation of credit balances alone, without a physical correlate). You would be right to think so if the government (theoretically, us) got that value. It/we doesn't/don't. Remember, the government gets two cents per bill, regardless of denomination. The value for money creation goes into the pocket of private citizens, mostly not even American citizens, either: the stockholders of the Federal Reserve Banks, which are neither Federal nor banks.

"The regional Federal Reserve banks are not government agencies. ...but are independent, privately owned and locally controlled corporations." Thus spoke the court in *Lewis vs. United States*, 680 F. 2d 1239, (9th Circuit, 1982)

"The Federal Reserve Bank is an institution owned by the stockholding member banks. The Government has not a dollar's worth of stock in it." (Governor W.P.G. Harding of the Federal Reserve Board, testifying before Congress in 1921)

Nor do these central banks have any reserves, as evidenced by the sales of gold that have taken place. Fact is, these institutions quite simply are not banks, in any sense of the word as known to the world at large. When they need money, they simply print it.

These (not)Federal (no)Reserve (not)Banks take the currency printed by the U.S. Treasury and then hand it back to the Federal government in exchange for promissory notes in the form of Treasury Bills and Notes, upon which interest is paid to the (not)Federal (no)Reserve (not)Banks. So, these guys who own the (not)Federal (no)Reserve (not)Banks pocket the interest paid on the "debt," then, eventually, the full face value of the Federal Reserve Notes initially given back to the government, when they come due. Pretty sweet (for them), huh? Wouldn't you like to be able to invest 2 cents and receive 4 or 5 cents each year on your investment, then a full dollar a few years later?

"(Every circulating FRN) represents a one dollar debt to the Federal Reserve system." (*Money Facts*, House Banking and

Currency Committee)

"Oh, come on," you say, *"it can't be that way - that's simply criminal, if so. I must be missing something. I must not be capable of understanding the finer nuances of international banking."* Wrong. You understand just fine and you aren't missing a thing.

Like Gallagher says of the Sledge-O-Matic: *"Yes!! It can be just that easy!"* This would be a good time for you to go back up and read the quotes at the beginning of this chapter...go ahead...I'll wait right here.

"When you or I write a check there must be sufficient funds in our account to cover the check, but when the Federal Reserve writes a check there is no bank deposit on which that check is drawn. When the Federal Reserve writes a check, it is creating money." (*Putting It Simply*, Boston Federal Reserve Bank pamphlet)

What's more, there is nothing unique about this arrangement. All the central banks in the West operate this way.

"In its major principles of operation the Federal Reserve System is no different from other banks of issue, such as the Bank of England, the Bank of France, or the Reichsbank." (W. Randolph Burgess, of the Federal Reserve Bank of New York, speaking before the Academy of Political Science in 1930)

Ok, moving right along. Let's see now: Money can be anything, money can be nothing, fiat money is what its issuer says it is, American money really is debt owed mainly to foreigners who give (almost) nothing in exchange for that debt. Only gold is real money.

Depression I

As if things weren't bad enough, they get worse. Much worse.

Hold on to your chair for this next one: The Great Depression (soon to be renamed The *First* Depression in honor of coming events) was caused by the (not)Federal (no)Reserve (not)Banks withdrawing money from circulation...intentionally. The banks then foreclosed on countless American homes and farms, then shortly thereafter found a fresh profit opportunity in worldwide war. *"As soon as Mr. Roosevelt took office, the Federal Reserve began to buy government securities at the rate of ten million dollars a week for 10 weeks, and created one hundred million dollars in new [checkbook] currency, which alleviated the critical famine of money and credit, and the factories started hiring people again."* (*Secrets of the Federal Reserve*, Eustace Mullins, 1993) Needless to say, Eustace Mullins is viewed as *persona non grata* by the Zionist masters of America.

Depression II

Well, that's pretty bad. What could be worse? The *next* Depression, The *Second* Depression, that's what. When was that, you ask? Soon, grasshopper, soon. If the money supply had been stabilized as recently as 1995, it could have been averted. Even Alan Greenspan, then-and-still Chairman of the (not)Federal (no)Reserve (not)Bank, cautioned us in 1996 about the stock market's *"irrational exuberance."* Didn't stop him from pumping in lots more money since then, though, causing the dollar to lose a great deal more of its value and leading to runaway inflation.

Inflation? Where, you ask? The stock market, that's where. Greenspan issued his caution as the Dow Jones Industrial Average (the Dow) crossed the 4500 mark, enroute to well over 11,000. As of this writing, it sits in the 10,000s. Fundamentals dictate a value for the Dow somewhere between 4,000 and 5,000.

Fundamentals? Glad you asked. Hardly anybody has, for years now. Fundamentals are what square up stocks as an investment with other investments. Above the level dictated by fundamentals, a bubble is in operation, which is a kind of pyramid scheme dependant upon a greater fool coming along to rescue the last fool who happened to buy a stock.

Mind you, the classic definition of inflation is an increase in the money supply beyond any increase in the production of goods. The *symptom* is the increase in prices. More dollars chasing the same amount of goods, in simple terms. When the stock market bubble *partially* burst at the turn of the century, the bubble moved on to real estate, then bonds, both of which now show signs of declining from their record highs. Kind of like the early 1930's, after the first stock market crash in 1929.

Before central banks decided that limiting and stimulating production via the money supply, which requires a debt-based, fractional-reserve banking system so as to effectively amplify monetary policy actions, the supply of gold and silver increased modestly each year, in approximately the ratio of the increase in production. That's why the dollar was stable for the entirety of the 1800's. Then came "The Fed" and all that changed in the blink of an eye.

Many don't seem to know it, but the stock market came almost all the way back in the early 1930's, before it really fell out of bed. The other shoe has yet to drop for us today, just like last century. The Great Depression was a process; it didn't come on all at once. We are in a similar process today. Given the criminal conduct of the (not)Federal (no)Reserve (not)Bank in recent years, each day of further delay merely compounds the misery through which we all must pass eventually.

The cycle we are in is non-interruptible, too. Even if they wanted to, the central bankers could not stave off what now has become inevitable, because they have exhausted the means of supporting the economic bubbles they created: lowering interest rates (already negative when inflation is factored in) and expanding the money supply (Herculean quantities were added in early 2004 with no effect other than to maintain the status quo for a brief additional period –

raining money down from helicopters would be the next step, but that would lead to hyperinflation just as surely as will interest rates already set to rise by demand of the world economy).

Record personal and corporate bankruptcies are occurring. In the face of a real estate/mortgage bubble, America is experiencing record foreclosures by banks of their loans to American homeowners, ranchers, farmers and small businessmen. Bad though that already is, *what it portends for the future is positively hair raising.*

There is No Hope

The die is cast and the outcome is certain. One need look only back to last century in order to see how things will play out. Let's review a number of things in play as this is being written which, taken together, guarantee Depression II.

The federal budget deficit runs over a half trillion dollars annually, with no reduction in sight. An increase in interest rates will devastate the federal budget, as tax receipts increasingly become earmarked to interest payments for the national debt. Defaulting on the debt is not an option, as that would destroy the dollar overnight.

America's balance of trade deficit runs over a half trillion dollars annually, with no relief in sight unless and until a massive devaluation of the dollar occurs so as to make what little America still produces relatively attractive to the world market.

Massive manipulation of the securities and currency markets by both the government and the major banks is taking place, masking to a large degree the volatility that free market forces create on a daily basis.

Economic and labor statistics issued by the government have become as phony as those issued by the Soviet government as it entered into its death spiral.

Monstrous, even humongous, levels of financial derivatives exist at major banks throughout the world and are growing at many times the rate of growth of any country's gross domestic product.

The stock market bubble migrated to the bond market, then to real estate.

Record levels of real estate foreclosures are occurring in a time of apparent prosperity.

Record levels of personal and corporate bankruptcies are occurring in a time of apparent prosperity.

Local, county and State governments all are scrambling to fund budgets that have outgrown their respective economies and tax bases. Ironically, those same governmental entities have massive investments ($60 trillion, by some estimates) which they cannot liquidate to finance current operations, as that withdrawal alone would collapse both stock and bond markets.

Floods of money sweep from country to country, seeking the best rate of return and/or the safest haven.

The central banks have artificially depressed interest rates to record lows and simultaneously flooded the financial markets with record increases in the money supply, thereby fueling the various inflations that have occurred.

Price inflation now is taking hold with a vengeance.

Real wages, adjusted for inflation, have been declining in America for years.

America's factory base has been decimated in the rush to overseas locales where wages are a fraction of those paid to Americans.

Higher level jobs in America which can be outsourced to foreign countries are being sent where educated and articulate people perform them for a fraction of what their American counterparts have earned from those same jobs in the past.

America's low-level jobs are being taken by a flood of immigrants, a great many of which are illegals.

Today, the two-income household is standard, whereas a single breadwinner was the rule before Depression I. Twice the opportunity to be sucked under is the result. Only one need lose a job for the household to be unable to pay its bills.

Oil is hitting record price levels, triggering both a restriction in growth and an increase in deficits at all levels.

The dollar's role as reserve currency of the world is under direct assault by a world increasingly worried about the shaky American economy. Because of the weakening dollar, as evidenced by rampant price inflation throughout America and guaranteed by America's ongoing trade deficit, some foreign countries are beginning to demand payment for oil in Euros, rather than dollars. Russia is beginning to price its oil in Euros in order to tighten up its relationship with Europe.

The only thing saving the dollar at the moment is the ongoing willingness of foreign investors to hold investments denominated in dollars. But that, inevitably, is about to change.

An increasingly-weak dollar makes foreigners less interested in underwriting America's billowing national debt. This will mark the end of the dollar as the world's "reserve currency" and precipitate a flood of dollars being repatriated to America, thereby starting the hyperinflation that now is inevitable. America could raise interest rates, causing its debt to be more attractive to foreign investors, but that would precipitate the long-overdue fall in the equity markets and dampen economic activity all across America due to the upward pressure on prices for all goods and services. Immediately, similar upward pressure on the prices of goods from the world's producers from whom America buys would occur, as well, with the cycle then repeatedly feeding upon itself. Once the price inflation begins, those dollars in foreign hands will come flying back and lead to hyperinflation.

Things will get particularly ugly for those with savings and/or on fixed dollar incomes, as the value of their wealth and/or income radically declines as a result of foreign investors dumping their dollars in exchange for anything of value in America. *Hyperinflation.*

Don't count on American military might to rule the day economically, either. It just doesn't work that way. Military strength derives from economic strength, not the other way around.

Finally, in a clear tipoff of things to come, corporate insiders have been unloading their shareholdings at a pace which sets new records every day. *Nobody* is buying, either, absolutely not one single American corporate insider.

The average American investor may think he has his finger on the sell button and will be able to liquidate at the first sign of a meltdown. He is wrong. On the way down, there will be NO buyers. Not until rock bottom is hit and, once underway, we will get there in a hurry. Most will not sell, anyway, having been lulled into complacency by the "buy-and-hold" malarkey peddled by stock brokers and the so-called analysts on television. Most will ride their losers all the way down, then wonder what happened after the dust settles.

Central Bankers Never Have a Bad Day

"We are completely dependant on the commercial banks. Someone has to borrow every dollar we have in circulation, cash or credit. If the banks create ample synthetic money we are prosperous; if not, we starve. We are absolutely without a permanent money system.... It is the most important subject intelligent persons can investigate and reflect upon. It is so important that our present civilization may collapse unless it becomes widely understood and the defects remedied very soon." (Robert H. Hamphill, Atlanta Federal Reserve Bank)

Central banks are creatures of inflation. Deflation is their mortal enemy, especially the sort that results from collapsing debt, because then they lose control of the money supply altogether. Only with constant inflation can a central bank effect controlled movements in the money supply. Deflation stands the multiplier on its head. America's entire money supply is created by borrowing. Once a panic is started, as by a major bankruptcy, it can spread like wildfire, with the result that nobody wishes to borrow any more. The system grinds to a halt, with the end of the very borrowing upon which it relies and must have in order to reinflate a collapsing money supply.

Without a steadily-increasing money supply, somebody necessarily runs out of the money with which to pay interest on outstanding debt and the dominoes fall ever faster.

The central bank's one trick is inflation, the creation of money through the act of lending. When there are no borrowers, the central bank becomes powerless. You may think they don't know this. You would be wrong. You may think they haven't anticipated this for years. Once again, you would be wrong. Inevitable though the process becomes at this point, it simply is a part of the process of "harvesting" that occurs periodically. Can you say "moo?"

The withdrawal of money from circulation, which precipitated the First Great Depression, now is guaranteed by the runaway inflation for which the (not)Federal (no)Reserve (not)Bank is responsible. They have no choice. The alternative is a US dollar worth about what the Zimbabwean dollar brings today: less than the value of the paper upon which it is printed. Even so, a bout of hyperinflation is inevitable, given the dollars in foreign hands that can be expected to be repatriated and compete with domestic dollars for the purchase of available assets.

But the Rothschilds and their fellow travelers have done quite well, thank you. They'll do even better after they acquire our homes and farms again - the homes and farms that it has taken us three generations to earn back since the last economic apocalypse. Then, of

331

course, there will be another monster profit opportunity in the arms trades required by the worldwide war that inevitably will follow. The script was written long ago. It worked then and it will work for them again.

"Some people think the Federal Reserve Banks are the United States government's institutions. They are not government institutions. They are private credit monopolies which prey upon the people of the United States for the benefit of themselves and their foreign swindlers" (Congressional Record 12595-12603: Louis T. McFadden, Chairman of the Committee on Banking and Currency (12 years), June 10, 1932)

"Whoever controls the volume of money in any country is absolute master of all industry and commerce." (James A. Garfield, President of the United States, 1881) Interestingly, a short time after making this statement, President Garfield was assassinated, though no link between his murder and his view toward central banks ever was established. At the time, however, there was strong agitation by the elite banking families and industrial magnates for establishment of a central bank in America. It was nearly 30 years before they succeeded in having President Woodrow Wilson establish the Federal Reserve System.

Here is an extra-credit question for you: Which ethnic group is grossly disproportionately represented among the ranks of the owners and the managers of all Western central banks, including the (not)Federal (no)Reserve (not)Bank? Something tells me you got the correct answer this time.

"It is loosely and unofficially estimated that the Rothschilds control almost three fifths the world's wealth of about $500 trillion in fiat money through the indebtedness of world governments, while about another $100 trillion of the world's wealth is controlled by the Rockefellers. Another 11 rich and powerful banking families, as well as wealthy individuals, families and governments, control the remaining $100 trillion of the world's wealth." (*The Zionist Connection – An Unholy Tripartite*, Ted Lang, EtherZone, May 24, 2004)

What's more, there is nothing to stop the cycle from repeating endlessly into the future. Nobody alive today recalls what the world was like before America was given over to central bankers by Woodrow Wilson early last century, when he allowed formation of the (not)Federal (no)Reserve (not)Bank system.

Today, it seems perfectly normal that there be a large, centralized government, massive federal credit, stupendous national debt and ongoing inflation. Very few seem to see the need to dismantle the central bank, eliminate fiat money altogether and get back on a "pay as you go" basis in life. Nor would the central bankers, who already own virtually everything, stand still for such a move. As I said, *it's hopeless*.

Bridging the Gap

What to do? Well, there a number of things to do which can afford at least some protection. For the more adventurous, fantastic profit opportunities may be in store.

Remember, money is whatever people agree upon. The dollar did not always exist. In fact, measured against its own purchasing power of a century ago, it barely exists today (less than 1% of what a dollar was worth in terms of comparable goods then). Of course, that was before the system was turned over to the Zionist international banking families. Increasingly, a great many people, people knowledgeable in economics and finance, disagree whether the US dollar even will survive. That should give anyone pause, especially

333

those living on fixed incomes and who therefore face the single greatest problem with the upcoming troubles.

Some on fixed incomes can effect a change in the source of their income and should do so immediately, by moving completely out of equities and bonds and into hard assets or the very next best thing, even contrarian mutual funds. Those on Social Security are the least secure, of course.

I fully contemplate that it may well be too late to do anything anyway, by the time this book comes to market late in the summer of 2004, particularly since it no longer seems necessary for them to get Bush reelected, otherwise the status quo would be guaranteed until nearly the end of 2004.

There is one thing, however, that I have seen virtually everybody agree upon: gold will hold its value as a form of money, just as it has since the beginning of recorded history. Gold can be held in physical form (bullion coins, as in the US Gold Eagle), stocks (shares of gold mining companies - Gold Corporation, GG, has been one of the better-performing stocks over the past couple of years) and contrarian mutual funds (like Prudent Bear, BEARX, which bets against the market and invests in gold, to boot).

Gold is not a true investment, mind you, because it just...sits there, like I said before. It produces no return outside of an increase in value which occurs while it is held. However, gold is a great refuge. Sometimes, you can make a killing in gold, but that simply is a windfall and not what I call investing. Investing requires the use of money to produce something; gold just...sits there, don't forget. You can invest in a gold mining stock. Purchasing physical gold, however, is taking refuge.

I mentioned that, as of this writing, precious metals, particularly gold and silver, appear to be grossly undervalued due to market rigging. If true, then a fantastic profit opportunity may well exist for those who can afford to buy and hold gold through the coming difficulties. Should the government decide to outlaw the private ownership of gold again, so as to devalue the dollar against it in a massive fashion, those who decide to hide theirs should be prepared to hold on to it for quite some time.

Safekeeping is an issue for any precious metal. With new laws, whereby banks must report the contents of safe deposit boxes to the government, a home safe of some sort really is the only recourse. Do not allow others to hold your precious metals and, if you simply must, ensure that they are segregated physically and plainly marked as being yours. Never take a deposit slip or the like and allow those holding your metals to hold them in their own, or "street," name.

Gold Pricing Pressures

Gold has some industrial uses, but very little by comparison with silver, which currently is massively undervalued when compared to the price of gold, versus the historical relationship which has existed between the two. In fact, above-ground stocks of silver, generally produced simply as a byproduct of mining for other ores, principally copper, have been depleted to the point of nonexistence recently. Silver, in particular, seems poised for a serious breakout once the rigging stops, as stop it inevitably must.

Gold, too, seems susceptible of a demand-pull increase in price. Much of the world's gold is mined in South Africa, a country which has reverted to Black rule and increasingly is unstable and irrationally managed. South African mines have been "high grading," meaning that they pull out the easiest-to-get-to ore first. Most mines do a proportional extraction to avoid the very bind in which South African mines find themselves today, with the cost of extraction rising and the value of their currency plunging due to their government's incompetence.

Workers always are the first to feel the effects of a business downturn, with both job and pay cuts. In the current political environment of South Africa, White mine owners who cut worker paychecks will be tempting nationalization of the entire industry, which could leave investors with nothing and lead to a further serious downturn in production, to boot. That is why gold mine stocks in general, and those in South Africa in particular, can be risky investments, even in times of rising gold prices.

Meanwhile, China just has made it legal for its citizens to own gold. Strong demand is coming up from all around the world and yearly production simply isn't keeping up.

The markets for both silver and gold are relatively minuscule. For example, there exist thousands of people, each of whom could buy every single ounce of silver that exists above ground today. The short derivative positions for both metals never could be met by physical delivery. In a meteoric rise, wherein every buyer demands delivery, some significant holders of short positions simply will go under, leading to still more chaos in the marketplace and an increase in the frenzy to acquire the physical metals themselves, rather than the relatively valueless derivative positions then going unfilled. Result? A bubble with prices going to the stratosphere. Is this certain to happen? No, but the circumstances certainly have come together to *allow* it to happen.

Incidentally, a crash in stock and bond prices, which likely will happen, could *also* destroy the derivatives market, with the scenario just described playing out just as given.

Before 1929, one could buy stocks on margin, with as little as 10% down, so that the market declines of the time created margin calls that literally wiped out many investors overnight. They try to tell us that today's increased margin requirements prevent a reoccurrence. What they don't talk about are the truly massive positions in other asset markets held by firms that need only 5% equity, as in mortgage-backed securities. A 5% decline in bond values will wipe out completely the equity of many investors. Result? A crash that will make the one last century seem like a hiccup.

Truly major individual players like Warren Buffet and George Soros (who individually is credited with destroying the currency of one country with his past trading) have moved into cash and very few, very selected direct corporate investments. After the crash, just as in Depression I, there will be buying opportunities of a lifetime, in both the equities markets and in real estate. But, only those with cash will be able to avail themselves of the bargains. If the dollar goes into hyperinflation, even cash will not afford its holder the opportunity to snap up the bargains. That is where the "barbarous relic" precious metals become indispensable.

Why is the price of silver being rigged, along with that of gold? To keep you bought into the concept of fiat money as being the only game in town, that's why. Can the market stay irrational longer than you can stay solvent? Perhaps, but then you likely always can sell your gold and silver and be no worse off than when you began.

Some will tell you that times have changed and that gold and silver are the aforementioned "barbarous relics." Don't be fooled. These people will be the ones selling apples and pencils on street corners this time around.

How safe is Gold?

What is gold really worth today? Well, the accurate answer simply is *whatever someone will pay for it.* However, there are historical measures which indicate that it is seriously undervalued. Could it stay that way? Only if the central bankers are correct in what they tell you about gold and also are correct that economic depression and monetary hyperinflation are things of the past. Even so, it will require ongoing rigging, because there are a great many people around the world who quite simply don't believe any of that – and with good reason.

I'm going to go through a quick analysis of the value of gold, one of many ways in which a price for it can be derived, I might add. It almost certainly will require you to read through it a few times to really get the drift, because it is not the point of this book to be an exhaustive treatise on gold or investing, after all. Rather, I wish only to construct an argument for it being used as a defense against the economic war being waged against us all by Zionism – in yet another display of wicked and undeserved anti-Semitism, most Zionists will say, of course.

To date, 193,000 metric tons of gold have been discovered and mined, worldwide.

In 1945, 63,570 tons existed. In 2003, 144,092 tons existed, a 127% increase.

In 1945, the price of gold was set arbitrarily by the government at $35 per ounce. In 2003, the spot price of gold was $330 per ounce (approximately $390 as of this writing), a tenfold increase.

In 1945, 68% of all gold was in central bank vaults. In 2003, 12% of all gold was in central bank vaults.

The total outstanding value of gold outside bank vaults in 2003 was about 100 times the total outstanding value of gold outside bank vaults in 1945.

In 1945, the total money in circulation throughout the world was about $300 billion. In 2003, the total money in circulation throughout the world was about $30 trillion, a one-hundredfold increase, which itself suggests a proper price for gold in the range of $3,500 per ounce (100 x $35).

Expressed as a pro-rata portion of the total money in circulation in 1945, gold accounted for $147.48 for each ounce of gold then in existence. Expressed as a pro-rata portion of the total money in circulation in 2003, gold accounted for $6,506.26 for each and every ounce of gold then in existence.

Some would call the analysis done at this point and claim that gold is worth between $3,500 and $6,506 per ounce. I am not one of those, some of whom use alternate analyses to derive values of up to $20,000 per ounce.

By the way, some actually suggest that the correct analysis is to divide the total money supply by the number of ounces of gold in central bank vaults, since that represents the extent to which outstanding money is "backed" by gold. In that case, the per-ounce value of gold turns out to be an incredible $54,218.94. However, this neglects to calculate a similar figure for each country with money outstanding, then weight each result appropriately. Some countries, such as America, have almost no gold left in bank vaults, though none will allow inspections.

America's Consumer Price Index (CPI) in 1945 was 18. The CPI in 2003 was 183, representing a 10X increase.

America's Gross Domestic Product (GDP) increased by 9X from 1945 to 2003, after adjustment for inflation (CPI).

The world's money supply, expressed in dollars, increased 100X from 1945 to 2003. America's broadest definition of money, M3, increased by about 36X during the same period.

Note that the money supply increased significantly faster than did either GDP or the CPI or, for that matter, America's population, which has doubled.

The Dow increased by 10X during the same period, too.

While American post-WWII productivity increased by about 3X on a per-capita basis, the money supply (M3) increased beyond productivity by a factor of ten, which squares with the CPI increase. When I was a child, those purple first-class postage stamps cost 3 cents, but today they are more than ten times that amount, an external validation of our statistical analysis. I recall today's $1 ice cream cones costing but a nickel a scoop.

In other words, our money has been robbed of 90% of its value in the last fifty years by excessive expansions of the money supply, with most of the loss taking place in just the last 30 years. Meanwhile, the per-capita supply of gold actually has declined by about 40%. What's the problem, you might ask – after all, gold went up from $35 to $330 in the same time period, approximately the amount of inflation. Here's the problem: at both points, the price of gold was being artificially constrained by the central bank, both directly and through its surrogate, the American government.

The real question is what happens to the price of gold if the bank loses control of it and, particularly, if the dollar swoons significantly, as seems to be occurring at the time of this writing.

Executive Summary

Yes, this is the way financial analysis is done. Assemble all the relevant statistics, analyze them with statistical devices like regression analysis, adjusting for extraordinary events and external manipulation. Move them around on the table before you, trying the pieces in different positions, like a jigsaw puzzle.   Eventually, a picture emerges. Usually, a rationale then is developed to fit the result that one intuits.

What I have done herein is a very clumsy approximation of that procedure, if indeed it can be dignified with so organized a word as "procedure."   Nevertheless, a picture has emerged and I am pretty confident of its parameters.

Clearly, the current price of gold represents about the lowest it ever has been, when adjusted for the various factors we have considered.   Therefore, it represents an eminently safe vehicle for getting through the coming economic meltdown. The wild card is its up side, which could be significant. It seems safe to say that gold will see some serious swings, but that they all will be upwards and almost certainly never again below the current value.

In Roman times, an ounce of gold could buy you a good suit of clothes, it is said. The same was true in 1929. Today, a good men's suit will cost between $1,000 and $2,000. By the "suit theory" alone, gold has a long way to go.

If gold were to take over the job of money in today's economy, all other things being equal, its value most assuredly would go to somewhere between $6,000 and $10,000 per ounce. However, there are other vehicles of value that would also pick up the slack, such as silver and platinum and backhoes and seed corn and...well, you get the idea. But gold needn't step into the breach; the dollar need merely abdicate its position in the world, as it inevitably now will do. Gold will be revalued to the levels that it would assume if it and the other precious metals were the only medium of exchange, even though some form of fiat money inevitably will be thrown into the breach.

I spent a lot of time in my earlier life analyzing stock and bond price movements, then financial statements from both a corporate treasury standpoint and that of a bookkeeper and an auditor. I learned that, like everything else, accounting and finance is an art. I cannot articulate precisely how I calculate the ultimate value for gold that I have, but I feel pretty good about its validity. The danger of exact formulae is in the likelihood of error creeping in. Broad-brush analysis, such as this, keeps the entire forest firmly in view at all times. Yes, I could throw some calculations down here and derive the very numbers I am about to give you, but in honesty that would be contrived.

I believe that gold will spike to as much as 3 or 4 thousand dollars per ounce in terms of today's dollar, no later than 2010, and probably much sooner, then settle in at around $1200, in terms of the dollar's 2004 purchasing power. I see $800 as the likely bottom of the possible ultimate range, which itself provides a profit potential of 100% over today's price.

341

Checking Our Work

A "sanity check" of this range can be made by updating the price of gold from some past point in time to today, using something that reflects the general decline in the purchasing power of the dollar. Problem is in getting accurate figures. Roosevelt pegged gold at $35 in the 1930s and kept it there through the end of the war. Many believed that to be a fair price at the time. If so, then simply multiplying $35 by the 36X increase in the M3 money supply yields $1,260 per ounce. Pretty close.

Another "sanity check" can be derived from the price of gold in the mid 1970s, which ranged around $150 per ounce, probably a pretty good free-market-driven price from just prior to the massive inflation of modern times. The Dow-Jones Average bottomed out in 1974 at about 575 and likewise probably was a pretty good derivation of free market forces. Today's Dow is hopelessly bloated by the monetary inflation of the past several years, so cannot be used directly. Fundamentals dictate, via traditional price-earnings ratios, a proper level today for the Dow of about 4,500. This quickly can be calculated by simply dividing the traditional "square-up" price-earnings ratio of 12 by today's average price-earnings ratio of about 28, then applying the resultant fraction to today's Dow. Fundamentals, remember, are what square up stocks with other forms of investments. Applying the interim increase in the Dow of 683 percent to the 1973 gold price of $150 yields $1,025, a conservative figure in that the earlier period's bottom for the Dow is used in the calculation. Using other Dow figures from the 1970s produce today's gold value as ranging up to around $2,000 per ounce.

Since gold will, as pointed out above, likely spike well above $1,200, if one chose to bail out at, say, $3,000, then real estate likely will be the safest transition investment at that point. If the stock market has crashed, as in 1932, then buying a bundle of penny Blue

Chips could prove to be very advantageous in the long run. Staying in gold, of course, is the sure bet, just as always.

The Real Allure of Gold

Is gold safe? You bet. In fact, it looks to be one of the best investments around just now, with silver's fundamentals even better. But the central bankers sure don't want you to know that. Possessing gold and silver in some form is an excellent way to practice defensive racism against the predatory nature of the international Zionist banking system just now.

This becomes even more urgent if one takes the view, as do I, that we have seen America's "last hurrah," with other nations, particularly China, assuming the ascendancy in world financial affairs as we move into the future. Stripped of its value, the dollar likely never will recover. An emergency "escape pod" from the trap that the American economic system is becoming is a necessity today. Gold can serve as that escape pod.

If the New World Order succeeds in forcing the entire world into submission, then all bets are off. A single world currency, issued by a single central world bank (guess who will own it) will be the first order of business. The price of gold will be driven to next to nothing, in that event, to ensure that it never again challenges the supremacy of fiat money. Of course, at that point, the price of gold will be the least of our worries.

We began this chapter with a quote from the premier foreign Jewish banking family, one that has profited so handsomely from overseeing the American money supply. It seems appropriate, somehow, to finish with another: *"Give me control of a nation's money and I care not who makes it's laws."* (Mayer Amschel Bauer Rothschild)

Chapter 18

New America

"Each individual of the society has a right to be protected by it in the enjoyment of his life, liberty, and property, according to standing laws."
--- John Adams

"We must understand clearly and firmly that the dominant authorities...not only do nothing to conserve what most of us regard as our traditional way of life, but actually seek its destruction..."
--- Sam Francis, *Revolution from the Middle,* (1997)

"Those who profess to favor freedom, and yet depreciate agitation, are men who want crops without plowing up the ground.   They want rain without thunder and lightning..."
--- Thomas Paine, Common Sense (1776)

We are a distinct minority of people living in America today. Biologically, we are American but socially and environmentally different from most living here.

We used to be the majority. Our forebears founded America. We are mostly older, though some in the younger generations have awakened to the problems we face.

We are overwhelmingly Christian, White and of European extraction.

We grew up in a far different country. We silently stood by while America was reshaped, thinking it would endure, as it seemingly always has. *We were wrong.*

Strangers in a Strange Land

We have suffered affirmative action and all that it meant, due to a false sense of guilt engendered in us by others about the treatment of Blacks that we never knew by Whites with whom we have nothing in common except skin color. We didn't realize that we merely were trading places with those discriminated against in the past.

We have endured the spectacle of renaming schools in cities like New Orleans after Blacks, both notable and unmemorable, thereby erasing the memory of our founding fathers. We have allowed streets, buildings and all manner of public property to be renamed, taking off "Washington," "Jefferson" and the like, to be replaced with "Martin Luther King, Jr." and others whose primary contribution to American society has been their skin color.

Not a single one of the founding fathers has a holiday named solely for himself. Martin Luther King, Jr., has one, though. *We know why.*

We suffered removal of the Confederate flag from public venues. Now we see the American flag become a mark of "oppression," as evidenced by Black Florida firefighters refusing to ride on fire trucks because they bore the stars and stripes.

We witnessed the spectacle of a statue of modern American heroes, three firefighters captured forever in a photograph raising the American flag over the WTC ruins, mongrelized in the name of diversity, whereby two of the three White figures were displaced by a Black and a latino, respectively. *We know the truth.*

Schools teach to the bottom of the classes and we pretend to wonder why we have to keep lowering the standards so that students appear to be as smart as ever. *We know why.*

We have sacrificed our children to a false sense of guilt, in pursuit of intellectual parity that can never be achieved without genetic restructuring. *Nobody left behind means nobody out in front.*

346

We suffer massive levels of crime that did not exist even thirty years ago, overwhelmingly at the hands of "people of color." Though our media and government do everything they can to skew the statistics, we know who is to blame.

School shootings. We know why.

Victim mentality. We are tired of the whining.

Massive immigration but no assimilation. No longer the melting pot, but now the potluck free lunch, and we know whose pot is being provided.

We are witness to a massive movement by Mexicans, called *"La Reconquista,"* the objective of which is secession of southwest America, to be rejoined to Mexico or established as a country in its own right. They even have a name for it already: *Aztlan.* We have all but given it to them, but now they pursue us to the poor and inhospitable locales of America to which we have retreated. Now they demand a share of those lands, as well.

"Americanism is a matter of the spirit, and of the soul...The one absolutely certain way of bringing this nation to ruin, of preventing all possibility of its continuing to be a nation at all, would be to permit it to become a tangle of squabbling nationalities...each preserving its separate nationality.... The men who do not become Americans and nothing else are hyphenated Americans.... There is no such thing as a hyphenated American who is a good American." (Theodore Roosevelt, 1900)

Welfare, food stamps, school and free medical care for illegals, primarily paid for by us, though many of us can no longer afford to feed our own kids properly.

Some of us haven't seen doctors in years because we haven't the money.

Some of us qualify for welfare, but we are too proud.

We can't afford to send our children to college, the same college that provides free tuition and living expenses to those whose primary qualification consists of skin color.

Yet our government lobs million-dollar missiles at empty caves and camel dung in places we don't care about. And sends billions in foreign aid to countries that hate us and actively work to subvert our dominance in world affairs.

We see political correctness run amuck. We can't read newspapers or magazines without having "hate Whitey"...er, diversity thrown in our faces on every page. That's why readership is declining. That, plus the general rise in illiteracy engendered by the failing social experiment that America has become. Even the advertisements now have massive overrepresentation of Blacks and Latinos, depicted in unlikely poses and occupations.

We endure the dismantling of Christianity and its removal from every public edifice. We see our pastors stand idly by, often lending a hand to those who seek to replace Christianity with other religions. We prohibit discussion of Christ in schools, yet California requires the teaching of Islam to seventh graders.

Movies and TV depict an America that doesn't exist...that never existed except in the wishful thinking of warped leftists, sexual deviants, cultural communists, globalists and other assorted control freaks.

Terrorist attacks and more to come, because we pretend not to know why. Because we continue to be the world's bully. Because we allow our government to do the bidding of others.

We have betrayed our grandparents and theirs. We have squandered our birthright and our heritage. We sacrifice our children upon the altar of political correctness.

This is not the country in which we grew up. Not the society that formed us. Not the future we were promised. Truly, *we have become strangers in a strange land.*

There is no place left in America for us. Every place has to be the same now, as dictated by those who would be our masters. Life comes in one size these days, dispensed largely through the TV set.

We deserve better. We demand better.

It is past time to say it: *we want a country of our own.*

It is time to stop being strangers in our own land, an increasingly strange land.

Hope Still Springs Eternal

America does not have to become the one described in Chapter 14, *"The Future."* If but 10% of America's population saw the danger and arose tomorrow with the resolve to change things, we could chart a new course and set things right. That isn't going to happen.

The Zionist cabal atop America quite simply will not step aside peacefully, nor will it allow the truth to be told to but a very few. They control the airwaves, the theatres, the newspapers and magazines. They own the publishing houses, which is why this very book you are reading found its way to you almost surreptitiously and certainly not via anything resembling a normal channel of distribution. Before much longer, they will have closed off the Internet and that will be the end of what little dissent exists in America today.

America's Zionist masters direct the efforts of the armed forces, both abroad and at home, which regularly are purged of anybody who gives the appearance of dissent. Police forces are under their direction and becoming increasingly militarized. Government workers of every stripe are being armed while America's citizenry is stripped of its weapons.

We will not be changing the system, because it has become impervious to change. Mere attempts to use what once was created

349

within the system to effect change marks one as a troublemaker, to be scorned as anti-government, anti-Semitic, racist or all the above.

The American judiciary and virtually all professions have become rigidified in ideological outlook.

Our educational system has been subverted to collectivist thinking, whereby our children are propagandized during their most formative years while we abdicate our responsibility as parents.

They have cobbled together a coalition of the immigrant, the weak, the needy and the avaricious into a false majority whereby we are subjugated in the guise of democracy.

In particular, they pacify and propagandize us *en masse*, via our television sets, while we are forced to take back our fellow free thinkers one at a time, through extended interaction and discussion. Overwhelmingly, the odds are against us.

There is hope, but it is a sickly flower growing amidst a field of destruction.

As shown earlier in this book, Zionists have done all this and more elsewhere, most recently in Germany and Russia last century. In all cases, though the native populations eventually rose up and threw them out, those countries have been wrecked in the process. It likely will be no different in the case of America.

Always, they overreach. Always, they get expelled. Always, they strip the country bare on the way out the door, then cause others to set upon their former host. *Always.*

Yes, this is a book about racism. But *defensive* racism, the sort erected to protect oneself and one's own from harm. Not the irrational sort of racism that calls for hatred of others merely because they might be different.

We have seen that there are some races with inordinate predispositions to violence. I advocate physical separation from those races. Separation by continent, as in the past, would be best, but that simply is not going to happen. I would be happy to be the one to go elsewhere, if there were but somewhere else to go. There isn't.

Multiculturalism has been just one of the devices by which America's new masters have divided us and robbed us of our will, while they stole into the corridors of power and seized control.

Interracial antipathy in America is but a means to an end for them and but a symptom of the fundamental problem for the rest of us.

In the long run, assuming we manage to get free of our Zionist overlords, our greatest problem will be to *stay* free of them. Unlike races which look radically different, physically they look quite like us. Interbreeding has further complicated the problem, though that same interbreeding has attenuated the genetic predisposition to control and exploit which is the *raison d'etre* of the Zionist.

First, however, we must have the opportunity to construct a New America. I believe that opportunity will come. Indeed, it will *have* to come because our ability to create it via revolutionary means simply does not exist. Nor will such an ability be allowed to gestate.

Ultimately, America will be brought low through its arrogance and overreaching, the singularly Zionist quality which always has been their undoing down through the ages. America has become a Zionist nation in its own right, not just in obeisance to Israel.

There is growing throughout the world at this moment an increasing awareness of the danger that America poses to all nations. Eventually, America will bite off more than it can chew and be defeated militarily by the concerted effort of much of the rest of the world. I would not be at all surprised to see Western European nations joining into that effort at some point.

Likely, this will occur after the coming economic depression has taken hold, causing social upheaval of epic proportions throughout America at the time that our government is decapitated.

There may well be a nuclear exchange, rendering great swaths of America uninhabitable. There may be an invasion and occupation, though I doubt it. Attempting to hold America would make America's recent adventures in the Middle East look like a Sunday School picnic. There simply is no country in the world capable of occupying even a demilitarized America.

Economic catastrophe now is inevitable. There is no avoiding it. Military catastrophe, of course, is avoidable but likely to happen anyway.

I have in this book covered in detail how to position yourself for the upcoming carnage, both economic and physical. Scoff if you will and ignore this advice. Even after the wheels come off completely, many will have a chance to get to safety. Even then, I suspect, a great many will not do so, as a direct result of wishful thinking and self delusion. They will become trapped behind enemy lines, because all of America will have become a war zone, make no mistake. *They will die.*

The Balkanization of America

I've heard it said that anybody with a globe and bottle of whiskey can be a geopolitician. Though I drink very little these days, I do own a globe. Let's test that thesis. My best take on how things might go in America when the dominoes start falling:

The battle lines will be drawn along what will be perceived to be defensible borders, coincident with natural impediments like rivers and mountain ranges. The lines will be drawn racially at first. A great deal depends upon whether America's metropolitan areas are left intact.

Aztlan will become a reality in those days and there is not a thing that anybody can do about it. In truth, there is little that could be done about it today, if the militant Mestizos occupying the future territory of Aztlan wished to take it now. Judging strictly by current population makeup and proximity to the Mexican border, Aztlan's border will stretch from the Pacific coastline across northern California, bisecting Nevada and Utah. The southwestern portion of Colorado will be included, along with much of Oklahoma and Western Texas. Arizona and New Mexico will go entirely, of course.

When reports of the carnage against non-Hispanic residents of Aztlan reach the rest of America with latino populations, the reprisal killings and violence will precipitate a headlong dash for the new border by all Hispanics not already in Aztlan.

Simultaneously, a similar scenario will be playing out in the deep South, where Blacks simply will up the already-simmering race war to a full boil. I expect that border to enclose the already-huge Black populations of eastern Virginia and eastern North Carolina. All of South Carolina will go, together with all but the far northern reaches of Georgia and Alabama. All of Mississippi and Louisiana will be included, together with eastern Texas, southeast Arkansas and southwest Tennessee. For lack of a better term, I have dubbed this new region, due to become a country unto itself, *"New Africa."*

I see a strong possibility, born of necessity for a gulf coast port, of New America dipping down through eastern Texas in a swath that encompasses both Dallas and Houston, thereby dividing Aztlan from New Africa.

Florida will become a special case, due to its large population of Cuban and Caribbean extraction. How it will shake out is anybody's guess, but it will end up being a White "no-go" zone, of that you can be sure.

Buffer zones of varying widths naturally will arise along the *de facto* borders of Aztlan, New Africa and what will become New America. Those will be the only relatively safe areas for those who find themselves welcome on neither side of the new borders, as with mixed-race families.

There will be outposts, strongholds if you will, of Blacks deep in what becomes White territory. Detroit comes to mind as an example.

What comes of them at first is anybody's guess, but, eventually, those people will migrate to New Africa.

If America undergoes change as a result of war, it likely will have been a part of World War III, and many of America's cities will have been reduced to rubble. Regardless, intact cities will become battle zones with the suspension of food deliveries, particularly, and devolve to the control of street gangs. The populations will spread into the countryside, where refugee camps will be erected and where the street gangs will be met and destroyed as they emerge, both desperate and hungry, from the cities.

If America is not preemptively decapitated, it will have responded in kind and national borders all around the globe will shift. The Chinese will move into all of southeast Asia, Indochina and, possibly, Australia and New Zealand. China can be expected to swallow Japan whole and take most of Russia east of the Ural Mountain range.

Alaska possibly will be seized by the Chinese at first, given China's burgeoning demand for oil and the prospect of its salvation looming just over the rise, beneath the Northern Slopes. China possibly even could establish a beachhold in the far west of Canada and the northwest tip of America, including Seattle, a region already home to a huge Asian population. Should this happen, expect general reprisals against those of Asian descent throughout what remains of America. They will, of necessity, flee to the far Northwest.

If a general war has taken place, Canada's capitol will be laid waste, as well, with the rest of Canada likely throwing its lot in with *de facto* White America. Eastern Canada possibly will choose to go its own way.

South America and sub-Saharan Africa will sink into a morass of crime, revolution, genocide and intertribal warfare, once free of their Western overseers.

Israel will be turned into a giant, self-illuminated glass parking lot by the Arab states it has tormented for so long. Likely, it will take large portions of the Middle East with it as it goes down. A new, Islam-based Muslim empire will arise from the ashes of the Middle East, stretching from India in the east to Turkey in the west and from Kazakhstan in the north well into Northern Africa in the south. Internecine fighting will keep the Muslims occupied for centuries to come, just as has occurred for so many centuries in the past.

Eastern Europe will erupt into regional wars, what with the removal of American and other Western influence. It will shake out eventually, as will America, along racial lines.

Russia will become substantially smaller and be occupied with fortifying its borders, provided it is not laid waste as a part of a world at war. Russia's greatest immediate danger may well come from the nuclear arsenal of an Israel caught up in the throes of death, though Russia's long-term enemy will prove to be China.

India and Pakistan will devastate one another with their nuclear arsenals, just as they have threatened for so long.

The northern reaches of Europe – Norway, Sweden and Finland – stand a chance of coming through unscathed, as do the alpine portions of Europe.

Western European nations, which have become as racially mixed as America, will share America's fate, and for the same reasons.

As America begins the long walk back from its own troubles, I foresee a schism arising between the western and the eastern portions as ideological differences manifest. The big-government, control-freak nature of many in the eastern portion of the US, particularly the remaining Zionists, will prove intolerable to free-wheeling and independent-minded Westerners.

Depending upon how things progress, Jews could become the focus of a great deal of anger by people throughout the world, particularly in America, if they are seen as having been the source of the difficulties, particularly a war that escapes the Middle East, then engulfs the world.

While I do not foresee a breakout of hostilities between the two regions in America, I do see there being a break of the sort that should have occurred in lieu of the American Civil War of the 1860s. This dividing line could well end up being in the vicinity of the Mississippi River. There could be further splits as America continues to Balkanize, much as the former Soviet Union broke apart.

For lack of a better term, I have dubbed the far eastern portion of what will remain of America *"New Israel."* The size of New Israel will depend inversely upon the degree of hostility to Jews and any requirement by New America that Jews be excluded strictly along racial lines.

I do not foresee Americans actually expelling any who have attained American citizenship, nor do I advocate such expulsion. However, just as Blacks and Mestizos inevitably will concentrate themselves in those areas which they currently dominate, so will Jews concentrate into an area centering on what already has become New Tel Aviv: *New York City.*

Because of the violent White overreaction to the murder of Whites in Aztlan and New Africa, *all* Blacks and Mestizos will end up south of those borders and all Whites who don't head north will be killed. I do not foresee anything of that sort occurring with Jews, but they are likely to find themselves singularly unwelcome in what remains of America.

The region which is left, including portions of Canada, is what I think of as *"New America."* New America will be bounded on the west by the Pacific Ocean, to the north by the far reaches of Canada's Yukon, to the east by New Israel and to the south by Aztlan, New Africa and the Gulf of Mexico along the current Texan coastline.

New America likely will stretch right through the Great Lakes region, incidentally, and encompass much of northern New England, as well, giving it an Atlantic coastline. The people of Maine, New Hampshire and northern Vermont are, for example, much more akin to those in the western United States than those in the Boston-New York-Washington, DC nexus. Eastern Canada could feel compelled to join, as well, simply to ensure its self preservation in a hostile world.

Thus, New America becomes pretty much a White European homeland, with its borders imposed upon it by others, in the main. Only the presence of Jews may be problematic and, by far, may prove to be the single most difficult task confronting New America, even in the face of all the chaos, death and destruction caused by and on behalf of Zionists throughout the world. This moral dilemma will prove so difficult, in fact, that I believe it likely to cause a further split of the eastern region, with the smaller portion going to those who demand ethnic purity by exclusion of all Jews.

There are rumors of agents of the Israel Defense Force (IDF) buying up huge swaths of land in southern Argentina, where monstrous sheep and cattle ranches have been on the market in recent years at rock-bottom prices. This makes me think that Israel has a fall-back plan should it need to exit the Middle East altogether and in the event that America also becomes inhospitable. Thus, it is possible that we would see Jews migrating to South America in large numbers, but likely setting up a government that most American Jews would find intolerable.

While I cannot advocate forcing the outright expulsion of any American citizen save those granted their franchise by virtue of their parents illegally entering America for the purpose of having one or more children born into citizenship, certainly I can support the idea of drawing boundary lines and requiring citizens to choose one side or the other so that different political structures can be erected in different states.

Starting Over

With the opportunity to start over, how do we do it? I can only speculate, which is all that can be done by anybody. There certainly is no magic formula and nothing I have read ever has made clear exactly how we pick up the pieces and put them back together so as to avoid the mistakes of the past. However, the failures apparent in today's American society certainly provide us some guidelines.

America's failures are directly traceable to the establishment of the Federal Reserve Bank system and the resultant handover to Zionists of the reigns of government. As time went on, the fabulously wealthy Jewish banking families saw to the takeover of America's media, educational system, judicial system, most professions and most of the significant governmental power points. They then employed multiculturalism and massive third-world immigration as a prime weapon to weaken and divide us. Any repetition of this must be prevented, at all costs, in New America.

The banking families will have to be broken apart, irretrievably scattered and their assets repatriated to the nations from which they were stolen.

Only by physical separation from Jews can we be protected from their fiscal avarice and compulsion to control us. Only by physical separation from Blacks and Mestizos can we be physically protected from their proclivity for violence. Perhaps after thousands of years of evolution it will be possible for the races to live intermingled. Not now and not in the foreseeable future, however.

Certainly, there must be a new central government erected by New America at the outset, for accomplishment of that which we cannot do ourselves, either individually or regionally. For the common defense, at a minimum.

Our single largest threat will come from China. In fact, I suppose that war with communist China is inevitable, though China will have its hands full just in consolidating its new holdings up and down the western Pacific Region and throughout the Far East.

I foresee an alliance between New America and Russia, and against China (remember China's certain move into the eastern portion of Russia, which is largely uninhabited at present), as being inevitable. In particular, a Chinese foothold in western Canada and/or the northwest tip of Washington State would prove intolerable from the outset leading us quickly to move to contain Chinese ambitions. Russia will possess an even more urgent need to face down Chinese forces during the times that I foresee.

Expulsion of Chinese occupying forces from North America, including the recovery of Alaska, if necessary, would be a priority both for our protection and to regain access to the vast untouched oil fields existing there. Middle Eastern oil may well be unavailable and may remain so indefinitely, due to radiation.

While WWIV, to be fought in the main by China on the one side and the new American/Russian alliance on the other seems inevitable, it also seems likely to be deferred for a generation or two, while all WWIII gains and losses are consolidated.

Form of Government

Both Thomas Jefferson and Mao Tse Tsung advocated ongoing political revolution, the first to prevent tyranny, the second to ensure it, it seems. Neither were correct, I believe. Nor do I believe that a particular form of government is the key to liberty and freedom.

Does it matter what form New America's government takes? There is endless debate today, as there has been down through the ages, as to what constitutes the "perfect" form of government.

Western nations unanimously tout democracy as the answer, though America's forefathers specifically eschewed democracy in favor of a constitutional republic. That was then, however - this is now.

The interesting question now concerns what form of democracy America has assumed today, with *"by public opinion poll"* the leading contender in many circles.

Historically, theocracies were the order of the day in most countries, a form of occasionally benevolent dictatorship. Theocracies have ranged from that uneasy alliance between church and state evidenced in European empires of a few hundred years ago to the harshness of Islamic fundamentalism seen at work in Iran and many other Muslim nations today.

Dictators typically have been in charge all through history, however, regardless of the ostensible form that any government has taken. Dictators have ranged from ruthless individuals (Idi Amin being a prime example) to committees of the elite, such as those found in most communist countries, and sometimes-benevolent institutions (church-states, for example). Dictators have ruled over mobs (Attila), fascism (Hitler), communism (Stalin), theocracies (pick your Pope or Ayatollah) and democracies (Zimbabwe's Mugabe comes to mind).

In essence, a dictator says, *"You do what I say. I couldn't care less what you think."* That is, to dictate, pure and simple. To some, it might seem that much of what is going on in America today resembles a dictatorship, given this definition. But ours still is a democracy, nonetheless. After all, the people get to choose their dictator.

Everything else, aside from pure anarchy (every person for him or her self), involves some sort of participation by the people governed (democracies and republics being the leading examples, with parliamentary governments designed to be a variation on the republic theme).

Self government is a relatively recent phenomenon for mankind, incidentally, though America was founded on principles of self government, first set forth by the Pilgrims with their Mayflower Compact.

And, no, it is not contradictory to see participatory governments as being dictatorial - how else could Hitler, Mugabe and countless others have ascended to power in the first place? Say what you will, it seems that most people quite simply want to be told what to do at every turn, with their real choice making reserved for the more personal things in life - mate, car, pizza, beer, etc.

The illusion of choice, as between Republican and Democrat candidates in America today, seems to satisfy the electorate, just so long as there are 47 brands of beer in the supermarket aisles. After all, most Americans don't even bother to vote any more (perhaps in recognition of the lack of choice).

So, there are democracies that act like dictatorships and dictatorships that can produce greater personal freedom than any democracy around. Does it really matter what form government takes? Perhaps not.

The Circle of Strife

There is a pattern which repeats itself all through the fabric of society, down through history. I think of it as the *"Circle of Strife."* And it happens everywhere, it seems, regardless of the form of government. Simply put, the Circle of Strife says: *freedom fosters tyranny and tyranny breeds freedom.*

Any nation's citizenry experiences absolute tyranny or near-absolute freedom, or something in between. And there is a cycling between the two extremes, seemingly independent of the form of government extant at any given time.

The Circle of Strife holds that only in a free country, as America once was, can tyranny find the space in which to gain a foothold and grow. Grow until, like the noxious weed that it emulates, every bit of freedom is crowded out of existence.

However, then the seeds of freedom left behind (memories, perhaps, be they actual or hardwired via some sort of DNA encoding) begin to sprout. And grow. And flourish. And, in a rush, to vanquish the tyranny that went before. Until freedom reigns supreme all over again, creating space for tyranny once more to gain a foothold. And so it goes.

We create our own opposition, in other words.

And revolution does not necessarily mark a shifting of the pendulum back along the course just traced. The Russian revolution last century was merely a stopover from the relative freedom under Russia's monarchy to the nightmare tyranny of the communists that very nearly destroyed that nation. Trading the devil you know for the one you don't is not always a good idea.

Men want to be led, for always we choose leaders, even though that choice sometimes simply is to allow someone else to assume control. Like nature, power abhors a vacuum. Wherever two or more people come together, always will one gain sway over the others.

Men want to be led benignly, in their best interests. That can happen irrespective of the form a government might take.

Democracy is Not the Answer

Democracy is not the answer. In fact, an argument can be made that democracy is one of the worst forms of government, since it always results in a form of mob rule. *Two wolves and a lamb voting about what's for dinner*, as Benjamin Franklin once said.

Always, there will be a sizable minority in a democracy tyrannized by the majority, an ever-present fear of America's founding fathers, which is what led them to establish America as a constitutional republic.

America's founders understood mob psychology. Without predesigned structure, a large group of people will shed its morality and mindlessly follow primal desires, with a lynch mob being the classic example. Bottomless welfare rolls, predatory taxation and boundless inflation are the result of mob rule, an inevitable result when the majority of a group finds it can peacefully take the minority's wealth merely by voting it to themselves.

America has become a form of autocratic democracy. The American republic's safeguards have been abandoned through time, casualties of Supreme Court lawmaking, congressional sellout and Executive Order, all at the behest of America's Zionist masters.

Today, you vote for whichever dictator you want, then his government leads by following the polls, the results of which are preordained by the media in the first place. A form of democracy. A guided democracy. *A dictatorship, if you will.*

Make no mistake about the dictatorship growing in today's America, with the reins of power held by those who stand in the shadows, orchestrating the mob electorate to flow in predetermined paths. Consider the following:

Tyranny will increase time and again, as evidenced by the machinations of the Department of Homeland Defense, Ashcroft's calls for mindless unanimity, the Patriot Act and the administration's neverending war, ostensibly against the denial of the West "its" oil, but in reality to subjugate Israel's enemies.

And the fact that America has a much higher percentage of its population behind bars than any other country in the world...ever.

And the formation of a federal police force via the commandeering of each state's National Guard, the arming of virtually every uniformed federal employee and the militarization of all local police departments.

And the ongoing disarming and regimentation of private citizens.

And the implementation of thought crimes.

And...and...and.....

How long before the pendulum reaches its maximum travel toward tyranny in America and begins to retrace its steps? Must all true freedom be snuffed from existence, leaving only its seeds to germinate in the dark? Must it be that, like William Wallace, we demand *"Freedom"* with our final breath?

Eventually, true freedom will return to America - or whatever America becomes following the upcoming unpleasantries. What form the government then takes probably doesn't particularly matter, but a constitutional republic did work once. It's just a matter of time. It's all a part of the Circle of Strife.

A Constitutional Parliamentary Republic

When the time comes, what form of government should we choose? Time will be short and events pressing. Adopting something quite like that to which we have been accustomed will be easiest. After all, a constitutional republic worked once for America, before she lost her way. I believe it can work again.

Rather than directly re-adopt the US Constitution, I favor incorporating some modifications and guarantees, designed to absolutely limit the size and power of a central government. *Call me old fashioned.*

Democracy has proven itself to be grossly inadequate anywhere it has been tried, which is why America's original founders opted for a form of representative government, a form which went out the window when the Constitution was amended to allow for the direct election of Senators.

My personal preference is for a form of parliamentary government, with a written constitution, so that minority voices always get a seat at the table of government.

The End of Empire

Thousands of Americans have been ruined by our government's invasive, intrusive and tyrannical behavior. Thousands more, perhaps millions, will suffer a similar fate in the times ahead. Their experience of reality is different from those of us who have suffered nothing.

Many of us have refused to question our government's actions, fearful of the repercussions. We believe we have much to lose, yet already we have forfeited the most important of our rights in refusing to stand for the fundamental rights of our countrymen.

A government that cannot protect us, that cannot preserve the peace, is no government at all. Many have declined to foster confrontation, fearful of persecution or imprisonment. *We have ten times more to fear from the government that stands near the end of our current path.*

I take the part of those maligned thus far. If I were similarly situated, I could never support a government that so blatantly has torn asunder the lives of its own citizenry.

I despair of our ever attaining independence from our imperialistic government, nor do others seem to see their way out. Other countries will, at some point, find it necessary to divert America from the course she has charted. They will be met with armed opposition and find it necessary to topple the regime astride America. Unfortunately, this likely will be a part of World War III and result in a worldwide catastrophic loss of life and property.

It is the height of hubris that America today thinks herself impervious to assault from without. She is not. America's recent Middle Eastern adventures have shown her to be a paper tiger at worst and, at best, a deadly cobra which can kill, yet not consume, its prey. America continues in possession of the most awesome nuclear arsenal in existence, an arsenal that will be used in fending off would-be invaders. I anticipate that to result in a draw, though America's teeth abroad will have to be pulled.

A Plan for Tomorrow

In anticipation of an opportunity to start afresh presenting itself at some time in the future, I offer the following:

Let us form a New America, forged from as much of the country as wishes to join us. Let there be a parliamentary form of government, with the current Constitution modified to serve as its charter, the modifications to ensure the very limited scope and reach of the central government.

Convene at first a Constitutional Congress for the purpose of amending and re-adopting the Constitution, with its membership chosen by popular vote, each member elected by a particular and equal portion of the general citizenry.

Upon adoption of the Constitution, this body to dissolve and legislators, governors and other elective officeholders to be selected by popular vote.

Let the States be more like sovereigns themselves, with no provision or necessity for overriding Federal statute or authority, save only as is necessary to allow the central government the performance of its limited duties of common defense.

Let the right of secession be absolute and evocable on the vote of 75% of the population of any definable geographic region.

Let us withdraw from the United Nations and demand that it withdraw from the shores of America.

Let the assemblies be annual, concern themselves solely with domestic affairs and their membership serve without pay or benefit of any sort. Let there be no recurring occupancy by any member, not even of differing position. No person who receives government benefits, either directly or indirectly, may occupy elective or appointed office, be allowed to vote or be given any other voice in government. These strictures are to apply to State and local elective office, as well.

Let the parliament or congress be of two houses: the Senate composed solely of men, two from each state; the House of Representatives, comprised solely of women, will total the same number as the Senate, with its membership elected by districts made equal on the basis of population.

Let the assemblies select the Executive, whose tenure will be for a single two-year term, and whose function will be strictly administrative and procedural, with no ability to negotiate with foreign entities or enter into treaties and no ability to originate or suggest legislation at any level. All foreign entanglements, which will be constitutionally discouraged, must be individually and unanimously entered into by the States as individual sovereigns.

The Executive may be removed at any time by a Parliamentary vote of "no confidence." The Executive, under certain well-defined circumstances, may dissolve Parliament and call extraordinary elections.

A similar representative form of parliamentary government is to be guaranteed to the states and local municipalities.

States' rights will be supreme, with the right to move between states absolute.

States may hold no more than 5% of the land of a state in local or state name. Central government landholdings expressly are forbidden. Current governmental landholdings are to be, first, awarded to compensate those displaced from their homes and lands; second, auctioned to generate revenue, with a form of homesteading reserved to that portion of the population that possessed no homes or lands at the time of the breakup of Old America.

Government pensions, welfare and individual or corporate subsidy of every type to be abolished and forbidden at all levels of government.

All existing practicing lawyers will be disbarred. All existing judges will be discharged. Neither ever again will be allowed to practice law or hold elective office. All existing statutes and case law to be forgone. New lawyers will read for their positions, in the time-honored manner of bygone eras.

Judges will be drawn from the ranks of lawyers, to serve in their area of specialization without pay or benefit each month, for that percentage of time necessary to satisfy the requirements of justice. Juries will decide all questions of fact *and* law, with sentences and verdicts executed immediately. Lawyers will be forbidden from holding elective office. The right to a jury for any proceeding will be absolute, with secret proceedings forbidden.

Victimless crimes will not be prosecuted. There will be no hate laws or thought crimes. Prisons will be segregated racially.

English will be the official language, with all governmental proceedings conducted solely in English. Citizenship to require a basic facility with the English language and familiarity with the history and governmental system of the nation.

The existing school system will be abolished, to be replaced by community-based schools, with teachers compensated directly by the parents of students.

Civil rights will be absolute, with no preference to be shown by any government, at any level, to any individual for any reason.

Individual and private discrimination shall neither be illegal nor discouraged.

Immigration will be an issue for each State to resolve. Illegal immigrants and their progeny to be ejected immediately upon adoption of the new Constitution.

The rights to assemble, freely associate or not, travel, be free of governmental intrusion, privacy, bear arms, free speech and the free practice of religion in any and all venues to be inviolate.

Income, sales and property taxes will be abolished, with governments required to exist upon the proceeds of tariff and import/export taxes alone. A strictly balanced budget will be required of every government entity, especially the central government, each and every year. Local use districts may be formed upon approval of 75% of the affected population, with votes to be taken only at open and general elections via verifiable manual methods.

No business monopolies are to be allowed. Unions are forbidden. Death sentences may be meted out to corporations after public trial for grievous crimes, with their assets seized to compensate victims (excess distributed to shareholders) and responsible officers prosecuted individually. Media enterprise, particularly, is to be dispersed, with no concentration of more than 1% total ownership of a particular medium in any single person, group or entity.

All able-bodied members of society are considered potentially to be part of the militia, with participation strictly voluntary. A modest uniformed, all-volunteer military force will be maintained for the common defense only, and strictly prohibited for non-defensive use within the borders of the States.

All existing government debt of the old America will be repudiated. All indebtedness to government of any sort is to be forgiven.

The dollar will be repudiated, to be replaced by government-minted gold and silver coins. Any and all paper currency will be issued solely by the central government and strictly backed by 100% value holdings in silver and gold only.

Central banking is prohibited. Fractional-reserve banking is prohibited.

The practice of usury is forbidden. The collection of interest beyond the level of 3% is defined to be usurious.

Unpleasant Alternatives to an Unpleasant Future

A great many Americans see a wholesale revamping of America's government, if not America's outright breakup, as inevitable. The present course of foreign imperialism, welfare, citizen control (oppression), economic opportunism and privilege for the few leads inevitably to economic catastrophe and revolt.

Should America prove capable of withstanding an assault from without, it will prove incumbent upon us to effect change from within.

Many bewail the fact that we seem so few in the face of the overwhelming masses of government agents and employees. It is not in numbers, but in unity, that our great strength lies. Should the government move against us in wholesale form, masses of the American population will rise up in number sufficient to repel the force of all the world.

America has, at this time, the greatest military machine of any power under Heaven. However, when necessary, huge portions of the government's forces will refuse to fire upon us and, instead, will join with us against the sweeping tyranny then apparent for all to see.

The present government never will allow formation of an organized citizen militia. Witness what has been done in the face of small forms of organization, as at Waco. Never will we be allowed openly to organize or form an effective resistance force. Even now, the government takes opposition leaders, our leaders, into custody and jails them on sundry manufactured charges. What it fails to realize is that its enemy is an idea, a spirit, generated by its own tyranny. *For every leader taken away and jailed on trumped-up charges, ten more will take his place.*

At present, we have little to defend, therefore no defense is necessary. If we actually possessed a foothold for our people, the more would we have to defend - and lose.

Neither have we debts, for the massive indebtedness of the current American government is attributable to the very forces arrayed against us. When the time comes, the assumption of debt in furtherance of our cause will be worthy and worthwhile.

For now, to expend millions for the sake of getting a few vile acts repealed, and to rout the present Administration, only, is unworthy the charge, and is using posterity with the utmost cruelty because it is leaving them the great work to do, with a debt upon their backs from which they derive no advantage. Such a thought is unworthy of men of honor and is the true characteristic of a narrow heart and the peddling politician.

America is burdened with a total debt of nearly twenty-seven trillion dollars, for which she pays annual interest of over a trillion dollars each and every year. Another twenty-two trillion dollars' debt burdens private American companies and individuals. Somewhat less than another trillion dollars' interest, for a total of about two trillion dollars in interest alone, paid primarily to bankers, most of them foreign, a sum equal to the entirety of the American government budget today and approximately one-third America's total annual economy.

America's current budget deficit is one-fourth that paid in interest each year, or about five-hundred billion dollars. A similar figure is the amount by which America's foreign trade deficit grows each year, representing the outflow of American assets to foreign shores. Another four-hundred billion dollars is spent on America's military, primarily in support of foreign imperialism and intervention in the affairs of other countries; funds spent on destroying other economies, all while many of America's citizens do without the necessities of life.

A cancer both foreign and hostile to America sits astride her, sucking her dry and directing her policies and government to ends inconsistent with those set forth by her founding fathers. This is our real enemy, make no mistake. Most of those employed in the service of the American government are ordinary people, like any other, people who will rally to our cause when the time comes.

That portion of the American government which will oppose us past the point of open and notorious tyranny is small. We will have a force greater, by far, should that dark and fateful day befall us.

Some say that we can reform government - just pass the right bill, repeal the appropriate act, elect the right President. Then, once we have made it up with the federal government, it will protect us. Common sense should tell us that the very power which has endeavored to subdue us is, of all others, the most improper to defend us.

The average American's knowledge of government tyranny and oppression, both domestic and foreign, hourly is improving. From the federal government we can expect nothing but ruin. While it holds sway over us all, this country increasingly will not be worth living in.

The economic fortune of the average citizen, perhaps, has not yet declined sufficiently to engender a passion for change. Trade being the consequence of population, men become too much absorbed thereby to attend to anything else. Commerce diminishes the spirit, both of patriotism and military defense.

History informs us that the bravest achievements always were accomplished in the birth of a nation. With the increase of commerce, America has lost her spirit. Notwithstanding her numbers, America submits to continued insults with the patience of a coward. The more men have to lose, the less are they willing to venture. The rich are slaves to fear, and submit to courtly power with the trembling duplicity of poodles.

Youth is the seed time of good habits, as well in nations as in individuals. Now is the time for New America to be formed and separated from those who wish to continue the policies and plunder of Old America.

When William the Conqueror subdued England, he gave them law at the point of the sword. Until we form a New America, immune to the tyranny and oppression now afoot in the land, we shall be in danger of having the seat of power filled by some true and awful despot, who will treat us in the same manner. Then, where will be our freedom? Our property?

Some say that despot already has assumed power, thus more the need for us to move swiftly. President Bush and his henchmen engineered passage of the Patriot Act and the Homeland Defense Act, blueprints for tyranny passed by Congress without even being read. Should the general American electorate know the contents of these Acts and the manner of their adoption, it would not hesitate a moment to think its elected representatives unworthy of their trust. Immediate necessity makes many things convenient, which if continued will grow into oppressions. Expedience and right are different things.

Many reasons can be given to show that nothing can settle our affairs so expeditiously as an open and determined declaration for separation of New America from America.

Under our present denomination of American citizens, we can neither be received nor heard abroad. The custom of all courts is against us, and will be so, until by independence, we take rank with other nations.

Just as America allows Mexicans to hold dual citizenship, that of Mexico and America, and Israelis, of both Israel and America, so should we now designate ourselves citizens of both America and New America. We must concentrate ourselves geographically in those portions of America most likely to be allotted to a New America in a breakup of the country, just as Mexicans have concentrated themselves in Southwest America, which they have taken to calling Aztlan. Already, fully a quarter of the productive White population of California has left in the past decade, resettling mainly in Northwest America, thereby providing an example to us all.

Until a separation is effected from that portion of America over which the federal government will continue to hold sway, we will feel like a man who continues putting off some unpleasant business from day to day, yet knows it must be done, hates to set about it, wishes it over, and is continually haunted with the thoughts of its necessity.

The Spirit of New America

We must effect a change in America. We might not succeed in making that change, but *we surely can deserve to succeed.*

Make no mistake. We are at war. War for our very existence. If there must be trouble, let it come now, so that our children might live in peace. Let us fight the fight. Let us suffer defeat, if defeat it must be.

To win a war, one must risk death. That might seem scary, but to have nothing worth dying for...that is not living at all. Put aside fear. There is a limit to physical pain and suffering, but there is no limit to fear. In 20 years' time we will regret what we didn't do here and now far more than what we did do.

It was William Wallace, as played by Mel Gibson in the movie *Braveheart*, who said, when rallying his army to fight the British:

"Aye. Fight and you may die. Run and you will live - at least, a while. And, dying in your beds, many years from now, would you be willing to trade all the days, from this day to that, for one chance - just one chance – to come back here and tell our enemies that they may take our lives, but they will never take our freedom?"

I cannot advocate a violent revolution. But, that's exactly what the likes of William Wallace, Thomas Jefferson and George Washington would do today if they were still among us. I like to think that, if we were to bring them back to life today, tomorrow they would buy a road map, a red Cadillac convertible and a bazooka, then set out for Washington, DC.

What I advocate is being prepared and awakening others to what is coming. What is coming? Not worldwide empire, American style. What is coming is America's comeuppance.

I believe it will go badly for the NWO crowd and, consequently, for America, too. But that will create an opportunity we don't currently possess – an opportunity to start over.

Don't despair at how difficult the road ahead might seem to be. The most important things in the world have been accomplished by people who kept on trying when there seemed to be no hope at all.

The only real failure in life is in giving up, you know.

I'm glad you have stayed with me this far in this important work, which now has become *our* work.

We don't all have to be the same. We don't have to have the same abilities. We don't have to share the same beliefs. Dare to be different...even from one another. I don't know the key to success, but I do know that the key to failure is in trying to please everybody. Heaven knows that I don't manage to do that.

We all have a role to play. Don't despair at your own talents. Now, pay close attention to the following: Don't try to be better than anybody else. *Just try to be better than yourself.*

Do that one thing and they will never break our spirit. They will never silence us. They will never take our freedom.

Together, we can touch lives.

Together, we can make a difference.

Together, we can awaken America.

Together, we can take back America.

New America - an idea whose time has come.